# Torn In The New SA

Living, Loving and Leaving South Africa

# Torn In The New SA

## Living, Loving and Leaving South Africa

by

Bronwyn McIntosh

An Energy Organizer Book

© 2010 Bronwyn Desmé McIntosh

All rights reserved. The text and graphics of this publication, or any part thereof, may not be reproduced in any manner whatsoever without written permission from the author.

**Torn in the New SA**
Living, Loving and Leaving South Africa

Published by:   Energy Organizer Books

Cover design by Bronwyn McIntosh

Printed in the United States of America
First Edition

ISBN: 978-0-578-06239-6

For Jan van Zyl
   ...who has always been my Facilitator. Your intercedence brought James, and Anne, into my life. You gave me choices and opportunities that I would not otherwise have had. Your friendship has always been open, unfettered and quietly supportive and for this I am eternally grateful.


For Anne Oliver
   ...without whom the entire journey of the past 10 years would not have begun. You have changed our lives. I trust that our friendship will grow and deepen over time and will last forever.


For all
   ...who chose to correspond and share the intensity of their emotions and their stories with me. You served as my inspiration to begin and to complete this project. Your energy sustained me.


                              Thank you.

I voted with my feet. Three times.

The first was joyous; the second was unceremonious; the third was hard.

The first time I stood in line for seven hours under the African sky. By the time I entered the voting booth my feet were killing me, but I had made new 'friends' of many colours as we waited patiently, determinedly, to vote for a new, united South Africa.

The second time, in rural Riebeek Kasteel, was over and done with almost too quickly for something so important. I walked in, spoke to no-one, cast my solitary vote, and walked out.

The third time I walked out of the airport building and onto the aircraft.

The funny thing is that many people now remember me, not for queuing to vote, but for queuing to leave.

# Contents

| | Page |
|---|---|
| Forward | 1 |
| Caveat Lector | 7 |
| Telling Stories *by James McIntosh* | 9 |
| Love Gone Right | 17 |

**Part 1: The Article That Snowballed**

| | |
|---|---|
| 1. Universal Escape Artists *introduction by James McIntosh* | 21 |
| 2. A 'Dangerous' Article | 23 |
| 3. President Mbeki Lambastes Me | 35 |
| 4. The 'Racist' Replies | 44 |
| 5. No, Mr Mbeki, Telling The Truth Isn't Being Racist | 51 |

**Part 2: Loving**

| | |
|---|---|
| 6. Born Into Love *by James McIntosh* | 65 |
| 7. Loving Cape Town | 67 |
| 8. Out Of Love *by Eve Hemming* | 76 |
| 9. Dancing With Dogs | 81 |
| 10. I Miss *by Michelle Leech* | 85 |
| 11. Two Oceans | 93 |
| 12. F**k You, Emigrant *by Rob Dickens* | 98 |

**Part 3: Living**

| | |
|---|---|
| 13. Absentee Living *by James McIntosh* | 111 |
| 14. A Day Of Summer. A Life Of Crime | 113 |
| 15. Lizzie Wields Her Broom | 125 |
| 16. Paranoid For Life | 132 |
| 17. A Day In The Life | 144 |
| 18. Letter To My Parents *by BT* | 153 |
| 19. Living In My Kasteel | 162 |
| 20. From A Distance – Non-South Africans Speak | 170 |

**Part 4: Leaving**

| | |
|---|---|
| 21. The Long Goodbye *by James McIntosh* | 183 |
| 22. A Day Forever | 185 |
| 23. Leaving Cloud Cuckoo Land *by Anthony Krijger* | 196 |
| 24. Prelude To Leaving | 209 |
| 25. Time To Say Goodbye | 217 |
| 26. To Those Who Aren't Concerned *by Alison Wolfson* | 226 |

|     |                                                    |     |
| --- | -------------------------------------------------- | --- |
| 27. | Saying Goodbye To Bracken On The Mountain          | 232 |
| 28. | You Have To Stay, Ben *by Kate Richards*           | 240 |
| 29. | On The Move                                        | 244 |

## Part 5: Learning

| | | |
|---|---|---|
| 30. | Paper Or Plastic? *by James McIntosh* | 257 |
| 31. | The Ring Of Safety | 259 |
| 32. | Learning A New Land | 264 |
| 33. | Waste Not. Want Not | 276 |
| 34. | Arguing With A Vagrant | 282 |
| 35. | America's Gift – My Children | 287 |
| 36. | Friends In Need | 292 |

## Part 6: Longing

| | | |
|---|---|---|
| 37. | Missing Is Easy *by James McIntosh* | 299 |
| 38. | Belonging(s) | 301 |
| 39. | Passion Lost | 308 |
| 40. | An Imported Product | 316 |
| 41. | The Immigrant *by Heather Claire Scott* | 323 |
| 42. | The Missing Mountains | 324 |
| 43. | Gatvol Is Not American English | 329 |

## Part 7: Lasting

| | | |
|---|---|---|
| 44. | Beyond Torn *by James McIntosh* | 339 |
| 45. | Attitude Is Everything | 342 |
| 46. | In Helen We Trust | 350 |
| 47. | Are We There Yet? | 356 |
| 48. | Staying The Course | 365 |
| 49. | Tapestry | 375 |
| 50. | The Way It Should Be | 377 |

| | |
|---|---|
| Invictus | 383 |
| Acknowledgements | 387 |
| Cast Of Key Characters | 388 |
| Biographies Of Main Contributors | 390 |

# Forward
That's right, 'forward'.
As in not going back...

This book is not really about South Africa. It is about all the people who have felt compelled to flee the land of their birth. If at any time during your reading of this book, you replace 'South Africa' with the name of another war-torn or strife-ridden country, you will find the same story (almost) applies.

There are so many of us now, leading uncertain lives, living in unknown places far from a place we called home. I do not speak only of South Africans. Across the world, there are millions of displaced people who have made a choice to leave their homelands, for various reasons. People all over the world are seeking a better life, for themselves and their families. This is a story of humanity, not a story of one country or one people.

South Africans have felt this loss, this fracturing of families and severing of ties, keenly because we are a nation of open-hearted, friendly, resilient and optimistic people enamoured with life. To have severed the arteries that bind you to your past, is to have severed a limb. Would you sacrifice a limb on a whimsical idea? Or would it be that when your fear is enormous, like an animal in a trap, you'd rather gnaw at the limb and leave it behind so that you could continue with your life – scarred but still alive.

In a 'normal' society, you wouldn't think about or consider such a thing. Leaving your friends, family and country would simply be an adventure – of choice. There is no normality in the current situation which affects rich, poor, black, white and the multitude of colours, cultures and religions of the Rainbow Nation. It's a forced adventure and no matter how much gloss we apply to this 'Grand Adventure' (the concept which I dangled in front of my kids constantly in the early days), it still rings hollow.

I've been criticized because I left even though 'nothing had ever happened to you'. By definition, I had to be caught in the trap first, I had to be scarred, in order to reach a level of martyrdom that would entitle me to leave with honour. I don't think so, I'm not that self-sacrificing.

Why are we any different from those (of any colour) who left South Africa during the apartheid years as their protest against the government and the system? Does that have greater moral fibre because they were protesting against a policy or a regime? We also protest against the government and its inability to respect us and provide for us, the people. If we had left during the Apartheid years, we would have been viewed in a better light because we didn't support the oppressive 'system', but as we've left more recently, we are 'traitors' or 'cowards' or, if Mr. Mbeki is to be believed, 'racists'. I don't think so. I voted with my feet.

This project has seemed too big for me for a long time. Once the deluge of responses from the initial article began to overwhelm me, it felt as though I couldn't withstand the tide. Then I did what I usually do, told myself to pull myself together and to take responsibility for my thoughts, opinions and reactions. I've tried to answer each correspondent individually, even those with negative comments.

Sometimes I see myself standing on a beach, the long white sands of Fish Hoek or Muizenberg, around 5 p.m. The sun is setting behind me, the water and the sand are cool, and the tide is pulling me out – the sensation of sand slipping away at my feet. This tide is pulling me under. There are so many people out there, so many who want my help, my opinion, my words. Their responses are not intellectual although some have that element. Their expression is of heartfelt solidarity, sadness, some of anger and some of regret. I can express my feelings, my opinions and my experiences but I cannot, and I will not, influence theirs.

Many South Africans who wrote to me, expressed a desperate need to return 'home' again. Many of them had been living overseas for five years or longer – none of them expressed a feeling of having fully settled into their new environments. They admire the place, the efficiency, the facilities and the security but the connection, the feeling, the interwoven familiarity with those peoples of their home culture is lacking. They have severed themselves and, unless the government takes decisive action regarding both the crime and corruption, they will choose to live with their scars, and to find a limited sense of belonging, in another country.

Many expatriates keep up to date with current developments in South

Africa. To silence their concerns is disrespectful to their humanity and their basic human desire for safety. (Even the Freedom Charter[1] recognizes this: *All people shall have the right to live where they choose, be decently housed, and to bring up their families in comfort and security.*) Do you truly understand that desire to walk in the streets and live in your home, unharmed? The fears and aspirations of ordinary people are the same. If the crucial issues were addressed, they would, I believe, return home in droves. They too, want to live, breathe, grow old and be happy in a safe place where they truly belong.

I've reconciled myself to the fact that there will be many critics of this book. I've thought long and hard about the topic, this book, the criticism, the people involved, the residents, the citizens and the expatriates. I am not a political activist, I am not a sociologist and I am not writing a thesis. I am simply someone who expressed a feeling and an opinion at a point in time and, in so doing, triggered a tidal wave.

There are many people who feel trapped by situations and events encountered in their daily lives in South Africa, many who wish to leave for the same reasons that we did. They do not have the means or the energy to do so. Many residents thanked me for giving them space to share their fears about South Africa. None of them are irrational. Each person, depending on age, culture, upbringing, education, the area in which they live and their economic circumstances, expresses this slightly differently. Despite this, you will notice the commonality of their concerns in the section entitled 'Living'.

Those who choose to stay, express passion, strong feelings and the powerful optimism that South Africa, as an emerging 3$^{rd}$ world (their words, not mine) democracy, will turn itself around. Their passion stems from love, sometimes an almost fanatical love and patriotism towards their country. I chose to put their commentary into the section on 'Loving' since their writings are another expression of belief in the country.

At its most basic, this book is about humanity. Everyone has hopes, fears, dreams and aspirations. This book is rooted in fear. My fear caused me to leave, following in the footsteps of those who had departed over the past three decades. However, my hopes and dreams for my life and my family also added to my need to leave. Everyone who lives overseas, on a temporary basis, or in self-imposed exile, or as an expatriate, has expressed intense opinions and the emotions that caused them to leave. I have

---

[1] The Freedom Charter as adopted at the Congress of the People, Kliptown, South Africa, on 26 June 1955.

chronicled these in the section entitled 'Leaving'. Whether they left yesterday, or 20 years ago, their feelings about leaving are still valid.

I have been asked why, now that I have left, I have begun such a negative campaign against my motherland. I've spoken my truth as I see it and others have spoken their truth as they see and feel it. The truth about the government, and its mishandling and abuse of the trust placed in it by ordinary South Africans, is negative. We are a deprived nation because, in 1994, our anticipation of improvement, and of the change to come, was great, and we have been let down, we are disappointed and we are angry. Some of that anger is being channelled into actions and responses which are slowly eating away at, and destroying the fabric of, the people of our country. We hear, from the government, that things are improving and that the tide is turning but, according to many of the people of South Africa, this is not their experience. When there is ongoing international news coverage of township demonstrations, in 2009 and 2010, protesting against a lack of basic housing and services, it serves little purpose for any individual to paint a negative picture of South Africa. I believe the government is doing an adequate job of discrediting itself, and the country.

As human beings, living anywhere on the planet, we are entitled to basic rights. South Africa is universally acknowledged as having the most advanced constitution in the world. Yet, this constitution cannot begin to guarantee basic rights to its citizens. The principles of the ANC's own Freedom Charter are not being met either.

I have included in every section bits of 'our story', since many who write to me have asked about this. I have included pieces of writing about our process, difficulties, and emotions generated by leaving. There are essays about our life here, our thoughts on living in the USA, emotions generated during the settling into a new life, my adventure with home-schooling my children (something I never would have considered in South Africa) and pieces about amusing situations that arose to make us starkly aware of our alien status.

I had my opportunity to speak my thoughts in my article in 2004 (see Chapter 2: A Dangerous Article). Sadly, some of my concerns about South Africa and the government have been vindicated (for me, at least). This comment from a correspondent speaks volumes: *I'm currently living in South Africa, never wanted to leave and I also thought people who left are cowards, but now I'm also seriously considering leaving for various reasons.* (FP - South Africa)

Every correspondent has shared strong thoughts and feelings about South Africa. This book honours those feelings and their words. I opened the book up to anyone who wished to contribute. These people are from all walks of life, all shades of humanity, and a variety of careers and professions.

> *A big thank you for listening and affording me the place and space to voice my fears!*
> CK - South Africa

These are their stories. Please read them in the spirit in which they were intended, allow people their space and their expression, try not to judge them, respect the inherent humanity and the fact that ultimately we are all different pieces of the huge jigsaw puzzle of life. Our connection (and our opportunity to work together for the country we all love so very much) lies in those very differences.

Thank you and Hambe Gahle.

Bronwyn McIntosh

∞ ∞ ∞

# Caveat Lector
(Let the reader beware)

This is not a book of data. This is a book of people. This is not a book about numbers or comparisons. Above all, this is not a research project.

The book is the result of more than 600 responses from people, of all shades and from all walks of life, who reached out to me either because of my original article, or the subsequent articles published in South African newspapers.

I have protected the identities of the people who gave permission for me to use their quotes and their stories. One only has to read a few of the very personal and often horrific stories to understand the need for this identity protection. However, I do have names and contact information for each correspondent – everyone is a 'real' person, not a single 'anonymous source' was included. The country or place linked to each person's initials was correct at the time the correspondence happened – they may have moved on by now.

These contributions are 'in the raw'. They have not been formally edited by my editor, nor have I changed their style or sentence construction, except to fix obvious grammatical and spelling errors (at least the ones I spotted). My role was to select the bits and pieces of stories that I thought most appropriate for the tone of the book.

I thank everyone who took the time to share with me, whether your contribution appears in this book or not. Please know that you touched me, deeply. I hope this book in turn touches you.

# Telling Stories

## Introduction by James McIntosh

*It is a dark and quiet night.*

That, surely, is the traditional way to start a good story. And what is tradition? It is the passing-on of customs and beliefs from generation to generation. Tradition is also something that is bound to get lost when you lose your country. Hence the importance of telling stories. To a great extent, our stories define who we are. We build our identity around the stories we tell and we craft our self-image with the stories we tell ourselves. How? Simply by deciding which we choose to believe and remember, and those we choose to dismiss and forget.

*It is a dark and quiet night.*

Of course it is dark and quiet. After all, this is in Richmond, Virginia, the United States of America, in a suburb where there are no streetlights, no car alarms and no gun shots in the night. The dark and quiet night is sometime in 2008. I am lying in bed reading, the kids are asleep, Bronwyn is in the bathroom performing her nightly ritual, the rest of the house is in darkness. And silent.

Suddenly, a loud crash echoes from one of the lower levels of the house. Then silence. Not a sound.

I carry on reading. Then I hear Bronwyn laughing in the bathroom. Her head appears around the doorframe. She is still smiling. "Isn't it amazing," she says, "How we now both assume that a sound like that is caused by one of the cats." How times had changed. In 1991 we also had cats in the house. Back then we could not, would not, have assumed that the sound we heard that night was caused by something as harmless as a cat. Here's how Bronwyn tells it:

*Christmas 1991. We had moved into the house on the mountainside in Sea Point a couple of months before. Summertime – that wonderful time of year in Cape Town where the early morning crispness is tempered with an elegant hint of warmth and the heat that is still to come. In the shade of the city buildings, you can still feel the coolness of the stone. Table Mountain stands implacable. Crazy things always seem to happen to us in threes. My father had his first heart attack; Christmas Eve found me developing a severe stomach ulcer that necessitated a doctor's visit to the house at midnight (back when doctors still did those things); and then during the latter part of that week – Christmas to New Year – we were in bed one evening, I was reading and James was already asleep.*

*The bedroom walls were pale blue, windows opened to release the heat of the day (no airconditioning – those were the days!), the house was old and had high, pressed ceilings and wooden floors, and the view from the window showed calm ocean water. I was inadvertently dozing and, as it was already rather late, I thought I should put my book down, turn off the light and go to sleep now.... I heard a floorboard creaking....*

Our stories are not always fully factual. We add and subtract minor embellishments as a ploy to keep our audience engaged – we tend to be aware of doing so. Sometimes our stories contain little lies we tell ourselves to keep us sane – for this ploy to work we must remain unconscious of doing so. (As you will appreciate from some of the stories in this book, these almost-truths are necessary, because sometimes full-truths are simply too raw to share... or even to acknowledge.)

This is why we tend to tell multiple stories about ourselves, depending on our audience. There is the short and sharp version we flip at strangers – name, age, place of birth, brief biographical basics. These are surface stories, the hard-protective-shell stories that must and can stand up to objective scrutiny – hence they tend to be factual. The next level stories are the more companionable stories we share with acquaintances as we feel our way to the common ground where meaningful connections grow. These stories have more warmth as we allow little peeks at our real feelings and inner selves.

With true friends and loved ones our stories take on the deeper, richer tones of hopes and fears. Because they embody our dreams and nightmares, these stories are simultaneously fully factual and fatally flawed. And then there are stories for very important people and very special occasions. To compose these stories, we dig deep and tell of things that shaped us. We tell of how 'I' became 'me'. The older you become, the more likely you are to tell these stories. Sometimes only grandchildren are willing to listen. But then, in the greater scheme of things (such as being torn from your land of birth), grandchildren are very important people and having them with you is a very special occasion indeed.

Of course, grandchildren take you straight back to 'tradition', the reason you are telling these stories in the first place. Because an important aspect of these kinds of stories is that they unify a group, whether the group is a family, a tribe or a community. Stories create shared emotional connections, and in so doing, encourage a belief in a common purpose.

Let's now get back to Bronwyn's story, the one I'm sure she will one day be telling her grandchildren as 'one of the reasons we left South Africa even though it made us very sad'.

∞

*I heard a floorboard creaking... and dismissed it as the 'cats' (of which we had four), continued reading, the floor creaked again. None of our cats were well-endowed enough, I felt, to create such a loud sound on the floor.*

*"James! James!"*

*"Uhh"*

*"James! Go and see what that noise is, the floor's creaking!"*

*"Uhhh, what? Go to sleep, it's the cats!"*

*"I don't think so, the cats won't make that much noise. Go and see, please!"*

*"Oh, for....!"*

*He muttered as he lurched vaguely, totally naked, out of bed. As my side of the bed was closest to the door, he had to walk around the bed, across the floor and past me, all the while making a considerable noise on the old, creaky floors. And walked out of the bedroom.*

*Then all went silent.*

*Directly outside our bedroom was a toilet. Being an older house, the toilet door opened outwards towards the bedroom, as opposed to inwards (as* most do these days). And still not thinking clearly, James walked out of our bedroom, looked towards the toilet door and wondered why it was closed.

'I know I opened it before I went to bed'.

He pulled the door handle but it held fast. And, in that instant, he realized that someone was holding the handle from the other side. Luckily, despite his dozy state, his brain was nimble. He remembers thinking, 'what now? I don't have any weapons!' (he was naked, after all) 'the only thing I have is my voice'.

Sitting in bed, in my lacy nightie, with my book, I heard the sound of the toilet door being yanked open and slamming itself against the wall and then, "WHAT THE FUCK ARE YOU DOING HERE?"

An unbelievable shout that I had never heard from him. If that's the cats, they'll need therapy after this. I heard the toilet door slam closed and then got out of bed to see what on earth was actually going on. Coming out of the bedroom, looking towards the toilet on my right, I saw James holding a pair of ankles, shoes, socks, as the person connected to the items was obviously hanging out of the window. It was a small toilet window – large enough for a youth or small adult to climb through and, again, being an older house, the windows were metal frames. James was holding the man's ankles and slamming them hard against the metal window frame. Then he let go.

As there was a concrete path about 7 feet below the window, we assumed the intruder had hurt himself and would take off in a hurry. James closed and locked the toilet window.

"Call the police!"

"Don't be ridiculous. He's gone. It's over!"

"No. Call the police and let them know what's happened in case he tries something else in the neighbourhood tonight."

"OK, fine...let me just put some clothes on."

Sighing to himself, he half-stumbled to the bedroom. Standing in the centre of the house, lights on in every room, I hadn't thought to cover my lacy nightie but from the vantage point of this hallway, I could survey everything, including the 2 outside doors. James' voice echoed mildly from the study, while recounting details of the 'incident'.

SMASH!

The noise jangled on my already tattered nerves. I ran towards the toilet, to see the recently closed window had been smashed and there was a hand reaching in to open it. I screamed.

"James, James, tell the police he's coming back again."

Grabbing the knob and slamming the door open and closed vigorously and as loudly and hard as I could, I tried to create a cacophony of sound and commotion while screaming.

The police, and dog, arrived within 5 minutes. I don't think the policeman knew whether he should dare laugh when he found me wielding a large knife – about 10" long – intended for chopping meat. I was still wearing nothing except panties and a transparent lace nightie. I told him: "Just let them come near me, I'll cut their balls off! I'll kill them!"

"Ma'am, it's OK, they've gone. They won't be back tonight. Please put that away."

They never found the perpetrators (surely, having the gall to return when the alert was sounded and all lights were on, either means that there must have been more than one or perhaps drugs were involved, to make them more brazen – I don't know).

Up went the security gates on all doors, an alarm at the gate and sensor lights around the property. Sometimes, at 3 a.m. the gate alarm would sound in the kitchen and I'd lie awake wondering, 'why did that trigger? Did someone come onto the property or was that a deterrent? Why would someone open my gate at 3 a.m.?'

Sometimes the house security alarm would sound from upstairs, a separate property with its own entrance. The owner was away during the week and we took care of it. James had to investigate and re-set the alarm. Meanwhile, he was gone, our front door was unlocked, I didn't know if anyone was upstairs waiting to waylay him. I'd give the code to the security company when they called, although he wasn't yet back, and pray that it was a simple false alarm and that all was well.

I never slept properly again until we moved to Riebeek Kasteel in 1995.

∞

As I said, that was then and this is now. There is a gap between the two happenings on two dark nights. The obvious gap is the gap in time. That is a 'quantity' gap - so many days, so many weeks, so many months, so many years. The real gap is so much more than time and so much more difficult to describe. It has a time element, yes, but one that feels to be 'so many lifetimes ago' because as I sit here and write I can no longer relate to the child-boy-man that I became back there and was back then.

My memories of that place-time and child-boy-man are fading to what my pre-digital generation knows as yellow-brown paper pictures. Those memories lack real colour and real depth, as if 'then' was not a 'real' time, and the 'me' equally unreal.

What does it mean? I think this means that I am no longer torn.

There are many things that I will never quite 'get' (like why no other country except the USA ever plays in the World Series Baseball competition) and times when I will still not 'fit in' (like handing out really, really cheap candy on Halloween). I know I will never be 'American'. Even so, I know I am no longer torn. How did that happen? A clue was hidden in the two cat stories; to find it I had to remember a third cat story, one about a much bigger cat.

The much bigger cat, a lioness to be exact, had the cheek to charge me. But that's another story. What matters here is that I lived to remember her when the memory of her could help me most. My three cat moments clarified for me what I was against. Clearly, I was against being eaten by a lioness and I was against becoming a crime statistic. Away from South Africa I was beginning to understand what I was *for*, because only from a distance could I see how different daily life could be.

This being-against or being-for holds the clue to being-torn or being not-torn. We are torn when we *leave* something; we are less torn when we *go to* something, willingly. (Did we leave South Africa or did we go to America? I am not torn because I *went to*; Bronwyn is still torn at times because she *left*.)

Those of you who are no longer living in South Africa, ask yourself, did you *leave* or did you *go to*? Think carefully, because it holds the key to crossing from torn to not-torn. Knowing what you are against makes you want to leave; knowing what you are for makes it easier for you to settle down, wherever your leaving has taken you.

If you read carefully the very personal stories in this book, you can tell who is remembering 'against' and who is living 'for'. In other words, who is still torn and who is feeling less torn. (Do we ever reach a stage of 'not torn'? I think so. But then, I'm an optimist.)

Being an optimist, I believe that we invariably tell love stories. We tell of people, places and things that we love or once loved. If a story appears to be about hate, then underneath you will find that it is a story of what 'bad' people did to that which we love. We don't easily tell stories that are purely about hate.  Our stories are really about love gone wrong.

And so, wherever you are now, in South Africa or scattered, my hope for you is that you will have the time and the inclination to create a story of love gone right.

∞ ∞ ∞

# Love Gone Right

I was a child of the 70's living in the Southern Suburbs of Cape Town and every home I lived in had burglar bars, fences and yet, we still had, ongoing burglaries. In 1977 we had 5 burglaries. It reached a point where my parents joked that there was an invitation outside the front door. None of those crimes, while disconcerting, were ever violent or hateful. None of those petty criminals ever came back to perpetrate worse acts on our family.

Yet, those very events coupled with Apartheid and the climate of oppression within the country led my father to investigate emigration to the USA, in the late 1970's.

I remember one day at school, in Standard 5, when the art teacher looked across the room and said,

"So, are you looking forward to going to America?"

I ignored her, confident that she was speaking to someone else.

"Bronwyn, are you excited about going to America?"

"Me! No, you must have the wrong person. I'm not going to America."

"Yes, you are. Your dad was here talking to the Principal. Oops, I'm sorry. It's probably a surprise."

My day degenerated further when I discovered that not only was I going to America, but I was going alone with my father sans mother and sister. The children in my class already disliked me and considered me to be a snob because I had joined the school after being at a private school for many years. They were a close-knit class and I was the outsider.

In 1979, during school term – September – my father took me on a business trip to the USA. While he attended business meetings, I sat in strange offices completing school assignments – try asking an American for help with an Afrikaans grammar exercise.

My father's greatest wish was for us to live in the USA. I was 11 years old and I had decided that I was not going to change continents. In 1980, our family – my parents, my sister and I – came over for a mid-year holiday in the States. We visited up and down the east coast of the USA. My father, a larger than life personality (loud, outspoken, brash and caring) loved the States – the fact that everything was bigger and better; the patriotism; the people. In 1981 he made a third and final business trip to the States and then I think he realized that his dream was not working out.

In 2002, three months after our arrival in the USA, I was in North Carolina, talking with a family friend. During our first visit in 1980, a brief encounter in an elevator in Washington had led to a friendship that was maintained through 20 years. She turned to me, and said:

"So, what made you decide to leave South Africa?"

"Well... the crime, the lack of security for the children, emotional and physical security of the family and the lack of economic opportunities for the future, for both James and the children. But mainly for the children, I could not imagine raising them in a country that condones the type of violence that is taking place there today. I am tired of living behind bars."

She turned to me, her face ashen, her eyes wide. "I don't believe it. This is déjà vu. It is quite uncanny. Look, I have goose bumps. I could be listening to your father. You've just said exactly the same things that he said to me 21 years ago. Here you are, with your children, doing what your father wanted to do for you and your sister, nothing has changed."

For many years in my teens I fought my father's desire to move to the USA and yet here I am, living his dream. Isn't it interesting how the wheel of life turns?

∞ ∞ ∞

# Part 1

∞

# The Article That Snowballed

*I hope your story and many others will drive South Africa to find solutions to many of our problems and ultimately bring your likes back ashore.*

JZ - South Africa

# 1

∞

## Universal Escape Artists

Introduction by James McIntosh

**W**hen Bronwyn first started her nonsense by writing 'The Article', I might have stopped her if I had known then that it would snowball. If the truth be told, I did not even know what she was up to. I had issues enough of my own, trying to understand Americans on their own turf. And let me tell you, some of these Americans are indeed difficult to understand. All over the world there are people dreaming of getting into the USA and here there is a website called Escape Artist[2] dedicated to helping Americans escape from the USA. I ask you!

That got me thinking. It seems that there are always people in the wrong place at the wrong time. In rush hour traffic, have you ever watched

---

[2] Here are a few snippets taken from escapeartist.com website: "A website that shows you how to restart your life abroad. Since 1995, we have been helping escape artists just like you restart their lives abroad. What is the function of a government? ...To protect us? ...From whom? ...How? ...is any government doing a good job? Are they a help or a hindrance? Many of us are now looking for what might be called a 'life.' Tomorrow we will live where the best real estate exists, where the least crime and repression exists, where population pressures have not decimated the environment and where business is encouraged and not hindered by legislation. We will live there regardless of that place's global location or its former political posture."

the cars on the other side of the highway racing in the opposite direction? There always seem to be many people who want to get away from where you are trying to get to. I have often thought that we should trade places – houses or jobs. It would cut out a cartload of commuting.

And border crossings. A border is an imaginary line on the face of the planet. It is a line in the sand, so to speak, often as arbitrary as that line we, as kids, used to draw in the dust. You know the one. "Step over this line and I'll biff you." And if the other kid was bigger and dared to put his foot over the line, then you would simply draw a new line and say firmly, "Step over this line and I'll bop you one." Well, sooner or later you were forced to back up your threat or back down. To make your stand in the sand, if you will. The minute I remembered those times, I understood the raison d'être of escapeartist.com.

We all have this line in our head, the one that our government keeps crossing. If our government steps over that line once too often, then we feel compelled to take a stand. Our problem, of course, is that it is rather difficult to biff the government and so we have little option, we feel, but to cross that other line, the borderline. The interesting thing is that exactly where the final line is drawn is different for everyone. You know that it is there for your family and friends; you think you can see its outline when they talk politics and things, but you never know what will finally make that person step over. With both feet.

I think that although Bronwyn crossed the physical borderline when she left South Africa, she finally stepped over the line in her head when she wrote the article for escapeartist.com. Read it and see if you agree. But then again, maybe your line is different from hers and you might see signs that she still is just a little bit torn.

Torn or not, when that article appeared, triggering many, many emails from South Africans all over the world, topped only by Mbeki's presidential 'endorsement', that's when I realized that maybe Bronwyn had set our bridges on fire, that maybe it would be a very good idea if we did not go back to South Africa just yet, and that maybe we should try really hard to get that green card.

∞ ∞ ∞

# 2

∞

## A 'Dangerous' Article

*My husband's parents were in concentration camps (during the Nazi horror) but escaped to South Africa. We have 'escaped' to the USA. Does this make us any different from all those others who leave their countries to settle and survive elsewhere?*
AMS - USA

While researching potential countries for our future, I stumbled upon a website called Escape Artist (escapeartist.com) and their related e-magazine called 'Escape From America'. I considered much of their information, about different countries, economies and lifestyle, when weighing up our options. As a subscriber, I continued receiving the e-newsletter after we were already living in the USA.

In January 2004, barely two years after our arrival, an article appeared which highlighted reasons for investing, living, or buying properties, in South Africa. I agreed with much of the information but I felt that the article was biased and did not accurately present the truth about daily life in South Africa. People who visit South Africa with a mythical idea that all is perfect become easy targets. I felt that if the article was not a balanced representation then could I trust any of the information contained on their website?

I wrote to the editor about my concerns. He asked me to submit my story, which I did and I left it untitled. They added the title 'Dangers of

South Africa: Fear of Crime'. After submission, I didn't expect to hear anything further. Imagine my astonishment when, within 24 hours, the letters began pouring in via email. My naiveté about the power of the Internet had led me into the depths of an unexpected conflict that raged in many psyches. I react quickly to things and I think later. If I had known the reaction, would I have submitted the article? I don't know.

I pride myself on having responded to most, if not all, of the letters I have received, even those which are negative or defamatory. I thank them for their opinions and I explain that my experience of South Africa is uniquely personal and it was written from that angle.

What follows is the original article, unedited. Since 2008, it appears that the article is no longer available on the Escape Artist website. I have contacted the editor but it seems that they are unable to repair the link.

## Dangers of South Africa : Fear of Crime

Do you know that feeling of awakening at 3 a.m.? Ah yes, we all know that well, the sudden knowledge that a loud noise has awakened you - the sound of a car starting, the sound of a gun shot, the sound of a scream, the sound of police sirens, dogs barking, the alarm on the front gate triggered by someone opening it, the outdoor security lights blazing in reaction to movement outside, the security alarm blaring.

These were the daily realities of living in a wealthy "white" suburb on the fringes of Cape Town. To sleep soundly, one had to be surrounded by security alarms (and companies working 24/7 to monitor them), and have alarms on the gate (why would someone open our gate at 3 a.m.? I frequently asked myself), movement sensor lights around the house. Was that our car starting? Is someone stealing it? All too often it was not our house waking us, but rather the sounds of the neighborhood, where there were frequent sounds of screaming, dogs barking and gun shots. Followed, of course, by the police sirens (sometimes!). If this was life in a "wealthy" suburb, can you imagine life in a township outside the city?

Eventually of course, one only sleeps fitfully, the slightest noise waking you. Yet you become accustomed to living like this, like caged animals, always wary, predatory, careful, watching your front, back and sides all the time – a constant state of post-traumatic stress disorder that eventually takes it's toll on your health and your quality of life. Still we had the occasional burglary, two of them happened while we were in the house and we were fortunate that they were not armed and the police were responsive. The third time we arrived home to find that the front door had been kicked in and the lock broken. Small items of little value had been taken but the absolute violation of our life and privacy was too much to bear.

We moved to a small farming community about one hour from Cape Town, in the midst of the Swartland wheat and wine region, Riebeek Kasteel. Although we were one of the few English speaking families in the town, life was paradise, we didn't lock our doors at night, frequently did not even close them and there were no high fences or security alarms, just two Belgian Shepherds for company.

Major crime in the area consisted of the occasional burglary of a neighbour's home – she would visit her daughter up north and 'locals' would break into her home, raid her freezer, cook the food in her microwave and eat it. This was a source of amusement for the townsfolk and was not seen as a real threat. The police station closed at 4 p.m. The only 'crime' was usually our noisy neighbor having an occasional party.

I drove to Cape Town and home again, a distance of some 180km daily. Roads closer to the city were more dangerous and I would not drive with a purse or cell phone visible. Stopping at red lights in the city, I'd be cautious of the car being surrounded by people, looking to make easy money of one kind or another. I walked every day to and from a derelict parking area behind my building – 8 a.m. I would arrive and 4 p.m. I would leave. Constantly scanning, checking in case of people walking too closely, watching too carefully, following too strictly. Have you ever walked to your car carrying your keys woven in between your fingers, points protruding, so that you could use them as a weapon? Have you ever checked underneath your car to prevent being ambushed? And then check the inside of the car, before unlocking, in case someone is hidden inside? I thought like that from an early age.

In small country towns, things have changed. Prior to our leaving Riebeek Kasteel, there were gangs from the townships near Cape Town (a 2 hour drive) coming to the village at night to steal cars. So, yet again, that breeze rustling through the leaves at 3 a.m. awakens one. Is it a breeze or is someone treading outside? Why have the dogs not reacted? Given the amount of gall needed to travel a 2 hour distance (4 hours both ways) along a highway with not much getaway space, it's a small stretch of imagination to visualize criminals arriving in the still of night, murdering your family and stealing your possessions, including cars. They would be safely home before anyone awoke the next morning.

When a mother experiences the world through a child's eyes, everything looks very different. Despite the problems in South Africa, I had been vehemently opposed to leaving for any reason. However, the birth of my daughter coincided with the horrifying early incidents of 'baby rape'. My feelings changed in an instant.

> There can be no keener revelation of a society's soul than the way in which it treats its children.
> Nelson Rolihlahla Mandela

It is extremely complicated when a simple trip to the grocery store includes two small children – eight months and three years. You have to watch your children, your trolley, cell phone, handbag, and your front, back and sides and keep your keys woven between your fingers. Accosted by 3 or 4 people (children/youths) asking for money, a job, or a cigarette, you know that if they put a knife in your side, you would give them your handbag, your car or the clothes off your back in order to keep your children safe. These things flash through your mind as you leave the store. Is this a way to live? Four pairs of hands try to help with unpacking your groceries into the boot while you check the car, open the car, close the trunk, strap the children in, give the helpers some coin change, and be alert for any other possible threat. Overwhelming sympathy, for these lost people who have no safety or future, consumes you.

My weekly visit to the bank was fraught with further anxiety. I withdrew R2000,00 weekly to pay wages for renovations at our house. In a country where people are murdered for R10 or for a cell phone and incidents of gratuitous violence prevail, R2000,00 would seem a fortune. Draw the cash and simultaneously check everyone in the bank queue behind me, look at them face to face, eye to eye, give them a once-over, "If you follow me, I will know you!". Does anyone appear to be taking too much notice, are they interested in my transaction, does anyone look suspicious? And then leave the bank and get to my car as quickly, quietly and carefully as possible, making sure that no-one has followed, no-one knows that I am carrying this large sum of cash. Countless incidents of people being followed, forced off the road and murdered for the money that they have just withdrawn.

Thinking about education for your children is to realize the falling standards, lack of resources, overwhelming bureaucracy and reverse 'racism' that is practiced in the education system in South Africa today. Coupled with the lack of interest in improving it. Private education is the way to go, say people, but so few can afford that. It is the educational equivalent of closeting yourself behind electrified fences and security alarms. Fixing the symptoms and not the cause.

We decided that we didn't want this future for our children. So we left, didn't pack much, gave most of it away and took essentials – CD's, books, bed linen, kilim rugs and a few much loved toys. It was, and remains, a tremendously freeing experience, to let go of all the 'stuff' that humans are prone to accumulate. I realized that I could condense my necessities into a backpack. Many people told us that they could never do what we did – they had too much attachment. For me, the 'stuff' was easy, the beloved animals, my garden, the mountains, the climate, the people and the scenery, was heartbreaking.

America, the land of opportunity. It has been a 2-year struggle to survive, build a new life and a new business. And of course a re-accumulation of stuff. I do things differently nowadays – I have learned to do my housework, iron my clothes, clip coupons, and buy at the Salvation Army and Goodwill.

And in-between, although I speak English, I battle to understand and be understood – I remain a cultural alien. I have learned to appreciate the small things, the little moments. The friendly clerk at the post office, the helpful staff at my local library, the yoga classes that keep me balanced and centered. Our bank manager makes me feel that the bank is home away from home.

I miss the land of my birth, but I recognize that this ambivalence will always be present in me. My children will never know the wonderful cross-cultural mix that is South Africa today. The trade is a life where I sleep soundly at night, I don't fear being raped or hijacked or murdered. I don't fear for my children any longer, they are safe and happy; they have great educational opportunities here. They are young enough to integrate properly.

And I, I will always be split in two – did I make the right decision? And I will ever have a life that straddles the ocean – a foot on each continent. I will not ever be completely whole again.

I have gained immense rewards, mainly a sense of humor and perspective. Viktor Frankl said "We who lived in concentration camps can remember the men who walked through the huts comforting others, giving away their last piece of bread. They may have been few in number, but they offer sufficient proof that everything can be taken from a man but one thing: the last of human freedoms – *to choose one's attitude in any given set of circumstances* – to choose one's own way." Though it seems tough, I remind myself daily that there are many who survive, thrive and rise above far more difficult circumstances. I chose this, I will do my best in every day and I will not look back with regret and wonder. I've learned to appreciate the adventure and not to focus on the material accumulation – or lack thereof.

South Africa is one of the most beautiful areas of the world. I believe that given time the problems will be resolved. The country felt more stable and positive under President Nelson Mandela – I fear that it is regressing under President Mbeki. Trevor Manuel – the Minister of Finance – is doing a sterling job of managing the economic future of the country. This is insufficient if the government drives investors away with their general mismanagement.

Life is cheap there, in many different ways! For foreigners, the climate, the scenery, the people and the opportunities available must seem boundless. If one considers relocating a family or business, one must be prepared for the reality of life in a country that has the highest murder, rape and AIDS statistics in the world. Were the crime alone resolved, I know South Africans who would return in droves to re-establish themselves and their businesses. I would love to return and take my children back to experience their culture and live the reality of it.

∞ ∞ ∞

*Your article says everything I have thought but don't know how to write down.*

EG - South Africa

∞

*Thank you for having the courage to speak out about what is happening to our country for all of us lost souls scattered across the world.*

SVB - UK

∞

*How you hit the nail on the head, yes, absolutely no sleep happens for me between 3 a.m. and 4 a.m. At that time I lie awake in bed listening to the sounds, are they getting closer? Was that breaking glass my house? My car? The neighbours?*

*Every day is the same, just don't try factor that time period into your* hours sleep per night. Hey, seeing as I'm awake at that time, I might as well go for a ride on my bicycle, at least then I needn't fear being splattered across the windshield of a minibus taxi enjoying the state of anarchy which allows him the ability to perform any life endangering feat he wishes on the road. But, alas this bicycle ride at that time of the morning can't happen either because then I would be running the risk of losing my life to whoever wants my bicycle.

So, I'll rather lie in bed, spray can of mace next to me and baseball bat under my bed. Anyway, it's only a short while before I embark on the very early journey to work to avoid the lawlessness of our roads.

PD - South Africa

∞

You hit the nail perfectly on the head. Your description of the stress and lack of sleep is perfect. I took my family to Northern Ireland after being robbed 45 times in 18 years, including a couple of violent attacks. Thanks for a great article.

PB - Ireland

∞

As a family man who has seen his wife car-jacked, four vehicles stolen, countless other criminal actions against us, I take my hat off to you! People like you take a stand against being politically correct – well done! I wish I could take my whole family and leave this disorderly country....

GP - South Africa

∞

I found your article on the escapeartist today. Thanks so much for your words. I can so relate to everything you wrote and reading those words gives me some comfort in believing that I too will reach a point in my life where I can find some form of peace within after the pain and turmoil of having to leave home 8 years ago and the feeling of not being able to return home. I also feel like I will never be whole again! I am convinced of that.

I want to understand and hopefully learn to live with these feelings of ambivalence as you put it that I too have. Until now I have not been able to control this.

My father didn't make it out of South Africa in time, he was shot four times in a failed hijacking four years ago; they got disturbed and left without taking anything. My two brothers have left South Africa, my mother has remarried and lives in a beautiful complex.

South Africa is in my blood, I love South Africa with all my heart and a day doesn't go by without me longing to be back at home again. I will be immigrating from the UK to Australia later this year. I am hoping and praying that some of these feelings of losing my home are going to be made a bit easier to live with while gaining what a beautiful country like Australia has to offer.

KH - UK

∞

Your article was spot on and I too have emailed many family and friends overseas to tell them about South Africa and I said exactly what you did. We live here, we know. You stated realistic facts and exactly what living in South Africa feels like and I couldn't have described it better.

AR - South Africa

∞

What you wrote touched me deeply. It puts things in perspective when you read someone else's experiences, which only another person from South Africa can relate to. I don't think those that have not lived there believe our daily 'norms'. We left Johannesburg 16 months ago. We love South Africa; we hate the crime. If the crime problem became controllable we would be on the first plane back. Sadly, I don't think it will happen. We think we did the sensible thing some times, but we are so homesick all the time.

Your account of life in South Africa is so accurate - it makes me face the truth and not the emotional longing I have for South Africa.   AMS - USA

∞

I'm sitting here sobbing into my keyboard having just read your website article entitled 'The Dangers of South Africa'. I stumbled across it in a desperate attempt to find a reason to return to South Africa. Like you, I live divided. We have lived in the UK for five years now and have a beautiful baby boy and I would wish nothing more than for him to grow up in the South Africa of my youth but we made the decision to move away because of the crime and although I know my little boy has a brighter future now I can't help living every day with the fear that I made a terrible mistake but the price of having my baby raped or murdered and growing up in fear is too high.

KB - UK

∞

Your article was the closest thing to truth I (we) as Ex-Pats have come across and I felt you deserve a small pat on the back for putting millions of Ex Pats feelings into one article.

CS - Australia

∞

I just wanted to say thank for writing 'The Dangers Of South Africa'. My family also relocated to America, I can relate to everything you describe in you paper. And I have to say there was a sense of panic that came over when I read it. It been so long since I have thought how life was in South Africa, and I never ever want to feel like that again. I take great pride in South Africa, the culture, the food, the sports, I miss having a braai, I miss going to a rugby match at Loftus, I miss being able to speak Afrikaans everywhere but I have adapted. I have learned to make my own boerewors and biltong and I have made many friends.

WJS - USA

∞

You described it so well - when I read your description of the rustle in the bushes, sirens and alarms at 3 a.m. - I had shivers run up and down my spine! How tragic that so many people are living in these conditions with such acceptance of their fate of 'it is not a case of IF, it is a case of When' is horrifying to say the very least.

T - USA

∞

Your wording and understanding of how I have felt for the past six years is so to the point. I left South Africa and my sisters six years ago with my husband and children to make a home in the UK. It has never felt like home but I feel we have no option but to stay and make the best of it.

Fear of crime and waiting to be another statistic was the only reason but as you said a big enough reason to flee. Anger at being forced from my home sometimes grips me but I never feel like I have made the wrong decision. But I quote from your article 'I will never feel completely whole.' Thank you for putting everything so into context.

MR - UK

∞

I read your article on escapeartist.com and I just felt that I wanted to let you know, I understand. My husband and I live in England and I always find it amazing to see that even if I don't know you, we feel the same feelings about this choice we made. I cried reading about how you feel split in two, always asking yourself, did I choose right? Every day I struggle with it, and I probably will until I return.

Your reflection at the end about how we can choose our attitudes is very inspiring and encouraging. In the end that is the difference, how we choose to deal with this choice.

JDP - UK

∞

I have been traumatised by crime and I'm often told by fellow South Africans that I must 'get over it' or that I'm too intense and must not 'focus' on the crime so much. It frustrates me. I just wanted to say how much I identified with your very well written piece.

NV - South Africa

∞

I am going back to South Africa (Durban) in February and was searching the web for a Durban Pilates trainer (which I couldn't find) and through the links, came to your article 'Fear of Crime'. Interesting how one thing leads to another and one wonders if it was 'just co-incidence' or was I meant to read your article? Hmmm.

We lived most of our adult lives in South Africa (Johannesburg, Durban, Cape Town) and had our own business there, in Johannesburg and Durban.... As the economy got worse and we started to really worry about the future, we decided to leave, hoping that we could go overseas, earn some 'decent/meaningful' money and return later when things had settled down.

We have been in Europe for three years and love the complete lack of crime and fear that you so eloquently refer to in your article. We fly 'home' at least once a year and immediately notice the difference between driving, living, going out at night, etc. in Europe and in South Africa. We'd been planning to retire back there, at the coast, but the crime factor was always a worry. I see you guys had the same worry!

We're now looking to see if retiring in Croatia or Thailand or Mallorca might be a possibility because I really don't want to go back to that panic attack at 3 a.m., as you say, wondering what the noise on the roof is and expecting it to be guys trying to break in. At the moment I know it's either my cats or the peacocks we have in our factory grounds (which sound like elephants with hob-nail boots on) and I just turn over and go back to sleep. Nice.

LM - Europe

∞

I've got tears in my eyes as I read your essay about leaving South Africa, as I see myself in everything you've described, the waking up at night and waiting... wondering and worrying... the keys as stabbing objects between my fingers EVERY TIME I get out of the car, whether to buy milk, get the post at the Post Office, to fetch my child from School. Pepper Spray cannister now in the pocket of my Golf's front door, but I don't know if I will be quick enough to use it if it is really necessary.

EM - South Africa

∞

My father was President of the Anti-Apartheid group in Scotland, he went to University in South Africa and started black scholarships there (it was a long time ago). It seems very sad that so much crime goes in South Africa and I read recently of white farmers and their families being killed and tortured in the north of the country.

I know exactly what you mean by post-traumatic stress disorder, living in such circumstances causes it in people who are sensitive enough to react to what is occurring around them. The current leadership in South Africa and their lack of any condemnation of the situation in Zimbabwe is really poor and does not seem to offer any hope for the future.

CC – UK

∞

*Dink jy voel net jammer vir jouself. Bly waar jy is. Hoop jy verstaan die Afrikaans want julle Engelse het nog altyd gehardloop. Dit maak my siek.*
(Think you simply feel sorry for yourself. Stay where you are. Hope you understand Afrikaans because you English have always run away. It makes me sick.)

JDB - South Africa

∞ ∞ ∞

# 3

∞

## President Mbeki Lambastes Me

*Africa will curse those who will leave it to rot.
I love mother Africa and I belong to mother Africa
and mother Africa belongs to me. Africa for Africans.*
RM - South Africa

September 2004 found our family in a state of fear and desperation. Having been formally notified by my husband's employer that his work visa would not be renewed at the end of 2004, the dire nature of our circumstances threatened to overwhelm us. And then, added to this, in the first week of October, I received an email from Angela Quintal, then Group Political Editor of Independent Newspapers in South Africa (now Editor of the Natal Mercury), who asked if I had seen Mbeki's 'defamatory attack' in his latest ANC online newsletter.

She sent a link to the web page and asked for my comment. Since this is the age of spam and clickable links to activate PC viruses, I found the email amusing, and original, and would never normally click on a link with such a ludicrous message. Yet, after copying the link into my browser, I found the email was accurate.

And so, nine months after the article originally appeared on EscapeArtist.com, it had triggered a diatribe from Mr. Mbeki's office via his weekly "Letter from the President" dated 1 October 2004. It was entitled, "When is good news, bad news?" Here it is, unedited, as it appeared at the time on the ANC's website:

There is a racist[3] article on the Internet entitled 'Dangers of South Africa: Fear of Crime' written by one Bronwyn McIntosh, a white South African who has emigrated to the United States. She says: "Do you know that feeling of awakening at 3 a.m.? Ah yes, we all know that too well, that sudden knowledge that a loud noise has awakened you - the sound of a car starting, the sound of a gun shot, the sound of a scream, the sound of police sirens blaring, dogs barking, the alarm on the front gate triggered by someone opening it, the outside security lights blazing because of movement outside, the security alarm blaring. These were the daily realities of living in a wealthy 'white' suburb on the fringe of Cape Town."

After commenting on the difficulties she experienced trying to acclimatise herself to her new surroundings in the US, she says: "Sure life is cheap there, in more ways than one! And for foreigners, the climate, the scenery, the people and the opportunities available must seem boundless. However, I feel that if one considers relocating a family or business, one has to know and be prepared for the reality of life in the country that has the highest murder, rape and AIDS statistics in the world."

Of course what she is conveying to the rest of the world about a "wealthy white suburb on the fringe of Cape Town" is an outright lie. But people elsewhere in the world who do not know our country, might take her at her word, having no reason to suspect that there are some from our country who will not hesitate to tell the lies she tells.

Having convinced her listeners that she fled from her white suburb in Cape Town, because the black savages were at her door, some editor in our country will then seize on her victory triumphantly to proclaim that "overseas, the perception remains that SA is one of the world's crime capitals."

∞ ∞ ∞

---

[3] The word 'racist' was used in the original version of Mbeki's Letter... and then quietly disappeared after my reply to him appeared in the newspapers.

*Daar is 'n verskil tussen 'n rassis en 'n reallis, Mnr Mbeki! (There is a difference between a racist and a realist, Mr Mbeki!)*  ADP - Australia

∞

*I don't think you a racist, more of a realist! I am an informed coloured bloke and know the difference!*  MC - Sicily

∞

*Bravo, you managed to get a response from him, congratulations, and your comment that this gives your article credibility is on the button! I get e-mails daily from people putting together petitions ranging from a call for a referendum to bring back the death penalty, to employing more police officers etc. This has been ongoing for some years now with NO response from the government at all. Again, well done! Maybe there is 'hope' after all...*  GW - South Africa

∞

*It is sad to see a leader like our president chalking up articles about crime and our personal experience to racism.*  AV - South Africa

∞

*You got to the president of South Africa because he knew that you were right. He is an educated man, well spoken. He knows that what you said will be heard and believed. Keep on writing, writing, writing! The pen is very powerful as you know. So powerful that you got the president to choke in his pipe!*  RVR - South Africa

∞

*After three decades of campaigning for sanctions and fulminating against the evils of apartheid as an exile in USA, I ended my exile and came home to vote for the first time in our first democratic elections. After the elections, I had to return to the USA and found myself fulminating against the*

racist media for harping on the crime in the New South Africa. I argued that the alleged upsurge was simply a matter of crime spilling out of the black ghettos to which the apartheid police had confined it. Now that whites were getting a taste of what their black compatriots had had to endure for decades, 'the world' had woken up to crime.

A few months ago I finally came home permanently and found, to my shock and dismay that not only crime but also corruption (which I'd hoped was also being exaggerated) were indeed at staggering proportions.

KC - South Africa

∞

I was born white in South Africa – this gave me privileges and advantages in life that I know I must be grateful for. I am not proud of those privileges, but I cannot go back and change them. I was born white, but I did not make the decisions that resulted in Apartheid. My skin is white, but I consider myself to be African in every sense of the word that matters.

RS - USA

∞

Don't listen to your president or to people who say you are a racist. You simply love your children and, as all the mothers in the world, if you can choose, you choose the best for them.

CT - Italy

∞

In our case, which advice did I wish I had known before going to South Africa? That the criminality was worse than we thought it would be. We heard and read about it, but it was even worse than we thought it could be.

NVR - The Netherlands

∞

I think that when Madiba left office we reached a watershed in this country. What has happened to all those promises that were made to the people? Sure, things were not great under the apartheid regime and clearly something had to be done about the situation. However, where are all those grandiose promises made by the new regime?  Where is this 'Rainbow Nation' concept?  Why is it that when a person of colour talks about violence or even discrimination it is acceptable, but when a white person does so everyone (and particularly the Mbekis of this world) scream 'racism'.

I am so tired of hearing that EVERYTHING is the fault of Apartheid.  There comes a point where governments have to start taking responsibility for themselves, their actions, and if needs be their non-actions.  Eleven years down the line is time enough for people to have put aside the apartheid excuse and to have got on with the business of governing responsibly.

JH - South Africa

∞

You have really made me feel a lot more positive about our move away from South Africa, and I thank you for that.  Don't listen to the negative e-mails you get, you are a inspiration to a lot of South African women who have moved away from home, and believe you me, they appreciate the truth!

NH - Australia

∞

The crime is out of control.  Violence is the order of the day.  And while the government officials tell us to "stop whining about it" all you need to do is live in a place where it doesn't exist to recognize it as a problem.

LRK - USA

∞

The crime and the level of violence that it takes place at is sickening to the point that sometime I wonder whether it worth trying to make South Africa a better place.  Will this ever happen?  When will ALL South Africans understand that any crime/violence against another person/animal is WRONG.  Please don't try to justify it!

DH - South Africa

∞

I moved to the UK three years ago with my wife and daughter and can fully understand and empathize with your feelings.  I was astounded reading the article in its entirety and comparing it with what President Mbeki had to take from it, and say about it, in his article on the ANC web page.

MB - UK

∞

I sometimes feel that I really want to share what is happening in South Africa with everyone out there, but fear that they will misinterpret it for xenophobia and racism when it is indeed not the case. I'm 35 and fought hard in a legal manner for a true democracy alongside the very same people who now push us out of jobs, rob and murder us and drive the country into a state of despair.

We had eight burglaries in two months on a small holding outside Pretoria and almost lost our lives in the last one. We moved to Lynnwoord, but have had several burglaries in past two years. They have recently hijacked a parent at our upmarket school, then stole the bicycles from the school and it goes on and on. I set my alarm for 2 o'clock and 4 o'clock in the morning, just to make sure that if someone is in the house - they would hear that I am awake and run off. We live less than 100 metres from the school, but don't allow our children to walk home because we fear for their lives.

Do people in other countries understand? I don't think so.

IG - South Africa

∞

Depression and dismay. I was a political activist for the ANC while at University and I feel depressed at the apparent lack of respect for democratic principles and the blatant racism of the new government. It is a disgrace that government forms still expect us to fill in racial classifications, that government ministers and ANC politicians and spokespeople refer to people of colour as 'not black enough'. There does not seem to be any accountability among anybody in positions of power or responsibility, and the most important criteria seems to be that people were 'comrades in the struggle'. That excuses any failings or excesses.

It is tragic that Mbeki will be remembered for his unwillingness to help the people of Zimbabwe and he turns a blind eye to their oppression and the abuse of human rights in that country. That is his greatest legacy;

very sad. And of course the Aids orphans and the collapse of health care in this country, the escalation of crime, the decay of Eskom... I'm afraid you can't blame it all on the previous government, who left power in 1994!

DB - South Africa

∞

I read the papers and listen to stories and I watch what happens in our streets, our neighbourhoods, our cities and I become a little sicker everyday. There is tension on the streets, the divide between have and have-nots grows and there is a brutality and violence that is increasing. Our president blithely calls anyone a whining racist if they complain, and everyday, lives are lost to this disease of crime. What kind of bestial nation tolerates a 400% increase in baby rapes? How many little girls lives are destroyed, their bodies destroyed because of ignoramuses who believe it can cure Aids?

SB - South Africa

∞

The (soccer) world cup in 2010 should be an interesting event. They showed us what part of the township they wanted to tear down and replace with better homes so that visitors would see an improved situation along the roadside. It's very unfortunate that the government functions as it does. Hopefully South Africa will see changes for the betterment of all South Africans in the future.

BF - USA

∞

I read your article 'The Dangers of living in South Africa' a number of times. I also know that Mr. Mbeki has lambasted your sentiments and even called you a racist. I am not about to do the same. You see Bronwyn, you left South Africa because you sought greener pastures elsewhere, and I hope that you found them. Still, there are millions of us, who don't have the luxury, or resources to make decisions that you and other expats made. Those of us who do have the resources, and have the liberty to explore beyond our country's borders, realize that our struggle did not end in 1994, and making our lives, and this country work, is a day-to-day struggle we can't turn our backs on. The point I'm trying to make here, and one I'm sure you've deduced from this letter's subject, is that we – meaning South Africans who are here and aren't going anywhere – can do better without having your negative sentiments cloud over our rainbow.

Please understand, you are entitled to hold the opinion you have of this country. But, you are not here. I am. I'm sorry that your life here was such a misery. You are not the only one. You experienced crime? I still do. Unemployed? Me too. Hated looking squarely at poverty's ghastly face? I don't bat an eyelid. Hopeless? I can't afford to be. Because there is no other home for me. Except this one. You forget that for millions of South Africans, life has never been better than what it is now. You see disintegration. I see opportunity.

As for the feeling that plagues you, of whether or not you made the right decision, by leaving South Africa, only you can decide that. If you believe that your children will fare far better by leaving in a land that is not that of their birth, then it is well.

Some advice... you will never be able to find the courage to return to us, if you nurture such hopelessness. You will never consider South Africa as home again, if you look down on us, as though you know something we don't, by being there and us being here. You will never be at peace with your decision of emigrating, if you keep one foot there, and one on South Africa's soil.

Your article evoked feelings of despair in me. Not only that. It made me sincerely angry. I believe that the only ones who qualify to denounce South Africa, are those who languish in it, and love it no matter what, every single day. God keep you.

AM - South Africa

∞

If one dares to challenge the government on any issue – crime, Aids, Eskom, lack of transparency, etc. – one is immediately labelled a racist. There is much corruption. The country is falling apart. I recall the days of apartheid. I was raised in a liberal home with parents who were more humanitarians than pro or anti black or white. They did not endorse the nationalist party and the rules of the country. My brother and sister were anti-apartheid activists at university. We often broke the law when my brothers had kids of other races sleep over who were fellow altar boys with them at church. We would be what was considered a liberal family. But what we live in today is not the idea of democracy and freedom. This is more like hell on earth. I am actively involved in charity work. I could write a book on the hypocrisy of this government.

The world knows what is going on in this country but refuses to report the truth. It is often said the last government in South Africa were the scourge of the earth with their apartheid laws and we lived in a police state. This government could teach them new tricks. They do not know the meaning of true democracy and transparency. They disgust me. And if all this means I am a racist so be it. LF - South Africa

∞

How come when a brother gets a load of crap, you call it racist, but when a white guy gets a load of crap, it's returning the balance? I would love to have a debate with a politician as to how I was brought up. I had NO advantages, so how come they paint me with the same brush? What if I took a blood test and it showed I had Zulu in my blood, do I take that to an interview and ask for an affirmative position? Go figure! PC - South Africa

∞

I was 100% non-racist and in fact refused to vote until all the people of this country were enfranchised. In 1994, I wasted my first vote on the ruling party and stood bawling my silly, idealistic eyes out. I'm still bawling, but now for a very different reason! LB - South Africa

∞ ∞ ∞

# 4

∞

## The 'Racist' Replies

*I sometimes feel that the minute I mention that I'm leaving the country, I'm branded as a racist, whining traitor to the 'African Renaissance'.*
MC - South Africa

I felt nauseated when I read the 'Letter' and I decided to address Mbeki, and his defamatory statement, by emailing him directly. I asked Angela for his contact information. In turn, she replied that I should copy my email to her. During that same week of October 2004, Independent Newspapers published my email to Mbeki, nationally, in their stable of newspapers.

Below is my email as it appeared in many South African newspapers. It was even translated into Afrikaans and published in Afrikaans newspapers. It is worth noting that I received no reply from Mbeki but the word 'racist' was quietly removed from his on-line 'letter'.

Dear Mr President,

I am flattered that you would take my opinions and emotions so seriously: your doing so gives them value and credibility.

I am neither a writer nor a journalist. I have subscribed to a website called Escape Artist for about 5 years now. This website has information about life in other countries but is aimed mainly at people who want to 'escape' from the USA. The articles are interesting and informative, and have made me want to visit the country concerned.

When South Africa was portrayed on the site as a veritable paradise for investors and retirees, I began to wonder whether the articles were unbiased. I know the truth about the daily challenges of life in South Africa. This, in turn, made me wonder if I could trust anything I had read on their site. I contacted the editor about this. They invited me to write about my life in South Africa.

I wrote the article from my heart, expressing factual experiences of life in Sea Point (1991–1996) and Riebeek Kasteel (1996–2002), expressing emotions and opinions clearly personal to me.

My experiences relate to the crime I directly encountered and to the way I had to adapt my lifestyle and behaviour in order to survive. I know that many South Africans have far worse experiences and suffer daily. I recognize my 'privileged' status and I do not expect pity.

Since publication, I have had a steady stream of communication from people in England, Kenya, Nigeria, Macedonia, Panama, Eritrea, Zambia, New Zealand, Australia, the USA, Switzerland, Canada, Romania, Ireland.... The response has been overwhelmingly positive and supportive of my essay. However, most of their stories, in their intensity, eclipse my minor experiences – at least none of us were murdered or raped.

Many letters are from expatriates saying that I had expressed their exact emotions about leaving and relocating and how completely they relate to everything I wrote. The letters are from diverse groups – age; ethnicity; culture. All of them tell how desperately they miss their life in South Africa. Other letters were from people who lived either in South Africa or Africa for some time, long enough to state that the experience had profoundly affected the rest of their life. Without exception, all say how much they want to return to live there.

Some of the letters were from investors seeking to relocate themselves and their families to South Africa and wanting to set up a business there. Sadly, this often does not work out. This quote from an American businessman, who wrote to me after taking his family to South Africa in April 2004, says it all: "We loved SA, but the investment climate is very poor. Tried every way to make it happen, with no luck. The numbers just would not work with the government requirements in hiring and wages." The same businessman is now using his investment funds to invest in the USA.

I receive letters from people, not South African, who are planning to live there for some time, or permanently. Some have married a South African, some have fallen in love with South Africa itself. And because I am currently in America, I get letters from Americans who are going to South Africa to work or visit friends or family, or simply to see the country.

I reply to every email. I tell everyone to go, visit and enjoy the country, it is a fabulous, beautiful, dynamic place. I tell them that they will be inspired and will fall in love. The people are warm and caring, hospitable and cosmopolitan, very interesting and diverse. I spend hours replying and expounding on everything that South Africa has to offer. I refer them to South African contacts, to places that I have visited and to people who may be able to assist them or show them the positive side of that glorious country.

But I do tell them to be careful, South Africa can be dangerous. I tell them to cultivate a streetwise awareness of what is happening around them but try not to let it detract from the magic.

In my response, I say that since writing the article, I can now see clearly through my anger about leaving. After 2 years in America, writing the article was a catharsis. I tell them that I would like to go back to South Africa and raise my children there. I've come to believe that I would rather deal with 'real' issues in South Africa than the commercial, consumer-driven, approach to life here.

I tell them that in ways I didn't appreciate, South Africa is an advanced country. I suppose I had to leave in order to see it.

We have not emigrated and do not wish to. I am African, my children are African. Being a foreigner here has its advantages – we don't have to subscribe to the American culture.

The hardships I have endured here (which I wouldn't have experienced in South Africa) have made me stronger. Now, I have skills and resources, emotional, mental and physical, that I can use to give something back to South Africa and its people.

If we had not taken this opportunity to spend time in America, I would not be the person I am now. I would be part of the complaining masses. Instead, I find myself focussing on South Africa's opportunities and how I can contribute to the country.

You should be proud to be president of a people who care passionately about their country and who take the time and trouble to vote and to voice their opinions. In 1999, there was an 89% voter turnout. In America it will be a struggle to get people to vote next month. It must be embarrassing to the president of the world's most powerful democracy to know that only about 50% of those eligible bother to vote.

We are in the US on a temporary work visa. I follow developments back home closely because when the adventure is over, I hope to return. If half the good news is true, then there is hope and perhaps the situation is improving.

∞ ∞ ∞

*I also love to live here. This is MY home too! My great grandparents came to South Africa with their parents – but when you become a mother, your fear for your children is always top of mind and I'm not prepared to martyr myself or my family just to be politically correct. This crime is NOT ok. We are a population under siege and you had every right to voice your opinion on the matter. That was your experience after all – you didn't make it up.*
CD - South Africa

∞

*I remember one day a DJ on one of our stations was talking about the load shedding that had been occurring lately, and he stated that as citizens we have to pay for our own private medical aid (the public hospitals are death traps), our own private security (to ensure we can sleep safely at night... most of the time... since the police are non-existent), our own private schooling (to ensure our kid's educations are on par with those overseas) and recently we would now have to fork out for generators so that we could generate our OWN electricity. We as citizens are looking after our own needs... so what exactly is our government doing for us?*
KK - South Africa

∞

*I have now happily returned after over two years in the UK and am very happy back in South Africa. One of the things I realised while I was overseas though was not the amount of crime that South Africa has but the forced perception that we need to panic about it all the time. Ever since I have returned to South Africa 1½ years ago I have removed my alarm system, discontinued my 24 armed response and stopped locking up my* house like Fort Knox. I now leave valuables outside in my Lapa and have no problems sleeping because I don't expect someone to steal my car or break into my house.

This change in perception has helped me the most and I am very happy to say that since I have been back in the country I have only had one run in with crime and that was when my wife's cell phone was stolen (possibly lost) in a shopping mall by a pickpocket. People seem to enjoy forcing fear down our throats and trying to blame it on the ANC government when in fact all crime has been steadily decreasing in the past 10 years.

GM - South Africa

∞

Sure, we as Whites lived a privileged lifestyle growing up, but we miss ALL the people of South Africa. I personally don't care who runs the country as long as he/she does a good job. When returning on holiday it is so heart-warming to witness Black and White students walking home from school, chatting to the most fabulous Black people and just generally noting that the spending-power now belongs to all. This is good change.

Of course the only issue that remains is the crime and this was your point. It is ours here too. Even while visiting Johannesburg two years ago, we were unlucky enough to be caught up in a home-invasion. Luckily no-one was hurt but my Aussie boys were terrified as they had never been exposed to this and had only heard all the horror stories from people in Perth.

As a result they refuse to stop in Jo'burg to see family and of course the fear is that Cape Town will eventually go this way too isolating families further.

HL - Australia

∞

Yes, I'm African and this may seem irrelevant to me, but the lovely country you advocate people can fall in love with because of its beauty can only strive for the better if our European counterparts who still hold the intellectual resources stay in this country to make it a truly beautiful country.

As a South African and even as I don't know you, I love you. It is because this feeling was entrenched in me as a child from the day I was born, to love thy neighbour. And it is when you conduct such articles as this one that I feel you will fuel my beloved country's loss in thousands of its profitable assets that I ask myself, when you grew up, what did your mother teach you?

Nevertheless, I shall love you no less but I will always ask the questions about you, would you be so kind as to tell me why do you still continue with your campaign?                                              JZ - South Africa

∞

Most surprising thing about relocating? Through all the troubled times in South Africa, one was often lead to believe that the eyes of the world were watching our every move. NOTHING could be further from the truth and in fact, the vast majority of people where we live now, don't know too much about South Africa other than the fact that it is on the African continent and…Nelson Mandela.                                                                                  SK - Ireland

∞

The challenge is that government is unable to deal effectively with crime. Period! The problem is that the Mbeki government wants to be seen to be successful and unfortunately they are not. It's like a person with low esteem who wants praises even when he is wrong, because he feels better. That is not how to respond to your constituency. We voted the government in power, and they are accountable to us.

If I were president, I would test the return of death penalty through a referendum! I am very sure that the government can resolve the crime problem…they just lack political will to do it.                                       DM - South Africa

∞

With due respect, I think you made a life changing decision of moving out of beautiful sunny South Africa and now you can't live with it. To try and console yourself you have engaged on a smear campaign to justify your actions to your family and the rest of the world. We in South Africa, black and white, love our country and we are proud of it. It hurts us to see you badmouthing it at every possible opportunity just to 'prove your point'.

South Africa, just like any other part of the world has its own share of challenges. Go to the US, UK, Australia etc, they all have their own problems.

*I am not gonna call you a racist. I think you are simply one of those who were misled to believe that soon South Africa will be sinking like the Titanic and you decided to jump ship. Now that the ship is not sinking, you are trying your best to help sink it and save face. Everybody can see through your bias and the so-called research that you are conducting will lack credibility. It does not take a rocket scientist to figure out what your findings will be.*

*You are a fellow South African and we love you. Everybody makes a mistake. Bring your family back to this wonderful country, home of the Springboks, your home.*
NL - South Africa

∞

*I sometimes feel that the minute I mention that I'm leaving the country, I'm branded as a racist, whining traitor to the 'African Renaissance'. I like to think I'm a rational person who has looked at the situation, weighed the pros and cons, and decided that it is worth taking some risks and making some sacrifices to try and improve my long-term situation.*
MC - South Africa

∞ ∞ ∞

# 5

∞

# No, Mr. Mbeki,
# Telling the Truth is Not being Racist

*Terrorists and bullies,
whether in the form of governments or gangs or cults,
are responsible for making people leave.*
AMS - USA

The extra publicity generated another surge of correspondence and emails about the original article. There have been interesting emails, of a negative or pessimistic nature, and sometimes I had difficulty dealing with the anger that spewed over my keyboard via email. I've been called a 'racist' (yes, thank you, I have that T-shirt already), a white bitch, a coward and many variations on that theme. I've been invited to join the Freedom Front in order to preserve 'my nation'. (Uh, exactly which nation is that?) That response certainly provoked some interesting thoughts. How did the person in question decide that I would be in favour of such a movement? For every one correspondent who expressed anger, there have been fifty correspondents to counterbalance this; fifty people thanking me for expressing their feelings, for giving them a forum and for easing their pain.

After years of responding to the emails and correspondence generated by the original article, I decided that it was time to write the book, this book that you are reading. Once again I made contact with Angela

Quintal, of Independent Newspapers, to share the idea of the book with her. She suggested that I write a follow up to my original articles and give details of the forthcoming book. This article was published in April 2008, nationally in various South African newspapers. Here it is unedited as it appeared originally:

"I will always be split in two – did I make the right decision? And I will ever have a life that straddles the ocean – a foot on each continent. I will not ever be completely whole again." These were my words written in an article 4 years ago. I wrote of feelings personal to myself and my experience, never for a moment thinking it would trigger a deluge of emotion.

The passage is the most quoted by expats who correspond with me. It aptly communicates feelings that never leave them. A continuous stream of emails arrive weekly, from all over the world. The ebb and flow depends on the time of year and events on the political and economic stage. In 5 years, this has never stopped. Many describe their intense emotional upheaval upon leaving South Africa (and the experiences leading to their decision). They feel torn at 'having' to leave. Families are torn apart by their departure. Others remain in South Africa (and want to leave) but describe ambivalence - they ask for help and guidance with their decision. Their desire to leave is triggered by fear for their future.

Fear fuels most departures. The major fears are economic coupled with crime – many people have experienced violent crime or been touched by it in a myriad of ways. Families or friends who've been burgled, mugged, hijacked, raped or murdered - the stories flow on and on. They tell me that these days fences are higher, steel bars and safety doors have multiplied and are stronger and the criminals are becoming cleverer. Despite their precautions, people feel it's 'a matter of time' before crime will affect their family, and they want to stay ahead of the statistics. That is, of course, if the economic situation doesn't consume their life.

South Africa draws passionate responses from people. Students, tourists, businesspeople who've visited the country for short periods of time write about how deeply the visit affected them and, in some instances, changed their life. These people want to return.

Others write and thank me for changing the course of their life because they read my article and decided not to visit or live in South Africa. Do I feel good about that? No! That was not my intent. When I receive letters asking for information about visiting the country, I encourage them to go and experience South Africa. I explain that I haven't lived there in six years therefore I cannot give them advice about safety. I tell them that South Africa is a unique country and culture and they will fall in love with it.

The economy is also mentioned by most people - the economy and the prohibitive business and employment laws. They are drawn to the lifestyle, the scenery, the ambience and the culture. They want to live in and build businesses in South Africa, and contribute to the stability of the economy. However, the crime precludes this. Many people simply want a better future for their children.

Survival, prosperity and a need for safety are primal human needs. Once those are met, people turn their energies to other endeavours. Many correspondents would return to contribute to and bolster the economy, if they were assured of a safe, stable infrastructure and basic services. The irony of their perception is that South Africa is not a place where they can secure a 'better life' (the ANC's tagline, when I left, was 'a better life for all'). This is why they leave and do not come back. Since publication, the article has generated enormous controversy and correspondence.

President Mbeki drew further attention to the article by calling it 'racist' in his ANC newsletter in early October 2004. I responded via email and my response was published in national newspapers during that week. University students asked for permission to use it for various course submissions. A British man used it to file a motion against his ex-wife taking their daughter to live in South Africa.

Did I anticipate this? No! I didn't give it a moment's thought. I didn't intend to draw attention to myself or become an 'expert' on anything, I recounted my personal experiences and expressed my feelings as a woman, wife and mother. The article has blessed my life in that hundreds of people worldwide have made contact with me. Complete strangers have offered friendship and hospitality. If I began a world tour today and visited each person for a day, I would travel to every continent and it would take two years or more.

I decided to honour the avalanche of correspondence by collating it into a book, to be called 'Torn in the New SA'. This is my opportunity to give a voice to all the correspondents - the expats, the 'should I stay or should I go' people and those who adamantly refuse to leave. Many people have strong feelings and this is a chance to express their emotions about living, staying or leaving South Africa.

"There is not much talking now. A silence falls upon them all. This is no time to talk of hedges and fields, or the beauties of any country. Sadness and fear and hate, how they well up in the heart and mind, whenever one opens the pages of these messengers of doom. Cry for the broken tribe, for the law and the custom that is gone. Aye, and cry aloud for the man who is dead, for the woman and child bereaved. Cry, the beloved country, these things are not yet at an end. The sun pours down on the earth, on the lovely land that man cannot enjoy. He knows only the fear of his heart." (*Cry the Beloved Country* by Alan Paton.)

We cannot speak of the beauty of South Africa without contrasting the fear that it evoked in us. South Africa remains a part of us but our self-preservation instinct or neurosis, say some, outweighed our love for the country. It's easy to say we're racists or cowards, I call us survivalists. We are modern pioneers, forging a better life for our family in an uncertain world. Sadly, we have become the true 'Scatterlings of Africa' - a casualty of our heritage.

∞ ∞ ∞

*My father was a refugee from the Spanish Civil war in 1936 and was shipped to England. My husband's parents were in concentration camps (during the Nazi horror) but escaped to South Africa. We have 'escaped' to the USA. Does this make us any different from all those others who leave their countries to settle and survive elsewhere? Whether it is from Cuba, or Columbia or Korea or Vietnam or Ethiopia, or Russia or China or India or Pakistan, or Serbia etc, the list is endless. Terrorists and bullies, whether in the form of governments or gangs or cults, are responsible for making people leave.*

AMS - USA

∞

*As an immigrant into South Africa from the UK, of Polish descent, your article resounded with my spirit on many levels. My mother, in particular, was never settled here. She always longed for Poland her beloved, albeit ruined by World War 2, home country, longed to return yet saw the benefits of having left there, even though that wasn't really a choice then.*

*The sense of being split between two places is so real and displaced is a word that comes to mind. I wonder if it's more specifically pertinent to*

South Africans who have left or whether the same principles would apply universally? It is a topic that fascinates me and I will forward your article to all my overseas friends and see how they respond.

I believe in survivorship and in the face of reality think that anyone who leaves isn't racist in any way, merely a realist.

ARDR - South Africa

∞

I hope your story and many others will drive South Africa to find solutions to many of our problems and ultimately bring your likes back ashore. But with that I hope for people to be objective, as their subjectivity has caused many to believe that this country is filled with monsters and demonic humans, while there are wars going on worldwide, exploitation at its height and even more countries with worse crime issues that those of South Africa.

JZ - South Africa

∞

I found the article interesting and it really touched an inner part of me – my family and I are in the process of trying to decide on whether we should stay or whether we should go. A job offer in Brisbane beckons, but I am a South African, a patriot, and have all my family and friends here – I am rooted here. But the crime which has each year become a greater factor in our daily lives and the recent political developments and infrastructural meltdown are challenging the tenacity of those roots. I fear that I might decide to stay, but may regret this if my family or I become victim of violent crime in the future or if the ships sinks and the opportunities and door to Australia are no longer open.

I detest the opinions of some people who believe that I need to apologise for Apartheid and that I benefited from it because I am white – I have worked extremely hard for everything which I currently have, at one point having three jobs at the same time. I never voted for the National Party and therefore never supported apartheid – my first vote was for the referendum which gave the National Party government the mandate to put in motion the steps which led to our first democratic election.

I am a good person, as are my wife and two young children, and we have a lot of value to still add to South Africa. My wife's small business and our household provide employment for six black people, all who are paid way above the minimum wage, so there is no taking advantage of anyone. We helped our domestic buy a house in Zimbabwe. Yet the sentiment of the government and the citizens who cannot apply logic and rationality when opening their mouths in public or the press is that the white man is not needed or wanted here. If I leave, I will be seen as a racist – I like your term 'survivalist' a lot better!

AJVN - South Africa

∞

"I call us survivalists. We are modern pioneers, forging a better life for our family in an uncertain world. Sadly, we have become the true 'scatterlings of Africa' - a casualty of our heritage."

I am a white man (even though I despise that term) living in South Africa and I take great exception to the above paragraph. I never read your initial essay and so I cannot comment on that. You say you are a casualty of your heritage? What exactly in your heritage makes you a 'casualty'? My reading of white expats over the years has left me largely embarrassed that they represent South Africa. All I ever hear is complaints about the problems in South Africa which 'forced' them to leave. Crime is obviously the favourite topic. Every expat speaks passionately about how crime impacted them without ever making reference to the context of vast inequality that has spawned that crime. I never want to downplay the impact that crime has on people but we should never divorce ourselves from the context. It's a little known fact that there is a strong correlation between inequality and violence, and South Africa is one of the most unequal nations in the world.

And where does the wealth lie? Well, largely with white people – we the beneficiaries of injustice. I find it amazing that white people expect that life should just go on, that apartheid is a 'thing of the past'. Legally it is, but in every other way it is not. Many of those beneficiaries of injustice have packed up and left furthering the injustice – removing resources from this country that could have made a difference. I hate to say it, but whites by and large have done very little to right the wrongs of 350 years of oppression. This is not about guilt but about responsibility. Every white person, presently, has benefited from Apartheid, especially in education and access to opportunities.

And what about the crime that makes life difficult. Has it ever occurred to you that those most affected by crime are the ones least able to leave. Yes, it's the poor who have to deal with crime but they don't have the choice to leave. And every time someone with financial and other resources leaves this country, taking their wealth with them, means the battle for the poorest gets harder.

Please do not be deluded by referring to yourself as a 'survivalist' or a 'pioneer'. The grandmother in a township, who ensures, against the odds, that her children and grandchildren have food on the table, is a survivalist. A pioneer would be a person choosing to leave the suburbs and go to live in the townships or the rural areas. Virginia, USA, is hardly a place of survival and even less pioneering (perhaps 400 years ago but not now).

And lastly, it is entirely wrong to call yourself (and other expats) the 'Scatterlings of Africa'. Exactly at what point did someone force you out of your home, dump you in a place you don't want to be? Do you actually feel you can align yourself with all those people that were forcibly removed from their homes and land during apartheid? Or those across Africa who are forced to flee otherwise they die? Or an exile, forced out due to political oppression? You, and every other expat, made, and had, the choice to leave. That is the difference.

As a husband and father I can understand the desire to ensure the safety and security of your family. But then I don't live in fear – I am aware of the reality but it's not fear. And I am not torn in any way. Not only is South Africa my home but it's also the place to give back. To whom much has been given, much will be required. As a white person I was given much and so were you.

GS - South Africa

∞

I do not think (that is my opinion) that the approach that you are taking is helpful. We all have different feelings about crime but I don't think that they matter much as compared to action that could be taken by the majority of those concerned to deal with the crime issue. Although I also agree that the authorities have to take action to deal with this matter, I do not think that their action alone will help the situation. It has been said a lot of times that everyone who is concerned should come together and do something but up to this far, myself included, I do not think that we have done much. Most of our actions are a knee-jack reaction to a crime that happens and after that we keep quiet.

My other observation is that, I do not think that the perpetrators of criminal activities get to read about articles like yours on the Internet and many others because they do not use these mediums, so we are perhaps talking to ourselves. There should be a concerted effort to take this to grass roots level and communicate these messages constantly for everyone to hear because criminals do not stay in bushes but in communities and houses. In my view we are tarnishing the image of a country but are not dealing with the problem and the perpetrators.

Let me give you an example. If big corporations can adopt either two police stations or schools or some socio-economic development projects in local communities, the impact of these initiatives could go a long way in making sure we deal with this problem now and in the long term. In my township, Temba in Hammanskraal, there is virtually no resources for young people to engage in extramural activities like soccer, tennis, cricket, rugby and so on; there is nothing – so all that people can do is drink and idle and this breeds a lot of wrong thinking.

So big corporations (government to some extent) need to really play a major role in making sure that people are provided with alternatives so that they do not sit and do nothing and ultimately become involved in crime.

KL - South Africa

∞

South Africa is my home and I love it. Back in 1994 I also stood in the queue for six hours participating and voting in the first truly democratic election in South Africa. I was one of those in a high state of euphoria, going all out and giving it all to make our country a shining example to the world. I had 60 people reporting to me, mostly black, and doubled my efforts to 'uplift' them, etc. I took enormous pride in the country, as we were a role model for the world: Mandela was a world renowned statesman and a celebrity, we won the Rugby World Cup and the African Cup of Nations in Soccer, foreign stars were competing to perform in South Africa, the party seemed to carry on and on...

I then (1994-1999) trusted the 'old guard' of the ANC with being in charge of South Africa, to make things happen. Naturally there would be hiccups, mistakes and problems to be solved during the transformation process. But I was never going to leave South Africa as South Africa was going to be one African country that would make it. I even convinced 'L' to come and live in South Africa, as we were going to make our future here.

The real revolution in South Africa might not have come about yet. If you do not mind this observation, the white elite has been replaced by a black one, the latter having the handicap of being totally inexperienced and 'too busy to get rich, get rich, get rich' (quoted from a speech by Mr. Mbeki). The ANC government has failed the people of South Africa and foremost and especially the poor.

Our esteemed president is quick to act and condemn those that do not share his views (i.e. the axing of the then Deputy Minister of Health for publicly revealing the truth on child deaths in East London's Hospital). He is quick to publicly point fingers on perceived racism by white journalists, but is blind (by choice) to the vagaries of his old friend Mugabe, who is regularly committing crimes against humanity to the people of Zimbabwe. Having been ousted by Mr. Zuma as the ANC president, Mr. Mbeki turned out to be a lame duck president who will go down in history as a loser, which he does not entirely deserve. Mr. Zuma, again has an irritating problem to deal with, one that so far refuses to go away – a large range of charges of corruption and related crimes... This is our face to the world!

'Cry, the beloved country' is the expression that is continuously in my mind. I read this book for the first time as a young boy of 16 or so and was greatly moved by it. Today, 'cry, the beloved country' as an expression is as valid as it was then, albeit from a vastly different angle. What would Alan Paton and his fellow protestors say and or do, if they were still alive and well today? Or is it irrelevant, since their skins were white anyway?

JVD - South Africa

∞

You speak of crime as if it is the one thing that is happening in South Africa. Yes there is crime in South Africa as in any country and I am also concerned but that is no reason enough for one to leave a country and bad-mouth it to proportions that you and your like are doing. From what we know, most of the people who left the country are white and they do so for a host a reasons but in the main, motivated by racism.

Let me take you some years back. We have been subjected to the ruthless, inhumane and barbaric system of Apartheid by whites but we remained resilient and fought the monster until the end – we did not leave the country under false pretences. Most of you did nothing to speak or even write a two paragraph article denouncing apartheid and calling for it to end. Our people have been denied the basic human rights like education, skills, economic participation under the system perpetuated by your like but yet we still keep our heads up.

The media, which is owned by whites, continues to write negative things even though there are a lot of positives that could be written about this country. Racist actions by whites continue to be published as if whites have and are pushed to do them by blacks. If a crime happens to a white family it gets massive media attention but criminal activities to black families are either not published or published as a by-the-way attitude. A farmer dragged a Black family man with his bakkie (pick-up truck) for several kilometres and killed him and all that he got was a fine. A young farmer shot and killed a young child and said he thought it was a baboon and this was not frowned upon. A racist young white boy shot and killed three people in Skielik squatter camp and he was portrayed as being mentally disturbed and so on. There are just too many of these examples but you all choose to ignore them and think that everything will be fine and yet when someone shoots one of your family members you climb the mountain and make a whole lot of noise.

Crime cannot just happen by itself but is as a result of something. If whites treated blacks equally and made sure that we all benefited from the wealth of the country, I bet my bottom dollar things could have been much, much better. I am not saying crime is good but it is as a result of the 50+ years of humiliation, suffering, economic exclusion, marginalization and whole lot of factors. Crime, however small, is not wanted but this is not possible on this earth.

The other contrasting fact is that when you travel in South Africa one part of the street you find a black township with shacks, people suffering, high unemployment, not proper public transport and so on. On the other side of the street you find a suburb with big houses, big cars, wealth and you then think that the people on the other side of the road will not envy the other?

You complain that there are systems that are excluding white people but fail to indicate that you cannot leave things to sort themselves out but need policies (BEE and so on), which the current government has put in place, to try and redress the past imbalances. Blacks in this country remain economically disadvantaged and most of them remain unemployed. Whites still make up the majority of rich people and control the economy but you do not mention this. If you look at the economic landscape, the majority of CEOs and senior managers who earn massive pay-cheques are white. Young white people get employed very easy because jobs are reserved for them by their fathers/mothers and so on.

 I hope that you change your attitude and assist to contribute positively to this and any other country so that at least our grandchildren can lead a happy and prosperous life and remember, do not throw stones when you are also in a glass house. KL - South Africa

∞

 Your article summarised everything I feel at the moment. Never, never doubt that your decision was the correct one – and a brave one too. Unfortunately, there is no safe or viable future in this country for us or our children and realising this fact hurts greatly. NL - South Africa

∞ ∞ ∞

# Part 2

∞

# Loving

*I LOVE SOUTH AFRICA!*
*You'll have to scrape me off it with a spatula.*
*The sad reality is, as crazy as it sounds, it is possible.*

EJ (a proud South African) - South Africa

# 6

∞

## Born Into Love

### Introduction by James McIntosh

I was there, in the operating theatre, when my son was born and I was back there, in the same place, when my daughter was born. Both times I noticed the same interesting phenomena. Although the procedure of bringing babies into this world must have been old hat to the doctors and nurses present for the Caesarian births, they all seemed pretty pleased to welcome our babes. Could it be that most babies, even the so-called unwanted ones, are actually born into love? I do mean 'into love', not 'in love' or 'through love'. Hate comes later.

Hate comes later because fear comes later. Apparently[4], we are born with only two natural fears, namely the fear of falling and the fear of certain loud noises. All other fears are learned, mainly through our ability to imagine outcomes. Fear is really just pre-judgement. We are judging what has not yet happened. This is why fear is time-based, but never in the 'now'. If we are afraid of something, then it is because we are afraid that it could happen. If we are afraid of someone, then this fear is based on what we imagine they could do to harm us. If we are afraid of something that has already happened, then it is because we are afraid of the future consequences of what has already happened even if we are only afraid of feeling guilty or

---

[4] I say 'apparently' because how can psychologists and other researchers really know what a baby is feeling, thinking and already knowing?

remorseful. (Once something is happening, there is no time to be afraid; there is only time for what is happening.)

I am now old enough to have learned that fear is the opposite of love, because all hate is born out of fear. My childhood was relatively fearless. I say 'relatively fearless' because I did not really know fear until I left home to do my compulsory military service. That's when I was introduced to fear and to hate. The men with stripes on their arms and pips on their shoulders tried to make me fear the 'faceless black terrorists' and to hate them enough to want to kill them. Instead, I learned to fear and to hate anyone with a military rank.

I had been reborn – into fear and into hate. And like any of the 'reborn', I was ultimately filled with gratitude. But that gratitude came much later when I realized how the South African military had turned me into a pacifist. Like many young men, I had to first confront what I was *not* before I could see what I am.

Some countries do that to their citizens. No, that is not correct. Countries cannot do that; only governments can. Let me rephrase that sentence. Some *governments* do that to their people and the South Africa government back then was no exception. Sadly, many people today think that the South African government during the first decade of the 21$^{st}$ century was also no exception.

Even so, even then and even now, there was and is much to love about the *country* called South Africa. So let us start the telling by sharing love stories.

As throughout much of this book, the contributors to this section express strong emotions about South Africa and what they truly, deeply, madly love and miss about the country and its people. Included are a few letters which can be perceived as negative and hateful. These are added to this section called 'Loving' for a simple reason. Clearly, these 'negative' or 'hateful' emotions spring equally from a deep love of Mother South Africa. This 'love' is also intense, but merely expressed differently. If you catch yourself reacting to a perceived negative expression, please read between the lines.

Never forget that for far too long in the old South Africa certain 'types' of love could only be safely expressed 'between the lines'.

∞ ∞ ∞

# 7

∞

## Loving Cape Town

*I'd much rather live in South Africa than simply exist in another country.*
RP - South Africa

**M**y soul is steeped in memories of a past life in Cape Town. An elusive scent on the air captures my attention and I am there again....

I walk up Long Street at lunchtime, absorbing the smells, scents, odours of life around me – people, slightly sweaty, heady perfumes and the clean smell of cheap bath soap – restaurants, rich, freshly ground coffee beans, pizzas, curries, spices and the pavement vendors selling hot dogs and burgers. By lunchtime I am drooling with anticipation at the thought of those burgers with overcooked fried onions and salsa. I don't know, or care, about trans-fat contents – I look forward, each day, to my lunch hour when I can cross Long Street and buy a chunky, delicious, fresh-cooked burger from the vendor outside the BP Building.

The shouts from fruit sellers advertising their sweet peaches, and other fruit, "mooi perskes, mevrou, fresh vannie boom va'dag" glance off my eardrums. The sweet scent of real fruit and vegetables, displayed in their wooden boxes, fills the air. Interrupting this reverie are screams from a well-endowed African lady who, spotting a friend two blocks away, begins a cacophony of yells and accompanying gesticulations as their melodic conversation carries across the street. I don't understand any of the African languages – only a smattering of Xhosa – but their sounds roll fluidly through my ears and fill my senses.

This eccentric mixture of people – business suits, elegantly tailored men and women jostling students in leggings with short spiky hair; bright coloured yellow, green, black and orange of ethnic, cubist, doodled print dresses worn by mamas with wide-eyed babies strapped tightly to their backs – engulfs me. The slivers of long, narrow stores draw me into their dim interiors. Peering into the windows as I pass by, I make mental notes of items – pewter, silverware, vintage clothes, funky hairstylists, a new store with ethnic underwear – and places to visit. The stores entice me with the density of their wares, seen through vague, dusty windows. A thin, lanky man, wearing traditional Muslim dress and a fez, strides past us, as I mingle with the clusters of people wafting gaily up the road. This teeming circus of life and people is my memory of Africa.

I awaken to the sounds of the muezzin in the early hours of sunrise calling the faithful to prayers at the mosque, in Wynberg. Although unable to understand the words, the purity of the sound rouses me from a deep slumber and focuses my day. After a breakfast of thick Maltabella porridge with milk and sugar, it is time to catch a train to Cape Town. Before I reach the train station, I have to cross Station Road, and pass Station Café. The early morning air is not yet saturated with the oily scent of fried food. I make a mental note to stop on my way home for fish and 'slap chips' soaked in salt and vinegar – a deep, pungent, sour odour that is imbedded in my being. I cannot get my fill of the multi-cultural foods available at cafes and stores all along the Main Road. Freshly made, hot, bredies, bobotie and samoosas at the Cape Malay café's, and Russian sausages and chips at the Portuguese café, with home-made chocolate fudge, wrapped in plastic, jostling cash registers in every store.

> *I love my country, love the animals the smell of the land and the diversity.*
> PM - South Africa

A ubiquitous array of childhood foods – Fanta Orange; Milky Bar; Mrs. Balls chutney with cheese on Duens wholewheat bread; homemade Cornish pasties; dry, chewy, ostrich biltong; samoosas; bobotie; Safari fruit rolls and squares and mebos bought at the counter in OK Bazaars; guavas and guava juice and loquats from a tree in the garden filled my life. Snoek – a unique fish I've been unable to find elsewhere in the world – smoked and eaten as pate on biscuits. I'd buy snoek at the co-op in Riebeek West and bake it with garlic butter, apricot jam and herbs. The sublime flavour of Koo apricot jam. And piccalilli which helped me to digest many unpalatable childhood dinners. (If I could reach a critical mass point where the amount, and taste, of the piccalilli superceded the taste of the revolting food item, I could swallow anything.) Home made pickled onions. The delicious smell of boerewors roasting on the braai – the spicy, crunchy coriander, flavourful, taste of real boerewors sausages made by the local butcher.

At our house, no braai was ever complete without toasted cheese and tomato sandwiches grilled over the smouldering coals. I remember my mother making the sandwiches and tying them together with coloured thread. Twisting the threads around, she would wind them carefully around each side of the sandwich and tie a knot in the middle. All the sandwiches stacked and ready for the braai were lined up like miniature food parcels ready to go to the post office. We had to be careful and remember to remove the threads, before eating, otherwise they'd end between our teeth like a form of delicate dental floss.

> Twenty years down the track the other aspects that I now realize that I miss, include the lifestyle, the foods, the fauna and flora and the history.
> 
> JH - Australia

The taste of homemade rusks dunked in sweet coffee in the early hours of the morning making it a time to sit and 'kuier' (visit) with friends or family, a time to wake up and catch up. The smell of rusks left overnight to dry out in an oven set on low heat or if I'd been particularly lazy, it was a time to eat *Ouma's* rusks instead of home baked rusks. My husband, being raised in the Boland by a mother who made superlative rusks, is very particular about the recipe and the manner of drying. I've long since given up believing I could ever match the skills of my mother-in-law (may she rest in peace).

In my family, there was always much excitement centred around summertime cricket matches. Which team would play against us this summer? The Australians, driven, manic, fast – I would scrutinize the newspaper articles, reading information about their players, their techniques, their mental approach - or the West Indians, tall, dark and handsome, with a wicked sense of humour that underscored their dynamic tactics. Who would it be? At the end of my matric year, I spent six weeks studying a book about cricket – idiosyncrasies of the game; identifying various styles of play; strategies of team placement; scoring; learning methods and decisions behind every ball batted or bowled; and the umpire's call – so that I, with my wealth of knowledge, would be able to understand the game fully during the summertime matches against Australia. I discovered that I knew more about cricket than the boyfriend who I was trying so hard to impress.

Everything was experienced in a keener fashion. There was a

sharpness to my interactions and a sense of living on the edge. Africa is full of surprises, and my awareness was heightened and constant. Is that youth or is that memory?

These are all South Africa to me. The childhood memories are ingrained and although I cannot share them with anyone here, they are still a part of me, a glorious, colourful, kaleidoscope that lives inside. All my formative events have been supplanted, and those familiar places and experiences I had thought to share with my children one day can no longer be. My children have lost their African heritage and replaced it with a part of their future life. It is my responsibility to create a new heritage for them in a foreign land.

My external life is narrower these days. I live two hours from a beach. I don't experience a melting-pot of cultures in every facet of my daily life. I am inundated with the security and the efficiency of services of a first world country, but there is also rampant consumerism and emptiness. My children have no appreciation of the intensity, the diversity of people, and the pleasures of the land of their birth.

Here the magic is missing....

Africa provided the colour in my life. The people of South Africa are dynamic and vibrant and colourful. I don't see that here – I ask if I've really looked for it? Or is it simply that my heart hankers for home and, even if I found the vibrant dynamism, I wouldn't recognize it because nothing can replace memories of the colours and intensity of South Africa.

> But we South Africans are a tough lot, and will 'tolerate' all the negative things because we appreciate and love all the positively beautiful things in our beloved country!
>
> JB - Germany

There is magic in the air in South Africa. The climate, sunshine, are different – even the light is different. Many years ago, when I was working in Cape Town, a client from the UK, heir to a South African estate, was visiting the Mother City for the first time. As an amateur watercolourist, he told us that he was surprised to find that he had to buy a new set of watercolours after arrival, "… because somehow the light is brighter here and my paints cannot capture the depth and truth of the colours."

*The light is brighter there.* That sums it up.

∞ ∞ ∞

*Cape Town is one of the most gorgeous places I've ever visited. With such natural beauty and such warm people, it's too bad that there still is so much suffering and inequity.*  
BF - USA

∞

*My story: I was proud and excited to vote in the 1994 elections. A day which I imagine most South Africans who were present will never forget. Nelson Mandela seemed to give us such hope and upliftment that we all bought into the dream of the new South Africa and its rainbow nation. The dream of a united and happy nation really felt possible. We simply love living in Cape Town, it is such a magical place. It will be a very, very sad day when we have to go. I could write so much more...*  
RW - South Africa

∞

*Everything! The sounds, the sights, the feelings, the tastes, the smells, the aromas. The laughter, the camaraderie, the N1 that took my family and I to all of these! As a Cape Coloured, I miss the realisation of the part of Nelson Mandela's Inaugural speech that stated: "Never, never and never again shall it be that this beautiful land will again experience the oppression of one by another and suffer the indignity of being the skunk of the world. Let freedom reign."*  
ANJ - Australia

∞

*The weather (sun-dried clothes!), being able to communicate in your mother tongue, the wide open spaces, the smell of a suburban garden, and the unique mix of western and African traditions.*  
AM - Austria

∞

*I love this country, and I love its people. I also love the opportunities we have here. I am one of four children – four girls. All four of us have had the opportunity to pursue tertiary studies, three of us have graduated (two with masters' degrees) and my youngest sister is currently in her final year of law studies. There are many countries where women don't have these* opportunities. In addition, three of us have found employment (the youngest sister is a full time student, so she is not yet looking for employment). I am working in government, and despite being white, I have moved up six ranks in seven years. Only once did I apply for a promotion – the other times my position was upgraded based on performance.

CC - South Africa

∞

My wife has settled back here, feeling safer, but I fear that I never will, I have come to the conclusion that once Africa gets in your blood it never leaves. After experiencing the UK for five years I feel that there is a simplicity of life in South Africa that you can never find anywhere else, I don't know how to explain it, it's just a feeling that I have. I don't think that you can really appreciate anything until you have lost it and what I know now I would never have left South Africa.

I miss the times when as a pipeline inspector I worked in the bush miles from anywhere and seeing the incredible sunsets when travelling home, listening to the sounds of the night out in the bush when staying over, these memories I will carry forever and hopefully if I can make enough money here I will be able to spend summer in UK and winter in South Africa then life would be really great.

PM - UK

∞

What you didn't ask is what causes the passion. The opportunities... whether explored or unexplored. The beauty... The group of people (regardless of race) that really are pure and true. The beauty (again). The climate! Family, friends. What a country.

TB - South Africa

∞

As a Christian, I am grateful to my God that He has allowed me the awesome privilege of being born and raised in South Africa. I wish my children could have experienced the same. Not having to see the police vans chasing black mothers carrying babies on their backs, running away because they did not have a 'pass', not the Casper vehicles chasing us school children with teargas.

*But the thrill of standing on the Cape Town parade, taking in the sounds and sights, the majestic Table Mountain with its 'tablecloth' and standing tall after conquering the Platteklip Gorge, the Sunday drives through Stellenbosch, Wellington, Paarl, Ceres, the loud family laughter at get-togethers, the church worship services, the hawkers comical persuasions, the Ultra Shell stops along the N1 with steaming coffee as the day breaks, the waving, smiling farm children along the way, the distinct smells of the different regions and provinces, the eruption in the neighbourhood when we won the Rugby World Cup!*

*Back then, migration was what birds did! It seemed that it came naturally. I wonder if they ever felt the way I did! I hope not. Maybe one day, like them, I can return.*
ANJ - Australia

∞

*It's quite simply really, I love my country (it truly is beautiful), I love the African sun on my face (it is true that the sun feels different in Africa!), I love the people, I love my family and want to grow old with them, laugh with them, cry with them and at the end of the day I don't really know what to do. It feels like I am waiting for something bad to happen which will just push me over the edge and help me to make that final decision. I feel total powerless to stop what is happening to South Africa. The only power I do have is the decision I can take to stay or leave and even that is difficult.*
NJ - South Africa

∞

*I love my country, and nothing bad has ever happened to me, my family or anyone I know. I have lived in a number of countries and don't fit in anywhere. Nowhere seems to have the same culture as South Africa. I don't see a point in going somewhere else and being unhappy, with no real friends for the rest of my life, rather than just being a bit more vigilant and living at home.*
CV - South Africa

∞

*Crime is well and alive in any country. What South Africa offers you as an individual outweighs whatever negative thoughts you have about this* country. Start looking at the amount of tourist arrivals if you want to have a thorough look. You are missing out on your country of birth. Cape Town for instance was voted in the top five of places to see before you die...surely. Our weather/climates must be up there with the best... eight months of winter in Europe... snow and hurricanes in North America... AND YOU BLAME IT ON CRIME!

You (are) real(ly) pathetic. My blood is South African. And stop scaring people away from our shores. At the moment I don't want to be anywhere else in the world!

JH - South Africa

∞

I loved the way our kids grew up without nappies on in the garden and on our beaches. The way the kids go barefoot to the store. I loved the school uniforms. The accountability at school. One is able to identify kids from the uniforms they wear. And if they misbehave in public we know where they're from. They can get into trouble for behaving badly and get flak for it. I used to, when I was naughty in public, happened only once, but that was enough!

RG - USA

∞

An undying love for South Africa. Despite all the bad news, I love this country and the greater majority of its diverse peoples. The overwhelming sentiment when considering to leave South Africa permanently is one of immense sadness. (But noticing the ongoing deterioration around us leaves one immensely sad as well).

JVD - South Africa

∞

We simply love living here too much. We love the outdoor lifestyle, the weather, the friendly people, the unique sense of humour, the exciting cultural diversity, the excellent educational opportunities, and the fact that our kids can grow up playing in gardens and doing sport, not sitting in front of cartoons all day because of the terrible weather or the lack of physical activities available.

I lived in the US as a young child and felt isolated, cut off from my home, and picked on for being different. I experienced a huge degree of intolerance from other kids and their parents, and even from teachers. I never want my children to experience that. I love the fact that they are growing up in an open, mixed society, that they don't even see colour, and that they are willing to embrace new people and new experiences, but remain well-grounded in their own home and values.

Both my husband and I have jobs we enjoy, with excellent growth potential, and have a good lifestyle that we can afford. Our bond is nearly paid off, our kids are enjoying school and have lots of friends in the neighbourhood, and we are excited about the country's future despite the troubling crime statistics and economic hiccups such as the electricity crisis.

Why would we swap this for foreign shores, where we would have to start over with no friends, no professional reputation and a seriously stretched bank balance? The bottom line is that we are African to the core, and South African at heart. We just wouldn't feel at home anywhere else.

PH - South Africa

∞

I LOVE SOUTH AFRICA! You'll have to scrape me off it with a spatula. The sad reality is, as crazy as it sounds, it is possible. As my dad always says, "One of two things can happen. Either it could get better, or it could get worse." And it's been going on like this for 14 years now... If it gets any better, I'll stay; if it doesn't I'll stay too. If it gets a whole lot worse, I'll go, but if it doesn't I won't. I reckon that sums it up nicely.

EJ - South African

∞ ∞ ∞

# 8

∞

## Out Of Love[5]

### by Eve Hemming

The world's a strange place; a bit like a merry-go-round. People migrate from one land mass to another. It's connected to humanity's free will and desire to conquer or explore new territory. My ancestors landed on this continent from the Outer Hebrides of Scotland and a few missionaries from Prussia. And the merry-go-round continues to rotate, as sure as the Earth rotates around the sun.

I'm heading off on that jet plane. And no, it won't be easy.

I love the sensory evocation of Africa, the smell of rain on dusty earth and the piercing prehistoric timbre of those sycophantic hadedas. I love the bold autumn hues and crunching on frosty dry veld grass. I love waiting for a purple Jacaranda flower to drop on my windscreen while I'm driving and slowing down for cows in the road.

I love buying Wilson's toffees in a trading store and smelling the African-print fabric, the aromas of incense and pungent Durban curries, and the ornate oriental artifacts in the Indian markets. I love the thumping

---

[5] This piece was originally published on 12 May 2008 as *Leaving South Africa on a Jet Plane* in *The Witness*, a South African newspaper. It is used with permission and the new title was approved by the author.

sound of African music emanating from that car parked down the road and the prayer chants wafting across from a mosque. I love the banter of indigenous languages that flows like a song that I can't quite understand after all these years, yet that sound as familiar to me as a mother's bedtime lullaby.

I love the smell of a veld fire, of sizzling chops on a braai, the salty after-taste of biltong when my body has shouted for salt and the Sharks. I love the sounds of yacht stays tinkling in the wind along Midmar Dam's shore and the crack of melodramatic thunder after a humid day.

I love our memorable family holidays – watching a golden orb setting across a gorge of silhouetted thorn trees, gathering handfuls of pebbles and shells on a south coast beach, the sounds of the Indian Ocean singing in my head, camping and picnics, and wide-open spaces.

I love the sounds and vistas from my childhood – the soothing coos of a rock pigeon, the sandstone farmhouse architecture, my Free State clouds, windmills and koppies. It's strangely comforting to think that if other things change, they'll remain constant for billions of years.

Loving so much has enriched my life beyond measure. The staff and children I work with are embedded in my soul. And I love my own precious children and grandchildren; even those chaotically noisy family suppers at Spur with that rather dire Happy Birthday song.

Where I'm going there won't be any of this. Instead, there are volcanic craters, magnificent, but alien vistas, geological delights and long winters. There's the Treaty of Waitanga and a whole different political arena. And there's the All Black's haka.

Why am I going if there's so much I love here? Because, that's why. I love so many things from my rich life here, that I want to cherish them in my mind before they metamorph into something that's no longer precious or familiar to me. I want to explore a new chapter because life's transient and unpredictable. I can live with periods of no lights, with exasperating delays and even some disorder. But I can never condone the prevalent, heinous and inhumane criminality and violence.

People like me may be searching for a Nirvana that's non-existent. We're all born with free will, but not necessarily all with the opportunity to create change. I have the choice. It may lead to material impoverishment, but then some of us are dreamers.

Nothing will be able quite to replace the passions which are at the core of my psyche. No new acquaintances will be able to reminisce about the 'remember whens'. But there will be enticing new chapters. And despite currently waking up each morning feeling gutted, I'm enormously optimistic.

I feel a profundity of abundance in what I've tasted in South Africa and absolutely no one can ever take that away from me.

∞ ∞ ∞

*So why do I stay put (when I've already had two home robberies which have scarred me financially)? It simply evidences the depth of my love... my love of the people and my soul-enriching experiences in acting out Christ's commandment of love here. I am becoming fully human, I'm coming to understand ubuntu. I have discussed my 'selfishness' with my wife, and she consoles me by saying she wants to stay too. This despite the fact that two of our four children are 'expats' as well now, and she knows she will not be able to have the in-depth relationships with grandchildren which her Irish instincts require her to fulfill.*

PVZ - South Africa

∞

*I am so ambivalent about all of this, and really it would take something hectically serious, like a civil war to change my mind, and then I wonder. I am so African – and I so belong here with all the faults and ups and downs, Africa remains magical. It will take a lot more than a lot of greedy, unscrupulous people and politicians to destroy the energy which is Africa.*

JH - South Africa

∞

*It was hard to leave behind family of course. I had many, many great friends who I still miss. But I also find that I miss 'the country' in intangible ways that I hadn't expected, and that I only fully appreciated when I returned home to Port Elizabeth for the first time after being in America for three years. The smell of the ocean, the colour of the light, the diversity of people, the way that people in South Africa understand the value of life – the issues they deal with seem much more 'real' than most of the issues Americans worry about. I miss the South African sense of humour (American television commercials are, for the most part, rather poor quality –they often verge on insulting the intelligence). And I do miss the sport – I miss watching cricket and rugby on a regular basis. And the beer. I miss the beer. American beer is puny and tasteless. You can get imported beer quite easily, but nothing beats a fresh, ice-cold Windhoek lager on the Port Elizabeth beachfront.*

RS - USA

∞

*South Africa has excellent infrastructure, plenty of space, plenty of sun, low need for expensive winter heating, plenty of raw materials, low cost of housing - no need to triple gaze and insulate houses to European Standards. School/University for my sons was still disciplined enough for a decent education. University was less expensive than equivalent UK university and they are graduating free of debt.*

JT - South Africa

∞

*The economy has been slowly but steadily been growing, the government departments have become more efficient, crime is on the decrease, tax has been dropping for the last couple of years, small businesses has been helped and given an opportunity to grow, our infrastructure like roads has improved in the last ten years. Broadband internet is still not on world standards, but we are doing a lot better than the rest of Africa. Our banks and financial sector is on par if not better that the rest of the world. Ever tried to do a transfer to or from America? Our biggest problem in this country is the American culture that has infiltrated our way of thinking and the moral decay that goes with that.*

WV - South Africa

∞

*I do a lot of overseas travelling and every time I get back to South Africa I rejoice at being HOME! I have considered leaving the country and if it was not for my wife who is strongly opposed to such a move, I would have been long gone myself. Mind you, I probably also would have been back here as well. I have seen too many friends emigrate to places like Australia, New Zealand, USA and the UK, only to return here within 2-4 years. The bottom line is that once an African, always an African!*

*I am positive, I have to be, I have an 11 year old son. He loves the outdoors, sun, beaches and everything else we are known for over here. I cannot see myself trying to raise him in the UK!*

It's October now, the most beautiful month of the year in South Africa, everything in nature is still the same, flowers everywhere, trees turning green almost overnight and that distinct smell of spring in the air. I try to look beyond the politics and be thankful for all the blessings that no one can take away.

Once again, thank you for your insightful article, it was most inspiring and effective. I hope you will bring your children back here to experience the magic of Africa!

GW - South Africa

∞

South Africa is alive in a way that I have not found in another place. Living there was to share in something larger, something to do with imagination and spirit and the essence of life. I find this hard to explain – I believe most South Africans will know what I mean. There is something about the people and culture of South Africa that is missing in North America.

SP - Canada

∞

Fortunately I've not had crime experiences over there, I have only good memories. I remember a 12 years boy, every morning at the traffic light going to work: he was poor, he lived in a shack with the family, but every morning he had the smile upon his face and told me and my boyfriend something good that made me cry. We gave him clothes and some money before coming back to Italy.

CT - Italy

∞ ∞ ∞

# 9

∞

## Dancing With Dogs

*I would never have survived emotionally
as long as I did without my dogs.*
SVB - UK

"Cher-ma-ver-ma-gilla-ma" The noise reverberated off our hallway walls, resounding off the excellent acoustics created by the 15 foot high ceiling, and echoed strangely like some ancient Celtic chant. This solemn intonation set off an equally loud, slightly hysterical howling.

"Ahr-Ahr-Ahr-ooooooooooooooo."

Keeping a balance between the two opposing musical ranges was more than my nerves could withstand.

"Bracken! Enough!"

A downcast look quelled my angry tone. He paused for breath.

"Sorry, I know you're channelling your wolfhound. Come! Outside!"

His musical appreciation extended through some of the Chieftains' other tracks (his wolfhound again) into Bruce Springsteen. I'd like to think he was a musical dog but actually I think the harmonica hurt his ears. He never reacted to classical, strings or any other type of music. Also, he never seemed to care much for the great European operas, but then my husband doesn't either (so that couldn't be counted against him).

Music first made an impression on him, at the age of eight weeks, when we danced the *Tennessee Waltz* (the Chieftains again) together. Well, danced, yes, sort of....

James and I were painting the guest bedroom a pale peach colour. A labour of love in our first home and the first thing we had tackled together. The puppies gambolled around our feet. Bracken and Rebecca (named after the characters in *Duncton Wood* by William Horwood) were large boisterous balls of fur and fun. The Tennessee Waltz began to play. I descended from my ladder and lifted Bracken off his feet. Clasping him close to my breast, his head on my shoulder, I began to sing to him as I waltzed him around the room. Nothing from him except little sighs of satisfaction.

It was at that moment that our hearts connected and we found love!

Dogs do love us unconditionally, despite our faults. Just like people, some of them love us more than they should and more than is good for either. Bracken and Rebecca grew into large, black Belgian Shepherds (Terveuren), long-haired, so there was always hair flying around and they needed shearing, much like the sheep in a neighbouring field, once a year in the summertime. Their stately commanding presence when closeted under a rich, dark, luscious black fur coat was overwhelming. Indeed, it evoked fear in many – much like those who cower in the presence of the ancient matriarch in her fur coat with her aura of wealth and power.

As soon as the heavy fur coat was shorn, leaving a light, breezy buzz cut, Bracken lost his regal bearing and presence (possibly also sheared off) and began to skip, hop and scamper around like a lamb in Spring – which just goes to show that one should never wear fur because it suppresses your natural spirit and exuberance.

Many locals were afraid of the dogs because of their fearful barking whenever anyone walked past our property. The dogs often chased one another to the fence, a game they never tired of and the loser would proceed to maniacally 'attack' the winner. To the uninitiated, this looked fearsome and gave them a certain 'rep' in the village. Our neighbour used 'day parole' prisoners from the tronk (jail) in Riebeek West. He supervised them while they worked a vegetable plot on our property. Usually, two gentlemen in green prison outfits worked for him and he would return them to the prison at night. One day, the one convict was heard to remark to the other about our large black dogs, "Djy wiet, ek sal never hier inbreek nie, want tjy klim nog oor die draad dan byt iets jou eit die donker en djy sallie eers sien wat dit issie!" (You know, I will never break in here because you will still be climbing over the fence when something will bite you out of the darkness and you will not even see what it is!")

I digress.

Bracken felt strongly about his role as my 'second husband' and, due to his natural herding instinct, would take a visual cue from my handbag and keys and frantically try to head me off and keep me away from the car. Anywhere but the car! Little nips on my buttocks and short, frantic barks seemed to indicate a much smaller dog of nervous disposition. Not this awe-inspiring lion of a dog who was now behaving like a 'stoepkakkertjie'.[6]

It soon became obvious that at times of great stress or upset in his life, Bracken reverted to this series of high-pitched, silly little barks that would be embarrassing if they weren't so amusing. This unusual and quirky characteristic would one day save his life and allow me to say a precious goodbye to him before I left the country.

Each morning, James would leave early for work. At the sound of the back door closing, Bracken would jump onto the bed beside me, put his head onto James's pillow and then, turning onto his side, he would sigh loudly, put his paw across me and begin to snore.

In America, many pets are treated simply as beloved family members. They are cosseted and pandered to much like children. To these owners, the idea that their little 'coochie' would be expected to protect them or to save their life, is a concept that is totally foreign to their experience. After all when your little mutt (pure-bred or not) has cost you $250 or more; wears a rhinestone studded collar; wears a winter jacket while walking in the rain; owns a bowl personalised with his name; a goose-down bed and has his own photo immortalized on a Christmas tree ornament, it's hard to believe he may ever be able to summon the courage to attack on command.

Once, sitting at a traffic light, I saw a car with a license plate which read "PETRUB". I often amuse myself trying to decipher licenses, so I thought *Hmmm, maybe her name is Petru B, or her initials are P E and her surname begins with Trub, perhaps it's a shortened name PET (like Peter) and surname RUB (like Rubel or similar)*. As the car accelerated, she drove past me and the graphics on the driver's door read, "Pet Massage" and I began to laugh at the thought of paying someone to massage my dogs.

Bracken and his sister, Rebecca were our first babies. And yet, from

---

[6] An Afrikaans word that, basically translated, means 'small thing that defecates on the verandah'. We used the word 'stoepkakkertjie' disparagingly and so often in America to describe small dog breeds that my daughter believes that there is actually a real breed called Stoepkakkertjie. She will point indiscriminately at small dogs who are yapping and say, "Look, Mom, a stoepkakkertjie!"

the beginning, these babies loved us with a ferocious intensity that kept us safe. Bracken and Rebecca might have a range of endearing behaviours like cuddling up to me in bed, nudging my son to drop dinnertime snacks or dragging items of baby clothing outdoors but, we knew, were we ever threatened, they would tear the throat of anyone who intended to harm us. Bracken and Rebecca were family by birth, mates by chance and an early warning system by design.

They were our beloved pets and our family, but they were also our chosen alarm, our guard dogs. I think that if a cosseted American dog ever visits South Africa, he may need his own South African pet for security. After all, that rhinestone collar would look very appealing.

∞ ∞ ∞

I will, however, NEVER be without a large, and fierce looking dog, as this acts as a primary deterrent for would-be criminals who, often, it seems will choose a softer target. I also keep my dogs indoors at all times – they go out into the garden when I am home – otherwise they remain indoors.

JH - South Africa

∞

Besides my direct family I miss all my old friends and my dogs, which are with our youngest son and wife. I miss the African bush terribly and the kopjes of the South African countryside and without sounding irresponsible, I miss traveling faster than the 100 kph allowed here in Australia especially as the road users are FAR MORE safety conscious.

BH - Australia

∞ ∞ ∞

# 10

∞

# I Miss

by Michelle Leech

I miss the first summer rains, where the day had been HOT and the smell of dust so familiar that we don't even know it's there. Then thick, heavy clouds roll in, the promise of rain finally realized. After the rains, standing on the stoep and breathing air so sweet and new.

I miss the thundershowers. Lightning lighting up the windows and thunder so loud it seems to shake the very foundations of the house. So awesome and powerful, yet what could be better?

I miss actually liking the rain! It was a satisfying interlude to the magnificent hot days, not an unending torrent that freezes you to the bone while your family in South Africa is posting photos of their beach holiday on Facebook. Ouch!

I miss buying mielies off the side of the road from a smiling lady whose baby sleeps nestled to her back.

I miss the sunsets over the grasslands, huge and colourful, like an artist's paint set tipped over and smeared by the hands of a child.

I miss the culture mix. The fact that so many different people, cultures and languages converge to provide something I am only now starting to appreciate, now faced with the blandness of some others.

I miss the game parks, water parks, theme parks.

I miss waking up ridiculously early in the morning and driving to Pilanesberg for our wedding anniversary. We stayed for the day and drove home in darkness – a perfect day of game viewing. Or we stayed for a week, a braai for dinner on our warmly lit stoep, looking out into the absolute blackness of the night. Listening to the sounds of Africa – the sounds of LIFE. Tingles down our spine... imagining what is out there in the darkness. What hides just a kilometre away? What hides just 10 metres away?

I miss the impossible beauty that is the setting for a life so real. Harsh sometimes, or even a lot of the time. But always the smiles. Bright eyes full of stories, eager to open up their lives to you. Feeling truly welcome.

The unbelievable sense of hope, and friendliness as well.

How is it possible for a land that has felt so much pain to go on in all its splendour, always striving for a better future? For a new tomorrow?

I miss the amazing people.

I miss my family. I miss so much...

In 10 years time I want to be home. A piece of land in South Africa where I can show my son the land of his birth. Where my family can gather to tell stories of our adventures over the oceans, and the new ones we will make. Watching the sun set over the distant hills. Peace. Quiet. The stillness of the night punctuated by the thousand wild creatures preparing... for bed, for the hunt... the birds settling in, the insects... the call of the jackal....

∞ ∞ ∞

The friends, the braaivleis, the rugby on Saturday. Castle and Mrs. Balls. Biltong. Going to Grandma's for Sunday lunch after church. Driving to Margate for vacation. I miss everything. There isn't just one thing. It was my whole world.

LRK - USA

∞

The landscape was hard to leave behind – I loved the Berg and the Natal coast and the veld and the Magaliesburg gorges and the Maluti Mountains and the rain and thunderstorms in Jo'burg on summer afternoons and the jacarandas – all of that.

I loved Yeoville and Hillbrow and Berea, and Parkview and the Melville Koppies and the Bird Sanctuary and Emmarentia Dam, and the Jan Smuts farm at Irene and the Easter cosmos and the mimosa trees and the dawn chorus of birds and the enormous and ever-present insect life of the evenings in a campsite.

And a few people tugged at my heartstrings – friends I'd made in Pietermaritzburg, old friends in Johannesburg and Cape Town. People have T-I-I-I-M-E in South Africa... so you can have friends in a way which is impossible here in the USA. There is all that life in the gardens and on the land – braais, and holidays by the sea, and in the mountains, and the naked physical impact of the weather – all that lightning and downpours, and unexpected snow, and wind and rainbows and hot sun. Despite the snakes, the South African natural world is much friendlier to man, more nurturing and welcoming and cocooning, than the American wilderness – no poison ivy, for one!

And on the streets at home there's life, a buzz, friendliness, warmth, helpfulness. One can share a joke; people aren't paranoid about contact with 'strangers.'

Being (a little) poor in South Africa can be an art form as well as a challenge – it can challenge one's creativity; (one) is at liberty to make much of little – a unique self can be expressed in the arrangement of a bunch of grasses and some home-made batik and a rickety chair and a box in a hot corner in the winter sunshine, with a mangy cat and dusty kikuyu grass and a commune of friends and some cheap red wine. An entire microcosm which costs almost nothing.                                                KW - USA

∞

Taking the N1 and driving for hours towards a little town for some peace and quiet. A place like McGregor. Or Prince Albert. Going wine tasting on off-the-beaten-track locations like Slanghoek (Worcester) or Jacaranda (Wellington) where you can also savour some cheese (from a single cow) or olives (from a single olive tree). Sunset on Llandudno beach. Lunch at Hout Bay Harbour. Dinner at Gordons Bay while the sun is setting.

But what I miss most is our people. Despite reasons to complain, many South Africans still manage to smile. And laugh. I think it has got something to do with coming from Africa. We just cope with life better than so many other nations.

    Biltong. A good braai. And a good argument over which wood creates the best coals. The smell of grass after rain. Seeing your children play in snow (Ceres). Being able to just visit friends or family within a few minutes... now it takes multiple connection flights...

    Ten years from now I want to sit on my stoep in the middle of nowhere in South Africa, once again finding peace in the simple things of life.

PM - Kuwait

∞

    There is so much that we miss - mountains, sea, the people, the Karoo, lazy afternoon lunches at a wine-farm, water-holes on a game-farm, solid work-ethics and competent staff... too long a list to dwell on. We have been all over the world in our travels – from uninhabited tropical islands to huge cities with 24/7 action – and no matter what beauty we find in all these places I find it is always tempered and sometimes blocked by memories of Africa.

BM - UAE

∞

    I miss the above-freezing temperatures, the howling winds and the rain of winter in the Cape. I miss being able to work in my sodden garden, laughing while bogged down in the mud. I miss the wonderful array of foods with no corn syrup added. The fish and chips and fried calamari at the Portuguese café in Malmesbury. The sandwich lady visiting our office every morning with a trolley laden with goodies for sale. Chewy, dried ostrich biltong with coriander seeds. Babies raised with a piece of biltong for teething. Droewors. Holidays in Hermanus and windsurfing on the lagoon. Meeting friends for tea. Sandwiches with cheese and Mrs Balls Chutney eaten at the beach, sand included free of charge. Nibbling on Safari fruit rolls. The squirrels in Cape Town Gardens and climbing onto the lions at Rhodes Memorial. I miss watching the thick gray cloud tumbling over Table Mountain like a tidal wave. Family picnics at Camphill Village market in Kalbaskraal.

    Old-fashioned glossy verandahs painted green, black, burgundy and polished till they shine. Hours of vicarious shopping in Greenmarket Square and the Grand Parade, and buying fabric at the Oriental Plaza in Cape Town. The scent of the Peace roses in my grandfather's garden. Wholewheat bread soaked with Lyle's Golden Syrup. Nothing matches the taste of Smarties and Chomp and Crunchies and Caramello Bears and Bar One chocolates. Choc 99 soft serve ice-creams with Flake in the middle. Playing board games with friends. Hanepoot and Jerepigo and South African Port and Old Brown Sherry, of course. Dettol and Vim.

I miss the eccentricities of a small town life. The rich Afrikaans accent and humour of people of the Swartland. Being proud of our local produce when buying fruit and vegetables from the farms and wines at the local cellars. Piet-My-Vrou. 'Kinders van die Wind'. The donkey 'Gringo' waking us with his early morning braying. The tantalizing smell of homemade rusks drying overnight in the oven.

I had to tap into these memories because I don't allow myself to think about them too much any more. A crazy mixture of thoughts and sensations which are lost to me somehow. And yet, there is a richness to these memories, to having had the joys of that life imprinted on me. An intensity of pleasure that cannot be removed by time. BM - USA

∞

What we miss about South Africa is, Biltong, boerewors and a good old Sunday Braai. SOR - UK

∞

What do you miss the most about life in South Africa? OUTDOORS, WEATHER, FUN PEOPLE, our humour! – just the relaxed way we live even with imminent danger around us. People sweat the small insignificant and inconsequential things here! LS - The Netherlands

∞

I think the most difficult thing for me was to leave the open spaces, and way of life. All our friends are in South Africa, after all these years in the UK we have not made any friends here. I miss my house, I miss knowing that the sun will shine, probably, all day, I miss seeing the Sharks at Kings Park, I miss the freedom of the road, the fact that traffic is nothing, compared to the UK. I miss my guns! My wife misses the house, but also her sisters and their families, our nieces and nephew, and all our old friends and colleagues. And, of course Maria, our maid, who did the BEST ironing!

I could write a book, not a paragraph. I miss the weather, obviously, the laid-back way of life, our friends, our dog, great beer, the vistas, the open fire in winter, our air-conditioned bedroom in summer, better stop now before I get too maudlin.

DH - UK

∞

Those stunning Highveld storms... meat cooked over a real braai, instead of these ridiculous gas-powered barbecues that seem to be a staple in Canadian back yards... Hunters Gold... Ouma rusks... the diverse scenery – the Karoo, Table Mountain, the Drakensberg, the big ocean waves... good dentistry (Canadian dentists – not great)... my Mom... Christmas dinner eaten at tables in the garden on a warm sunny day.

KJ - Canada

∞

'Family' get-togethers over long-weekends like Easter and Christmas-New Year. And of course, biltong and koeksusters!

SK - Ireland

∞

What do you miss the most about life in South Africa? Almost everything except the crime. It would be a hard choice but I suppose a good bottle of Roodeberg, a roaring fire in the hearth and a North-Westerly gale lashing the windows while we look out onto a raging sea after a lunch of kreef followed by Karoo lamb would probably rate right up there with a bushveld braai or a Drakensberg hike.

BM - United Arab Emirates

∞

Table Mountain, in the shadow of which I lived (joyfully for at least 20 years), and the sound and smell of the ocean that wafted through my (barred) windows every night; climbing Lion's Head and Table Mountain, grilled calamari at the waterfront. I would miss South African humour, kindly black faces, our accents (which I used to hate), if I didn't have my girls and their families, lots of new South African friends (including black ones), wonderful new American friends and fairly stimulating work to sustain me.

That said, I have a seemingly subconscious internal remembrance of my life in South Africa, good and bad, that plays out in my head, in my mind's eye, almost constantly. It's extremely painful. I probably have post-traumatic-stress-disorder.

EN - USA

∞

What I miss most about South Africa are my friends, my family, the familiarity, gas station pies, pools, braais, sunshine and Blacklabel. *sigh*

CS - USA

∞

I miss the 'popping' sound of opening a can of 'green' Cream Soda – and enjoying the best smelling cold drink in the world! I miss making balls out of putu pap (crumbly porridge) and dipping them into tomato and onion gravy with my fingers! I miss singing Shosholoza at a rugby game and getting tears in my eyes when my team runs onto the field.

TR - USA

∞

(I miss) so much. Other than friends and family. The blue of the sky, the scenery (Table Mountain), the people, the lifestyle.

CL - UK

∞

I miss so many things that the list may be long, but here goes... My Mom, my friends, my beautiful farm, my children running on the grass in open spaces on our farm and enjoying the rural life, my wonderful house-keeper who I still correspond with, Woolworths, the gorgeous vines in the afternoon light, the mountains, Table Mountain and the tablecloth falling over it, knowing and being familiar with the layout of the city, the roads, shops, doctor, dentist etc, as well as knowing where other places in my country are, the familiarity that you have when you were born in a country and know things about it that strangers don't, the sunsets over the sea in

Camps Bay, Primi Piatti, the colourful way that the coloured people talk and laugh (they have an amazing sense of humour), the wonderful interactions that one could have with black people, who are so interesting in their true cultural surrounds.

DM - Australia

∞

The empty beaches. Sailing or surfing in the afternoons after work. The beautiful people. Sitting around an afternoon braai with my old friends chatting about life in general. Kirstenbosch summer concerts with friends on a beautiful evening. Camps Bay sundowners. Driving from Camps Bay to Hout Bay. Lazy summer afternoons reading a book and watching the ships in Table Bay harbour. Lots....

AP - UK

∞

I will not miss my electric fence, the armed guard who patrols the property with a shotgun every night, the burglar alarm in my house, the bars on my windows, the fear of strange noises, locking the car doors and watching every intersection, hiding my handbag when I get into the car, not going out at night, avoiding hijack hot spots, crossing the road to avoid groups of strangers, not being able to carry cash, checking my driveway before leaving for work and before pulling in when arriving home, power cuts on a regular basis, stories of sewerage polluting our rivers and seas because of lack of maintenance and systems, water shortage threats because of lack of system maintenance and planning, fear that my children will not be able to get educational training and jobs they want due to their skin colour, knowing that my husband cannot get a job at a corporation as he does not fit the 'BEE' profile, the list is very long....

CH - South Africa

∞ ∞ ∞

## 11

∞

## Two Oceans

*I'm completely torn in two.*
TH - UK

**M**y sister and I would catch a train to Fish Hoek over the weekends – our Styrofoam boogie boards clasped close to our chests. Early on a Saturday morning, we'd walk to Wynberg station and catch the train. Wittebome; Plumstead; Steurhof; Diep Rivier; Heathfield; Retreat; Steenberg; Lakeside; False Bay – the names were a poetical backdrop as we chatted about school and, lulled by the clack-clack of the wheels, looked out of the window. Being early, we could always find a window seat before the train filled up with people at a station closer to the beaches.

Approaching Muizenberg station, the funny rows of old-fashioned, red, blue and green changing rooms, dotting the landscape like small beach houses, indicated that we had reached the coastline. We laughed and watched the sea water lapping the rocks, below the tracks, as we rode past Muizenberg, Kalk Bay, St. James and finally, rounded the bay, into Fish Hoek. We never worried about time and had no cellphones.

In those days, my fears revolved around the Great White sharks that occasionally terrorized the swimmers at Fish Hoek. I'd remember my father – a perlemoen diver in his youth – telling us about 'the Submarine' – the shark feared by all divers and swimmers. From the mountain slopes, he said, you could see the dark shape of 'The Submarine' cruising the area. It was said that he was 20 feet long. Once, just once, I was on my styrofoam board, in the sea at Fish Hoek – fairly far out, by my standards – when the alarm bell rang from shore to signal the presence of a shark in the area. Although there was not a wave in sight, I made my way back to shore in double quick time and prayed all the way.

Most of our male friends were surfers – clad in board shorts and cut off tees with envious tans and sun bleached hair – who hitched lifts, during the weekends, all over the coastline to catch the 'Wave of the Day'. It seemed that most of us had boyfriends who were constantly missing in action because, at that time, surfing surpassed the attractions of teenage girls. Sandy Bay was the beach where people tanned naked; Llandudno was the beach where my friends and I tanned topless in our teen years; Clifton was the place where you could never find parking and Noordhoek was the beach that you could walk on forever. Frequent visits to St. James Beach, with its array of rock pools, allowed me to spend hours refining my technique for catching rock fish – creating small tidal pools of my own with sand to trap them – only to release them later.

I spent a brief week in Donkergat, near Langebaan, with a schoolfriend, when I was eight years old. Each morning we'd awaken early, in the old whitewashed beach cottage on the shore, and race one another to the rock pools. We were intent on catching the tiny fish trapped in the pools by the waning tide. Carol, my friend, taught me to make 'bokkems'. This unique and interesting name means 'small, dried, salty, fish' – at least to me, it does. We caught the fishes, strung them, salted them, and then pegged them up onto the washing line to dry out in the summer heat of early December. A couple of days later, we simply unpegged the dried fish and ate them, crunching our way through their whitened flesh and bones, shriveled eyes and crisp innards. They were a rarity for me - unique cuisine, a form of fish biltong - and a taste still unsurpassed today. In later years, driving through the Cape Flats after visiting the beach with my parents, we'd drive past a bakkie and the fishermen selling fresh snoek and bokkems strung together in bundles – a strange, cured, brown shade of dried fish – and I'd remember Donkergat, and gag. The headiness of summertime, salt water, heat, freedom and youth combined to make everything an adventure. Sensations were heightened in such a space in time.

Water and the ocean were a formative part of my life.

Summertime, in the USA, has found us visiting up and down the coast of Virginia and North Carolina. Despite having viewed the Atlantic Ocean from a number of angles now, it always looks the same to me. However, being on the other side of the world, the Atlantic is no longer simply an ocean. It has begun to represent homesickness. My homesickness as defined by a large body of water.

In our first year at the beach on Chincoteague Island, we excitedly told the children, "Look! Look! Look at the ocean. Somewhere on the other side of the world, that same ocean is touching the shores of Cape Town, thousands of miles away." They looked distractedly for 10 seconds, graced us with their smiles and then dived onto their boards and back into the Atlantic.

I meandered along a beach in North Carolina during summer last year, picking up broken shells because the colours resonated with me – orange, purple, yellow, cream, red, brown, pink, grey, black and white. Glorious seashells, rolling ashore and dripping with colours as the water washed over them. And yet, removing them from the beach, they became vague pastels lacking depth or intensity of colour. Once removed from the water, they lost their lustre.

I wonder if that is how it is with me? I live two hours from a beach and I walk on the seashore, and swim in the sea, once a year for a week. Each year, I've tried to overcome my desperate desire to see that water again. I'd like us to visit somewhere else during the summer and see other areas of this huge country. I can't. Once a year I can clear my head and my energy and walk the unyielding sands for hours. And then it's over for another 12 months.

∞ ∞ ∞

*What is the plus side? The plus side is that across the board there are the most amazing people in this country – hopefully sufficient to counteract the effects of the new passengers on the gravy train – those who are making some of the most unbelievable decisions.*

*We have flora and fauna which is to be found nowhere else in the world, and we have amazing small towns where, in some cases (albeit very few) the old moral values apply - where people count and not the size of the bank balance, and where helping your neighbour is part and parcel of every day life and does not even warrant a comment beyond a simple: thank you.*

*We have Africa – which those who have been born here recognize as some indefinable something - you are forever African no matter where you live. Africa is a life force, it is a feeling, it is an energy, it is multifaceted, it is amazing.*

JH - South Africa

∞

*Coming Home Revolution played a major role in my return (which may be permanent or temporary– only been five months). My reasons: Having fun, I was time-poor overseas whereas now I can live it up and have loads of spare time to enjoy my youth. I couldn't identify with the Aussies and couldn't think of marrying one.*

GJ - South Africa

∞

*I love South Africa, I love its people. However, like you and countless others I have no desire to leave, but yet feel pushed to make the right decision and go away.*

*I commenced work in 1993 and so have not only lived through the Apartheid system as a child, but also worked as an adult through the reconciliation period from then and up until current date. It has been a unique experience to see borders between people come down, but has been negated by the walls that have gone up by all to protect against the rampant crime.*

*I have travelled to the UK for a month in 1997, have seen my relatives and instead I longed to return home to Cape Town. With my British passport by virtue of birth, I could have gone to live and work abroad many years ago. Clearly, South Africa is where I want to be. This country, it's people, both magnificent.*

*I believed I could make a difference by living out my life in South Africa (I am now 35 years old). I did not have a wealthy upbringing, but did manage to pay for my studies to become an accountant. I realise that with these skills I will comfortably find work abroad. Yet, I wish to stay in the RSA.*

*However, when I know of not one family member or friend who has not experienced crime and have no hope of things improving, surely I need to use logic and protect my family's future. Even if crime (I have left out all the other bad performers; Health, Education, Public Works, HIV Aids, the*

Defence Force, Housing, Social Welfare, Border Control, Zimbabwe) remains the same and does not get any worse, it would be madness to stay here among it all. However, I don't even see it remaining the same, just getting worse.

I wish you all the best and thank you for standing up for what is right and good about fellow humans caring about fellow humans. Anybody who still thinks complaining is about race or prejudice is blinded by the past injustices.

AW - South Africa

∞

What else has stopped us leaving? Braais, biltong, Mrs Balls, Ghost Pops, fresh calamari on the beach at Hout Bay, the smell of the air on the Tsitsikamma coast, the sight of Table Mountain viewed from our bedroom window each morning... And of course our family. Skype is not the same as a two hour flight to be with them when you're needed. We lost a young family member a year or so ago and at least we had the comfort of all being together and being able to support each other in person, not via email.

PH - South Africa

∞

It is heaven just to go out with our friends and the rangers on those great big game vehicles for game drives and to watch the game running wild and to stare in wonder at our beautiful African sunsets.

LT - South Africa

∞ ∞ ∞

# 12

∞

# F**k You, Emigrant[7]

## by Rob Dickens

All it takes for evil to prevail is for good men to do nothing.[8] I come across as a judgmental patriotic fundamentalist with an optimistic streak that would make both Gandhi and Mandela give me a slow clap. I come down on emigrants with great vengeance and furious anger. I judge them. It's a very sensitive subject because you touch on a nerve. You know that they have that niggling guilt. That's why they spring to their own defence like a tigress defending her young. They must justify their decisions, lest that niggling doubt become more than just a niggle. It's tough to leave your home. Really tough. It's a hard slog. A challenge and once met it can seem like a great decision.

A great personal decision that will benefit your life, perhaps your family's life too. You feel safe and comfortable, and you believe your family

---

[7] Originally published on his blog on mydigitallife.co.za - 22 February 2008. Used with permission. According to Rob, he wrote this piece "as an impromptu diatribe against the pervasive Afro-pessimism that plagues his beloved South Africa, but more so against the confirmation bias of your typical ex-pat. Psychologically, they must justify their reasons for leaving the place of their birth...unfortunately, this breeds a cancerous cynicism. Viva Mzansi, Viva!"

[8] The original quote is by Edmund Burke, a 19th century English political philosopher: *All that is necessary for evil to triumph is for good men to do nothing.*

to be safe and comfortable. And who the fuck is Dickens to fucking judge that decision? How the fuck can this asshole begrudge anyone the freedom to choose their own comfort level in life? What a plonker.

On an individual level you'd be right. I should not begrudge people a decision like that. They are free to do what they want. But I don't think on such personal levels alone. To me, I always, always see a bigger picture. Much larger than you or I, or my family and yours. Perhaps I start looking at a picture that is the size of South Africa. My home, all of its people. Hell, it's a microcosm of the developing world. It's a microcosm of every single battle that humanity has ever had to face: economically, socially, philosophically, religiously, politically. We have it all. A daily battle to prove that the evils of this world can and will succumb to the power of good.

All it takes for evil to prevail is for good men to do nothing. Worse still is turn your back and leave. This is bigger than just you and me. This is bigger than your family and mine. This is bigger than South Africa. This is humanity. The war wages between what is considered good and what is considered evil. This country is the frontline of that battle. History and fate have determined that this is where we bunker down. The Rainbow Nation, a melting pot of cultures. The foremost African nation. The chance to prove ourselves. The opportunity to be a part of history. To write it. To stare down the seemingly insurmountable challenges and succeed.

What a grand opportunity? Amazing. A gift really. An opportunity to literally be a part of history in the making. To write the lines in the history books, sentence by sentence, word by word. Or one could see this challenge and be overcome. One could see this challenge and decide that the effort and perhaps even the cost, is too much. You need to ask yourself what sort of cost are you looking at? You also need to ask yourself what sort of a life you are participating in?

You do a job, they give you money, you buy shit, you consume and you aggregate things, technological gadgets and a house. Every now and then they let you out of your cage to go on a holiday. Pre-packaged bullshit usually. Fast food leisure. You get back to your hamster wheel with vague memories and some good digital photos. Your little world is comfortable. Your little world feels safe. You feel happy. You will live out your years doing this repeatedly.

But what have you done? Nothing. You fled the country of your birth for the comfort of another culture. You turned your back on your home country and its entire people. You didn't think of anybody else but yourself (and your family). Did you ever actually make an effort to change this place? Did you ever actually help your fellow South Africans? Do you honestly think, when the history books are written that they will applaud you?

I don't do enough, but I try my goddamned hardest all the time to make a difference. I preach this gospel all the time. I fight a wave of pessimism that would dwarf the largest tsunami. I fight a surge of selfishness.

I wish the world could become more comfortable with selflessness. With civic duty. With that feeling that your fellow man is greater than you. Humanity is greater than you and suffering must be eased. Not just your own suffering... all suffering.

All that it takes for evil to prevail is for good men to do nothing. Emigration condemns us all. Stand and fight courageously or turn your back and leave.

I am a part of this country. I am a part of its people. An injury to one is an injury to all. We need to rally together to fight the minority. The majority has overcome hardship before. Three centuries of hardship. We can do it again. I ask people to think beyond your little world. Beyond your job, your house, your car, your family. It takes a large amount of guts to do that. To think of your fellow man. Your fellow South African. Let's improve our lot. All of us.

Two quotes resound in my memory: You have nothing to fear, but fear itself. Ask not what your country can do for you, but what you can do for your country.

I'm astounded to hear that the country of your birth, that nurtured you until you were successful enough to be able to leave. You tell that country to fuck off and die. I harbour no beneficent feelings towards that attitude whatsoever. I think it is selfish. You could have done something. You could have lifted your ass off of that fucking couch in front of your plasma fucking television and fought for this place. You could have done something. But you didn't.

All that it takes for evil to prevail is for good men to do nothing. I'm staying and I'm going to do something about it.

∞ ∞ ∞

*Look, it's not great, but it could get a whole lot worse. I like staying here. Crime hasn't affected me at all, ever. I feel relatively safe (I stay in a Northern Suburb of Cape Town). The incoming government is a bit scary (Zuma), but then again, we were all scared of Mandela and then of Mbeki.*

EJ - South Africa

∞

*I read your letter describing the horrendous crime circumstances in South Africa. It is unfortunate that you had to leave our Country because of your convictions and or perceptions. Yes, the crime rate is high and all that you have said is true, but do you really think running away from the problem will solve anything? We actually need strong people to make a difference here.*

*I am the owner of a Security Company and I am aware of what is really going on. Our city has it's fair share of problems, probably not as much as in Cape Town, Durban or Johannesburg. Making all you have said applicable to the whole country I feel is not fair.*

*My brother was murdered just before Christmas in 2003 and I felt the same way you did when leaving South Africa. I probably would have if I had the resources, but when the emotions died down I decided to start doing something constructive, instead of running away. Myself and others like me will work endlessly to make a difference, and maybe, through our hard work and commitment, cowards like you will feel welcome to return to our beautiful country and stop criticising.*

DR - South Africa

∞

*The whole country and its systems seems to be falling apart, but with our energy, and optimism, we may just succeed in pulling off a good turn around.*

LS - South Africa

∞

*I was one of those people who stood in long queues, waiting to get forms to apply for South African citizenship when F W de Klerk called a referendum to ask if we all wanted to move on from the bad old apartheid* days and have a change in politics. I proudly raised my hand, swore allegiance to South Africa and voted (on St Patrick's Day) for the first time as a South African and hoped the changes that were coming would make me proud. I never expected to want to leave that beautiful country as a result of how radical and unacceptable the changes would be and how much my life would change.

KLB - Ireland

∞

I will only leave if whites are banned and I can not fight back more than I would have at that stage. I love my country, which was fought for by my forefathers, in God's hand. No country is without dangers or problems. Those who have left South Africa are white cowards, who could not keep a promise, made to their Creator. They even left their parents behind. The economic situation is also hitting me hard, but none of these would drive me out of MY country.

IS - South Africa

∞

Optimism? Probably also my support structure of family and friends here, it's not an easy thing to leave. Besides, who says it'll be any better overseas?

Also, we're in vibrant and dynamic times. One day, when it's all over and it's a wonderful country to be in, I can say 'I was there'. Also, perhaps the thought that I have an opportunity to help, maybe change things, instead of just up and leaving.

I worry about leaving what's familiar to me. People feel more comfortable in places they know. And besides, moving to a different country is not insurance that you will never be a victim of violent crime.

PP - South Africa

∞

Apart from government I feel that business, churches and others should also take a lead to really drive a 'rebuild South Africa' campaign. Maybe we are each waiting for the other to tackle the issues. As I said earlier we need some strong leadership (apolitical if we cannot get it from the political side) that has a vision and can take us there. Although I can understand that individuals who have the opportunity to 'make a better living in another country' emigrate, I also feel that people should stay here and make a difference. If all the most able people leave it just becomes increasingly difficult for the remaining people to do the job.  PH - South Africa

∞

We remain upbeat about the economy and the ongoing prospects for economic growth. We believe there are many talented individuals in the upper echelons of government who will continue to steer a moderate course that sees beyond the political posturing and diabolical track record of some senior politicians.

We believe one day we will have a president who acknowledges and tackles the problem of AIDS head-on, instead of retreating behind academic semantics and putting his head in the sand. We believe one day we will have a health minister who is not a national disgrace. We believe Trevor Manuel has done great things for this country and has set the basics in place for whoever takes over from him.

We believe that the South African spirit is tough and resilient, capable of triumphing over the most daunting of challenges. We are making the best of the power cuts and enjoy playing Scrabble and backgammon and actually just talking to one another, instead of watching TV. The blackouts have been a great excuse to braai 5 times a week this summer!

We also believe that the crime problem <u>will</u> be resolved within the next few years. We want to stay and be part of the solution. We have had the privilege of growing up in a beautiful country with so many opportunities to offer, and we desperately hope that we will be able to offer this same privilege to our children. Thanks!  PH - South Africa

∞

I have lived in a number of countries and don't fit in anywhere. Nowhere seems to have the same culture as South Africa. I don't see a point in going somewhere else and being unhappy, with no real friends for the rest of my life, rather than just being a bit more vigilant and living at home. The crime is quite bad in South Africa, but I have had no experience of it myself. But then every big city in the world is plagued with crime, murder and theft.

When I lived in Dublin I was much more scared to walk around at night, than ever walking around in Cape Town at night. I never had a pepper spray during all my years in Stellenbosch, but bought one after a few months in Dublin and carried it with me every day.

The government has indeed instituted a reverse apartheid with the Black Empowerment Movement and Affirmative Action etc, and it is frustrating. I believe that the country just needs to move through the next 10 years to let the educated 'previously disadvantaged' generation make it into the work place and onto the sports field and none of that will be necessary any more. It just requires patience and support. The country's problems, prejudices and mistakes made in the past cannot be undone in a matter of years.

I don't know enough about the economic stability but when I studied it, it was a solid economy, with good growth rates (especially considering it's a developing country). People forget this and try comparing it to the UK, Australia, the USA, but it is a $3^{rd}$ world country and should be compared to the likes of Uganda, Colombia, India.

CV - South Africa

∞

I am however keen to play a role in South Africa's future and a close friend's comment just before I left made me wonder. She said, "You will travel the world and meet wonderfully interesting people and see exotic places. But remember that you were born in South Africa for a reason." I believed her at the time and continue to believe in a great South Africa. While looking for a job in London I am also considering some other entrepreneurial ventures in South Africa – time will tell.

HL - USA

∞

As all citizens I fear crime but every other country experience crime, the only difference is that our media tends to blow crime related events out of proportion. If you want to stay in South Africa you will have to deal with your fear of crime, always be alert and utilize security measures to the full.

The situation regarding the government is not as bad as what we have expected. I am working for a semi-governmental institution and have been treated exceptionally well by the employers. Lots of employees left during

*1994 due to racism related issues. Most of them have regrets as they could not make it on their own. The rising petrol price and inflation rate have a negative influence on the economy and the citizens of South Africa have to cut down on luxuries to survive.*

*In conclusion I would like to comment that South Africa is better off with the negative citizens who are emigrating. I believe that South Africa, with all its flaws, is still the best place in the world.*

AC - South Africa

∞

*I am a South African and an African. Like you I do not have allegiance to any other continent except Mother Africa. Do you remember the "I am an African" speech by Thabo Mbeki? I do not have uncles in Europe, Asia, America or anywhere else except in Botswana, Zimbabwe, Lesotho, Swaziland, Zambia and other any of the Countries above Limpopo River.*

*I will not leave Mother Africa no matter what, I am spiritually attached to Africa. I am naturally attached to mother Africa. I have been in England, Russia, Australia and Canada and I have always felt foreign in those countries. I have also been in Egypt, Liberia, Nigeria, Zimbabwe and Botswana. I felt at home in these countries. My ancestors see me closer, they can touch me, feel me. I can perform my rituals without any hinders or amusement from my neighbour. Africa is my beginning and my ending.*

*I will fight violent crime like I fought Apartheid crime. Apartheid crime was worst but we defeated it and I won't run away now, I will fight it like I did before.*

*Like I said I do not see myself leaving Africa and South Africa in particular. The government of the African National Congress has been the most democratic government in the south, we have an economic boom, the poor have never felt so close to their government.*

*The ANC is the government of us, it stands for the poor, it caters for the needy. The ANC has transformed itself from a liberation movement to a strong and credible political party for the people. The land has been redistributed to the original owners and the majority of South Africans and Africans in particular will never leave the country. People who are crying about crime are not patriotic and are mostly if not all white.*

*I have never heard a son of the soil or the daughter of the soil saying* he or she will leave the country because of crime. The reason is one, blacks only align themselves with Africa and you align yourself with Europe. Africa will curse those who will leave it to rot. I love mother Africa and I belong to mother Africa and mother Africa belongs to me. Africa for Africans.

RM - South Africa

∞

I do not condone nor do I support any sort of crime, I understand that for trade reasons there sometimes occur a need and a place for expat intellect in other countries. But I don't condone the idea of South Africans leaving as expats because of crime, this country is still a work in progress.

Yes, I'm African and this may seem irrelevant to me, but the lovely country you advocate people can fall in love with because of its beauty can only strive for the better if our European counterparts who still hold the intellectual resources stay in this country to make it a truly beautiful country.

JZ - South Africa

∞

I completely support all those who are emigrating and have already emigrated. I even appreciate the wisdom in this decision, as I question the government's ability to govern this country. But for my husband and I, family and everything else I have already mentioned, are just too great a deal to leave behind. I do not have the emotional strength to put all this behind me and start anew.

JW - South Africa

∞

It's easy to be negative but being positive takes more courage and perseverance. I prefer the latter. We have challenging times ahead of us but I believe in this country and it's people. I'm positive about where South Africa is going.

Please come back to South Africa because I truly believe you have so much to offer your country of birth. We are all South Africans forever and deep in your heart I know you want to come back. We need people like you here on the ground to help bring about change.

Most people run to countries with horrible foreign policies that inflict *so much pain and suffering in places like Iraq and the rest of the Middle East. It kind of reminds me of Apartheid where certain individuals did not mind about the rest of the world as long as they were taken care of. I have no problem with people who leave South Africa to better themselves and to improve their standard of living. My sadness lies with those who turn their backs on South Africa and slag it at every opportunity they get.*

*I have a problem with those who run away from the challenges that we face in South Africa and who want to come back when things are sorted out. That's just not right and you cannot live happily while others are suffering in the fight for peace and freedom.* RP - South Africa

∞

*I love South Africa. Leave? If I could, tomorrow!* SB - South Africa

∞ ∞ ∞

# Part 3

∞

# Living

*On behalf of those of us who chose to stay here,
please stop reminding us how bad things are here.*

*We know, thank you.
We live here, remember?!*

CC - South Africa

# 12

∞

## Absentee Living

Introduction by James McIntosh

One of the reasons 'Living' follows 'Loving' is because of our warped relationship with time. Many of us who have left South Africa continue to live in the past, in a country of memories. Many of those who are determined to stay in South Africa are living, mentally, in a future South Africa. Many of those who have not yet decided, to stay or to leave, oscillate between past and future.

How many of us, do you think, are living in the present, in this moment?

When our world is in chaos, we seek meaning in our past ('remember when...') and we seek significance in our future ('surely things will...'). We forget that the only time of meaningful significance is now, this present moment. And in that forgetting we waste the present time by not being *in* time. We tend to live in any time zone except the *moment*. Here's why – guilt and fear.

Guilt keeps us remorseful about the past; fear keeps us doubtful about the future. Together they keep us absent from the here-and-now. And so we fill today with regret for a yesterday that should have been different and clutter the present with dreams of a better tomorrow. We forget that guilt is second judgement. It is hindsight with perfect insight that makes you think you could have, should have, behaved differently. And we forget that fear is pre-judgement. You are judging what has not yet happened. You are afraid of what could happen or afraid of the future consequences of what has already happened.

"For Pete's sake", you might be thinking, "why is he going on and on about guilt and fear?" Because few things kill love as fast as guilt and fear. I, for one, don't want you to ever stop loving South Africa (one could argue that South Africa needs all the love it can get).

There is another reason I stress guilt and fear so much. Too much guilt and fear will stop you from making the right decisions...for you. Surely, what stops many people from leaving is guilt (about 'running away' perhaps) and fear (of the unknown). And many people who have already left South Africa will tell you that they feel guilty (about leaving family and friends perhaps) and are often in fear (for the safety of those left behind).

If we are truly honest with ourselves then we might just admit that it is not really death itself we fear. We fear not having any more time. No more time for those we love and what we love to do. Seen that way, leaving South Africa is a little death. The problem is that in our fear of dying we postpone our living. We fill the moment with remorse for a yesterday that should have been different and we clutter the present with dreams of a better tomorrow.

So please, in reading the stories in this section, remember your own memories of living in South Africa (past or present). Enjoy them, celebrate them, grieve for them if you must, but don't let them suffocate the life out of this moment. After all, it is in this moment that you create tomorrow's memories.

∞ ∞ ∞

# 14

∞

# A Day of Summer. A Life of Crime

*Can someone tell me what it is like to go outside
at night and walk around the block on a hot night?
'Cause I sure as hell ain't gonna go find out!*
SCVZ - South Africa

Sitting at the kerb, I watch the quiet afternoon sun dappling through the pine trees, creating tortoiseshell patterns on the tar. Carol picks up a rock – a large rock, about the size of my head. "Collect the pine cones," she orders, and I obey her. Seating myself back on the kerb, I place a mound of pine cones between us. I watch as she places the rock on the tar, anchoring it between her ankles. Her small, deft fingers forage through each cone with grunts or squeals following the finding of an empty cone or an intact pine nut.

I remain silent, watching her patiently, waiting to find out details of this latest adventure. The mound of pine nuts grows steadily into a small pile, big enough to fill our 9-year old hands. Finally, it's enough for her. I am still silent, watching the sun playing with patterns on the road.

She separates a nut from our precious hoard, picks up the rock and brings it down hard onto the nut – SMASH – and fragments of granite shell fly at me. The leftover seed and nut are mush, not quite as she intended. We don't care, anyway. "Taste it!" she commands, picking out the mashed nut and handing it over. I do, and the nutty sweetness draws me in.

"Mmmm, I like that. Are you going to do all of them?"

"Yes." She's already busy with the task. "Otherwise the squirrels will eat them all." Steadily, she continues her fierce concentration on the task. Smack! Smack! Smack! making a fine art out of each action. At the fifth nut, she seems to have figured out the mathematic and scientific precision of energy, action and reaction.

"Wow, you did it, you didn't break it!" I'm in awe.

"You have it, you can have this one." She's always magnanimous when she's in charge.

"OK"

Again, the fierce concentration takes over. Savouring the freshness of the nut, I roll it between my teeth, not wanting to eat the seed too quickly. A precious pit of flavour.

Smack! Smack! Smack!

"Hey, you're getting good at it. You've done three without breaking them."

I decide spontaneously to chew the nut. If Carol is that successful, there will be more to come this afternoon. I watch her, I watch the quiet road – no cars have come by at all. The rustling grass in the field across the road makes me think of snakes. I must ask Carol if there are any, she will know and, anyway, I'm not scared of snakes. And I look at all the pine trees creating an avenue on our side of the road. I wonder what enormous bounty of pine nuts those trees contain, awaiting our eager fingers.

It is Christmas holidays, it is summertime, we are 9-years old and the days stretch interminably. The gloriousness of these realizations overwhelms me – and I sigh.

∞ ∞ ∞

*When primary school pupils play games called 'Rape me!', 'Kill me!' – and do in fact kill and maim each other earning for the New South Africa's schools the dismal distinction of being, according to a widely quoted report, the most dangerous on earth, it is hard to exaggerate the gravity, the depth and the pervasive reach of the problem and the plethora of problems to which it is connected.*

KC - South Africa

∞

*I understand that the government is trying to rectify the past but in my case I was basically born in the post-Apartheid era. I have read the history books about the truly terrible events but I have never witnessed the apartheid years myself or been the one involved in the apartheid crimes. To me we have always been an integrated society, so why should I have to suffer now? What did I have to do with apartheid to deserve this punishment? Was my only crime being born white in South Africa?*

KK - South Africa

∞

*I cannot take it any more. I am the man in the house. However I cannot look my wife in the eyes and guarantee her that I will be able to stand up against two or three intruders with guns or knives. I can bench press 120kg without strain. I am genetically very strong, but it cannot stand up against a stolen 9mm pistol 2 a.m. in the morning.*

*I read a story one morning of a father that had his throat slit in front of his family because he refused to give up. It happened in Kayalami, Johannesburg. I managed to confirm this story by making contact with a relative through 'Die Beeld' newspaper. I was furious that it was not published in other newspapers. No radio station mentioned it on the news. I then contacted Radio 702 & Cape Talk. The lady in charge of the news desk, Lynn O' Connor, acknowledged that she knew about the story but admitted that she could only afford to mention a certain amount of crime each day.*

RVR - South Africa

∞

*We are planning to leave South Africa. We have already applied to Canada and our papers have been with CIC (Citizenship and Immigration Canada) for nearly a year already, we know it is a long wait. As I am thinking of all the reasons we are leaving, I have tears swell up in eyes. We wouldn't be leaving if the crime wasn't so out of control. Yes, we know there is crime all over the world but not the violent, senseless type we in South Africa have to put up with. Our children are exposed to this cesspool of evil and it is affecting them in ways that will only show in later years.*

*Like many other people in South Africa our family has been exposed to the criminal elements. My daughter and I arrived home at approximately 9:45 p.m. one evening. On entering our garage we were faced with five* armed men coming down our driveway. Before I was even out the car a driver was already in my seat. I was told to take off all my jewellery and walk inside and say 'Hi, Honey, I am home'.

By this time my husband had heard us arrive and went down to the bedroom. With a gun pointed at my daughter's head we were marched down to the main bedroom (my son was asleep in his room, we begged them not to wake him up). My husband didn't realize what was happening until he saw the men with guns shoved in his face. We were taken to the lounge were jackets were put over my family's face. A man was standing guard over my daughter with a gun at her head the whole time. I was ordered to the bedroom where they ransacked my cupboards looking for money and guns. It felt like a life time but was only a short 25 minutes. In that time they had packed both our cars with everything they could fit in. We weren't raped or shot but our emotional scars are deep. My daughter sees South Africa as a filth pit and everyday she wishes we were out of this country, no amount of counselling can make her feel any different.

Two weeks ago a 21 year old girl and her dad were walking their dogs in Shongweni (about 15km from us) when they were approached by five males. They raped the young girl in front of her father who they had tied up and shoved a cloth down his throat with a knife and called him 'a F####ing White C##t'. This young girl has 'forgiven' them but the community hasn't. This is the type of exposure to crime we have in this country. Enough is enough.

CAB - South Africa

∞

I have lost four friends through highjacking. I've lost a cousin to the abysmal medical system and nearly lost my step dad.

SS - USA

∞

Our time back in South Africa has been very educational. I do not think we realised just how bad the crime had truly become, until we were once again living here. This is despite my reading the headlines online most days whilst living abroad. We were burgled in January. But the most shocking result of that was how everyone – and I mean everyone, from the grocer, to every neighbour in our flat block, to the caretaker and his wife –

had a crime story to tell, most of them actually had more than one. And I don't mean they knew someone who knew someone, who had xyz happen to them. I mean they personally had ALL experienced crime within the last year. It was a BIG wake up call for us.

JW - South Africa

∞

After spending several months in the UK on a business trip, I was awakened to how people live over there – sleeping with a window open... walking around in the evening without expecting to be murdered and raped. I was angered by how we had been living in South Africa, with the constant fear of being burgled, mugged, murdered and violated. By that time, we had been burgled twice. We had had one car stolen and two cars broken into. A close friend had been gang-raped.

AH - USA

∞

My stepson has been hijacked twice off his bicycle, once at knife point, we have been attacked at our own home by two drunks who followed my husband home because he was on a motorcycle and they didn't like the lights, we have been hijacked, the list goes on and on. We have satellite tracking on our cars, good lord what else must I do to just feel safe. Can someone tell me what it is like to go outside at night and walk around the block on a hot night? 'Cause I sure as hell ain't gonna go find out! I remember it as a child only!

SCVZ - South Africa

∞

In the last three years we were there our car was stolen and we had three burglaries. My son and I were alone (my husband was away) in the house (2 a.m.) when we heard our dog bark. People were already in our home. The fear I felt cannot be described. Our Fox Terrier ran to the outside of our bedroom window and I was able to let him jump into the bedroom through the bars. He stayed in the room with us and when he eventually calmed down we cautiously opened the door. The only weapon we had was a baseball bat. The intruders had removed our sliding door to get in (we never heard it).

*After the police, etc came round and did their thing it was 4 a.m. and we were both too scared to stay home. We spent the rest of the night at the local medical clinic's emergency room. That single event changed us. Even though our local vet was killed in his surgery at 10 a.m. on a Monday morning; even though our local Portuguese café owner was killed for R100 (25 years old with a pregnant wife); even though four women we know were raped. Until it affected us personally we refused to be negative about South Africa.*

AS - USA

∞

*When a 96 year old lady was murdered a few houses down the road from my house for no reason I couldn't get it out of my mind. It was cruel and unnecessary. I kept on going over in my mind what she must have gone through and I didn't want to live in South Africa any more because I couldn't relate to that kind of senseless brutality.*

*Crime has touched the lives of everyone I know in South Africa. My son was attacked by a gang of thugs with a blow from a bottle to his head and glass lodged in his skull. My 81 year old step mother was stabbed in her own home and left for dead but she managed to get away and hide while her attacker was stealing her cell phone and she survived. She is traumatized. My friend was held up at gun point but managed to get away.*

SVB - UK

∞

*I moved to Johannesburg in 2005 to work at a premium Johannesburg law firm. I had worked hard to get to where I was and had earned the right to work where I did and earn the salary I did. In about June 2005 we were held up at gun-point in our offices. I was one of the victims. Although they didn't harm us it was not a pleasant experience to say the least. I guess it was because there were other people with me, or maybe because the robbers were 'professional' but the experience didn't affect me too adversely and in fact was some sort of relief. Having come from the 'dorp' I had always feared being held-up or hi-jacked. When it happened I guess I fooled myself into this line of thinking, "It isn't too bad, yes I felt fear when I had a gun to my head, but its only a few seconds and they either shoot you and its over, or insurance will deal with it." – Pathetic isn't it.*

Anyway I have progressed up the ladder with lots of hard work and found myself in the favourable position have being offered a job at a very reputable boutique law firm. The money is excellent and the environment is almost unreal. The firm is great and I have never been happier. Yes I'm getting to my point. In February this year, a week before my birthday I slipped out to Rosebank for a quick supper. It was in a busy area, where there a lots of tourists, etc. I had given a beggar R40 at the robot earlier that day and did not have any cash to pay for underground parking. I was too lazy to draw so I simply parked on the side of the road.

At about 9 p.m. I left the restaurant and returned to my motor vehicle. There were other cars around me and I had seen guards around. That in itself I suppose took my vigilance away (my 'fault') I got in and dropped my cellphone under the passenger seat. Whilst leaning over to pick it up, the interior light of my car suddenly came on and I came face to face with another huge gun. Long and short is I was robbed of my money, watch and cell-phone but allowed to keep my car (how noble of him). I even thanked him when I drove away. Now this experience was somewhat different. See, when you are in the seat of your car, with no-where to turn or run, I can't quite describe it... it does something to you. I almost felt a tickle inside my brain with fear. I will never forget his breath and the smell of gun-oil and the way he spoke to me was like one would imagine a violent robber to talk. I honestly thought he was going to kill me.

BT - South Africa

∞

I am in the process of immigration. My house is on the market and I am looking for a job in the UK. As I am over 32 and do not have a degree, I am struggling with immigration. I have no fear of going to a new country, the fear is staying here. My son was shot and killed in a 'hijacking' in October 2004. Nothing was done about his murder, no investigation at all. Because of this my daughter left to live in the UK. She has been there for 2.5 years. She came back last month for a visit and while she was here I had a 'home invasion' where they came into her bedroom shone a torch in her face and asked for her cell and her money. She never slept in the two weeks that she was here. A month later I am still waiting for forensics.

Criminals are protected in this country. I cannot wait to leave. My parents used to farm up until five years ago. They were attacked and so brutally beaten that my father had 50 stitches in the top of his head alone! My grandmother (aged 80) was beaten and left for dead on the same farm six years prior to that.

WB - South Africa

∞

I'm one of those messed up people who's had quite a few bad experiences with crime (and lucky enough to have come out unharmed each time) from break-ins to hi-jackings, attempted rape and assault. In my heart I want to run like hell from the place that I once loved (I want so much to raise a family, but it's too risky here) but my fiancé wants to stay because our families are here and we don't have enough money to immigrate.

I'm only 25 this year, but I'm torn between staying where I grew up, in a beautiful place I love and getting out and living while I can.

EG - South Africa

∞

In the previous five years or so my wife had been held up twice, I had been shot in an armed robbery at the house (all of which the children witnessed), my daughter had been involved in an armed robbery and shooting while at a friend's house, my son had been the victim of at least a robbery and possibly a hijack attempt (the passenger window of his car was smashed at traffic lights in Hyde Park and somebody was busy trying to get into the car through the window when the lights changed and he drove off, managing to leave the person behind, although losing his cell phone in the incident). We had a double electric fence on top of a 2+m wall and a guard patrolling the premises all night every night and still felt unsafe. GW - Dubai

∞

I have been living without proper sleep for only four weeks now, and it is dreadful. We live in an estate with 24 hour guards who patrol. We woke up 04h00 one morning to a youngster (maybe 21) attempting to climb through our window. We have guests staying with us at the moment and at the time of the incident, and the 'robber' was kicked and punched back out the window by our guest. Apparently this 'robber' then jumped over our wall into the townhouse complex behind us and attempted to break into another home! A few days after that we heard gun shots and screaming and it hasn't stopped since. It's like you say, every little noise causes you to wake up!

TP - South Africa

∞

We have five children, four of whom have been mugged... not once... not twice, but many times! They have come to accept it as normal!

CK - South Africa

∞

I have tears in my eyes for I just read your article on the Internet. My heart goes out to you and your family. I grew up in (small rural town near Cape Town) and have been living here for 22 years now, and I'm still not able to leave the place, for my love is too great. But my fear is starting to overtake me, and I am looking out for greener fields, not because of money, but to have the feeling of safety, that to me is worth much more than anything.

Like you, I also love my country and I always thought that as a South Africans we should stay and fight, but I have learned that one's life is worth much more than your pride. We are sitting ducks for crime, we know it is coming, we just don't know when. At first you read about violence and abuse in the papers, magazines, then you hear about it through the mouths of strangers, then you hear from your friends & family and then you are part of the crime statistics in South Africa. I am so sad, angry, hate all these emotions are combined, for we have this beautiful country, but we cannot experience it as citizens.

MW - South Africa

∞

I have come to realise how everyone, (especially my family), remain numb to the violent crime headlines. I myself read news24.com every day – and as a result often find myself lying in bed at night, reflecting in horror on some of the things that had happened to good families that day, almost always in front of young children. It deeply affects and depresses me, and I can't understand how South Africans seem to think that by not reading these headlines, or not reacting to them – that it will somehow make things better, somehow stop it from being reality, somehow stop it from ever happening to them.

I do not suffer from that illusion. My husband and I are all too aware that it is a high likelihood that we will be subjected to crime again – and we fear for that occurrence. We recently bought a house and have spent a huge sum of money on the best alarm and armed response we can afford, not to mention gates, walls, burglar bars and security doors.

However, and it's a big however, in South Africa we are 'somebodies'. We can afford a lovely three-bedroom home with a small garden. We can afford a lovely lady to help us clean the house once a week and share the load of ironing. We stand out as Caucasians in a crowd of African people as something different. Even more than that – we belong. We share a history with all other South Africans, of Black Cat Peanut Butter, Shaka Zulu, biltong, rugby and Afrikaans. We have our family and our friends. And we think that is worth the risk of continuing to live here.

JW - South Africa

∞

It has been remarkable that over the past few weeks almost every day there have been news reports that some of the most wanted criminals have been captured, crime syndicates have been busted, and criminals were caught red handed due to tip-offs from the public. I am sure these things don't get splashed worldwide like our sky-high rape statistics. Here you often hear that there were violent clashes between police and criminals where the police won the battle. This probably is also not sensational enough to reach international audiences.

I am a Christian of religion, and I believe that our Lord who made the universe, is much bigger than South Africa's crime problem. From various sources you hear that the average South African man or women on the street is turning back to the Lord, and when we as a nation turn back to God, he promised that he will restore our country. We keep praying for this. Maybe all South Africans living elsewhere should do the same.

In terms of the government– I am working in government, so I see a lot of things from closer than the average South African. Yes, we have problems with service delivery. Yes, we have a lot of things going wrong (mismanagement, corruption, etc.). But yes, we are doing something about it. As an example, I am involved in the training of public servants. We are developing training programmes that are based on international best practice and that can hold their own against the best in the world. We are reorganizing ourselves so that we can increase our reach five to tenfold, and our politicians are under tremendous pressure to show progress in the quest of a better life for all. I know. I often have to make input to the progress reports that are delivered at high level meetings.

In terms of our economic stability – I am no economist, but I can see that we are facing growing pains. However, these are also addressed and tackled as they arise. A friend of mine told me earlier this week that she was complaining about South Africa to a friend of hers who is living outside the country but who has a lot of investments in South Africa, and he reminded her that South Africa is one of very few developing countries who do not have foreign debt. We are in the process of preparing for the 2010 World Cup, and still we have not buried ourselves in debt. That says something about the health of South Africa's economy.

So, I guess the long and the short of my story is that I am (mostly) happy in South Africa. We have challenges, but who does not? I think it is time for people who have decided to move to other countries to make peace with their decisions, and to stop watching out for South Africa's failures in order to justify what they have decided. On behalf of those of us who chose to stay here, please stop reminding us how bad things are here. We know, thank you. We live here, remember?!

We are trying our best to turn the country around, we are trying to solve the crime, so that, as you stated in your article, "South Africans would return in droves to re-establish themselves and their businesses (t)here". You said that you would love to return and bring your children back to experience their culture and live the reality of it. We are trying to give our children just that.

CC - South Africa

∞

In my (medical) practice I see many victims of crime and I may add that what I see is done with hate and vindictiveness. Something I notice more and more when it is black on white. An example of one of many is a husband and wife tied up on a couch and tortured with a hot iron. The daughter was then raped by a group of black males and the parents made to watch. After all this the wife and daughter were executed (We don't even see this in war after the Geneva Convention).  Needless to say I treated the husband/father for his numerous fractures.  I see this type of hate crime more and more in my practice.

NB - South Africa

∞

My husband and I will leave South Africa as soon as we have managed to sell our home.  I have had 13 neighbours murdered (one of them boiled to death!) in as many months.  The thought of leaving South Africa is like having my heart torn out... everything I know and love is in South Africa including my family and friends.

Try as I might I cannot find anything positive to say about the future... it all just looks so bleak and a life lived in fear is no life at all.

CH - South Africa

∞ ∞ ∞

# 15

∞

# Lizzie Wields Her Broom

*My feelings have always been that when the women of this country,
irrespective of race, creed, colour, band together, stand as one,
and tell the government that they are TIRED of the violence, crime, etc,
and follow this by action – as only women can – then, and only then,
will things start happening here, and will we see progress.*
JH - South Africa

Donuts – an American tradition – are oily, fried lumps of dough, slathered in various sweet icing and are best bought when freshly made and still steaming. They always remind me of Lizzie, our maid, who baked delicious vetkoek in the afternoons.

I'd sit on the bench at the pine table in our kitchen, after school, and watch her voluminous bulk moving around the kitchen as she directed her energies into collecting ingredients and making the dough. Then the sizzling of the vetkoek as it landed in the hot oil, only to emerge quickly – dripping with oil – too hot to eat but delicious to watch with anticipation, as it cooled. A lumpy, misshapen ball of fried golden dough; I would salivate at the thought of the apricot jam soon to be smeared inside. Lizzie would only make a few each time (all the more reason to savour them) and then we'd sit together comfortably at the kitchen table and eat and talk.

She would tell me stories about her life in District Six, about her family's forced removal and transplanted life in Heideveld and about her daughter and her grandchildren. I was too young to comprehend the enormity of the sadness that lay behind her stories. She was always smiling, friendly, large, funny, happy, Lizzie.

My favorite food was potato salad – a taste which Lizzie would sometimes indulge by making it for me. In the summer holidays, I'd plead with her to make some for my breakfast. In return I would receive a lecture on the state of my stomach and how distressed it would be to find potato salad instead of breakfast porridge. And then, Lizzie predicted, I would have to go to the doctor with my indigestion. There was a time for everything and the time for potato salad was not at breakfast. After sitting through her lecture, she still made the best potato salad ever.

Lizzie also made home-made 'gemmer bier' (ginger beer) for us. My mother would collect the glass Coke bottles (those were the days before plastic became so fantastic) with their screw top lids and, when she had collected enough, Lizzie would brew ginger beer which we would store on the floor in our pantry. Occasionally, watching television at night, we'd hear a cacophony of sounds – 'bam! bam! bam! bam!' – and find that the ginger beer had fermented to such an extent that it led to violent explosions – shooting the caps off the bottles – and was fizzing all over the pantry floor. It never discouraged Lizzie; she'd just make another batch.

One afternoon when my sister arrived home from school, Lizzie was in the kitchen. My sister walked into our lounge to find a 'gentleman' hiding behind an armchair – the front door (a fair distance from the road) had been standing open. She screamed, which alerted Lizzie who rushed into the room.

"Hey, wat doen jy? Wat dink jy? Wat doen jy hier?" (Hey, what are you doing? What are you thinking? What are you doing here?) She shrieked at the man and, believe me, Lizzie in all her bulk and glory was not to be trifled with.

> *I know that if anyone were to EVER touch one of my children or other close family members, I will retaliate without a doubt.*
> CR - South Africa

"Ek soek werk," (I'm looking for work) said the gentleman.

"Hey! Jy soek werk? Agter die stoel in die sitkamer? Moenie vir my lieg. Uit! Uit! Buite! Weg is jy, jou skollie." (Hey! You're looking for work? Behind the chair in the sitting room? Don't lie to me! Out! Out! Outside! Away with you, you petty thug.)

And Lizzie chased him down the driveway, wielding a broom.

Ah, if only all it takes is Lizzie and her broom, then South Africa would have been swept clean of crime and violence long ago. And maybe, then, my kids would be growing up in sunny South Africa.

∞ ∞ ∞

*It was always the criminals behind bars with the innocent and free on the outside, but it is now the innocent and no longer free that are behind bars.*
MH - South Africa

∞

*Just this morning a 53 year old woman was shot dead in her driveway in Bergvliet (you should remember how 'safe' that little suburb used to be) and only her handbag was stolen. Life now has been reduced to the cost of a handbag or a cell phone. Nobody cares any more.*
DM - South Africa

∞

*Crime is a huge factor. We have already been held up for an hour in our home by armed robbers, and we fear we may not be so lucky next time (we were unharmed during the armed robbery).*
VF - South Africa

∞

*By far my biggest issue is with the violent crime in the country, the constant fear for your children's as well as your own, life. The fact that it is no longer good enough for criminals to hold you at gunpoint for material possessions, they now have to torture victims as well. Why is it ever necessary to pour boiling water on an elderly person, burn somebody with an iron, impale a defenceless child? The cruelty in the country makes me physically ill.*

*The government is a only interested in financial gain, power and pushing their own agendas. As they so adequately put it: 'if you don't like the crime, leave'. OK, thanks, guess we will do that then. I will take the pain now, so that my children can grow up in a place where they are firstly safe and free and secondly able to pursue whichever careers they want to.*

*The economic stability I don't think is insurmountable. I would put* up with everything (even the consistent power outs) I am just not willing to put up with the crime and violence one more second.

CJ - South Africa

∞

Victims have no human rights, only criminals. If you protect yourself and kill one of them, you are arrested and charged with murder.

SH - South Africa

∞

I think it's very sad that the population in general has lost their respect for one another. If you see your fellow man as less than you or as owing you something then there is no hope. I think that the lack of respect extends to all aspects of life there. Infrastructure is not maintained, that shows a lack of respect for structures, system and facilities that have been put in place for everyone to use and enjoy. The other problem is integrity, I think that a lot of people are not doing their jobs or living their lives with integrity. Cutting corners or playing blame games shows immaturity, irresponsibility and incompetence and this applies to many South Africans at many levels of income.

DH - Australia

∞

At the moment I am feeling that there is still hope for our country. Maybe if I was directly affected (hijacked; raped) it will then galvanize my decision to leave.

DOR - South Africa

∞

Life is pretty much the same as far as crime is concerned here. It seems to be so out of control. If there is a burglary the cops don't bother coming out to attend to it, so you don't report it and just carry on and count your blessings that you weren't hurt. We had a lady murdered by some garden workers about a year ago two streets down from where we live. I was totally unnerved by the whole thing.

And then they decided to target us. We stay on the perimeter of the complex with a high wall and electric fencing to protect us. No trouble to them – they sliced a piece of rubber pipe, fitted it over the electric wires and calmly removed them. That night I had got up to have some tea. I went to the kitchen, put the kettle on and made my tea. I never saw anything amiss as I am short sighted and without the specs I am as blind as a bat. As I got back into bed my neighbour's dog began barking. I woke up my husband and swore about the racket and the fact that the neighbour didn't get up to shut them up. Again I got up and put the lights on and that must have spooked them. They ran down the front garden and calmly jumped over the gate and ran down the road. Fortunately the next house in the complex they targeted had electric beams and as they got into his garden the alarms went off. The owner was awake and ran out to see four of them running down the road and making a hasty getaway.

Needless to say Fort Knox is now my home. We have beams all round the house, an alarm that wakes the dead and my husband is now going to put up sensor lights. Shit... how many times have we forgotten to deactivate the things before we step outside. Thank goodness we have healthy hearts that can take the strain.

My beautiful country has now been turned into a jail with huge walls surrounding our beautiful homes. Great big gates, and electric fences on each and every wall. I think I know what Madiba must have felt. My beautiful country seems to be going backwards but I have the right to live here too. I am an English speaking South African who also has the right to live in this beautiful country of my birth and don't see why I should be forced to leave because of a multitude of people who don't care. Hopefully we will be able to work something out and live in peace together as a nation of South Africans fulfilling Madiba's dream of a rainbow nation.      LT - South Africa

∞

I share your sentiments and my heart breaks... something I refer to as Cry My Beloved Country. South Africa is no longer South Africa and after coming back here against the advice, wishes and will of friends and family, I got hijacked (which strictly speaking could happen anywhere). But what tipped the scale for me is that not a single police officer arrived on the scene as they were fighting over whose jurisdiction it was. Insurance refuses to pay out saying we STAGED it and I am left feeling powerless at every single traffic light, intersection or dark corner in a country I once adored so much I cut short my 60 month work permit in the UK before I could naturalise.

Sad state of affairs and Thabo and every other citizen of South Africa living in delusion of where this country is at, can call you and me and every other SURVIVALIST (love that) what they like. The bottom line is that they are running this country into the ground, running anybody with any sense of survival and hope for life out of South Africa and what is going to remain of South Africa will be but a pale shade of grey resembling Zimbabwe.

NVR - South Africa

∞

I've loved the landscapes, the poor people which I've had the fortune of talk with, the game reserves, but I've had the impression of a country without direction, with a lot of crime and without the basic social helpers (medical aid, schools, nurseries). I've found a great distance between the rich and the poor and I've often thought that this distance would become every day bigger.

I felt the government was quite absent. The cops were corrupted and the crime was all around us, day and night, we could feel it.

CT - Italy

∞

There was a very interesting TV program on one of Nolene's shows (3Talk is on SABC3 TV) dealing with car-jackings, etc. They showed a video clip of a row of cars standing at a traffic light waiting for it to change in their favour. Two black (I emphasise this as they were black) thugs strolled down the lane of cars, one on each side. Spotting something they wanted in a woman's vehicle they smashed both front windows (driver and passenger sides), stole her handbag, cellphone, etc, slapped her alongside the ear, and sauntered off across the oncoming traffic discarding items from the bag which they did not want. NO ONE DID A THING. The point is NO ONE COULD DO A THING.

On this program they had a 'reformed' car-jacker talking about how the syndicates work in terms of cars which are earmarked for theft. When they join these groups, they are trained, and then as he said, one should never, never confront a car-jacker as they are always high on drugs before embarking on one of their carjacking trips; they are also always armed, and the slightest thing could make them jittery which results in the victim being shot. His comment was that many of them could not do this job without being high, and the 'bosses' ensure that they are.

Now my point is WHAT IS THE GOVERNMENT DOING ABOUT THIS?

JH - South Africa

∞

I think South Africa, like the rest of Africa, is a tragic and dangerous place. I see none of the hope I once saw; I have none of the joy I felt after democracy came about in such a wondrous way. I see crime, corruption, Aids, fat-cat whites and blacks partying away in good-old South African fashion while society crumbles around them.     EN - USA

∞ ∞ ∞

# 16

∞

## Paranoid For Life

*(Imagine) having a three year old tell you that she can't sleep in her room because there are no burglar bars on her window.*
SVDB - Ireland

I am paranoid. So what! Aren't we all? I've asked myself a number of times whether one is born paranoid or is it slowly inculcated as a result of exposure to the environment and people and experiences.

I have met people whose major concern is the protection of their family. They are determined to protect the family from any, and every, possible 'danger'. And, I do not mean the life-threatening kind of danger – a gun-wielding burglar or car-jacker. They do not have to worry on a grander scale about their very existence, so they become bogged down in the creation of a completely sterile, safe environment for their child or family.

These paranoea revolve around fears of their environment. Everything must be sterile, not a germ in sight, and monitored at all times. Children who wait for the annual flu vaccines to arrive, because their parents say "we must have them, we have them every year, so that we don't get the flu." Yet, this same child lives on junk food for most of the year. The next child eats organic food, drinks filtered water, wears natural clothing, but is shunted quickly to the doctor, for chemical intervention, every time he sneezes. I once overheard a mother tell her daughter to drink from her own bottle as she wasn't willing to share hers. And please don't let Johnny touch that counter top again until I've wiped it with the wet wipes impregnated with the anti-bacterial, anti-flu chemicals.

I'm sorry but I do start to laugh.

I call their children 'the Band-Aid Generation' because, while playing, they occasionally get a minor scratch, just some scraped skin. Since there is not a drop of blood, it is not something I consider an injury or even worthy of any attention. They rush indoors to find me and ask for a Band-Aid. They are visibly distressed when I tell them I don't give Band-Aids unless there is blood (a substantial amount of blood). "But my mother always gives me a Band-Aid." "Well, I'm not your mother."

I'm fairly unsympathetic, even to my own children, because I'm of the 'a bit of dirt never killed you' mentality. I'm sure I'm not the only one who has fond memories of a childhood where the refrain, "Mom, I've got a scratch," elicited the response, "well, put a bit of spit on it or lick it until it stops, and go and play." Ewww, I can practically hear your revulsion. I also remember applying my own spit to my sister's scraped shin one afternoon. She wasn't totally in favour of the idea but it worked – the bleeding stopped – and we could play again.

We have to teach our children that there are planetary evils and enormous dangers out there, but the onus is on us to put this into perspective, too. Yes, there is global warming, the Ebola virus, lunatics with weapons, vehicles that crash and people that die unexpectedly. If we teach our children to be paranoid about every door handle, counter top and food item, then they must assume that this world is a very dangerous place, where even food cannot be trusted to nourish you and there are germs lurking, and ready to ambush you, everywhere. What kind of mind-set does this create for their future? Do they grow into uptight adults, fearful and paranoid, unable to touch anything in the event that they may encounter a germ? Paranoia is the domain of those who have nothing else to be concerned about perhaps?

> We are digging deep into our survival instincts that people in safer countries don't have to do as frequently or as deeply.
> TW - South Africa

I've found my mind-set is slightly different. My paranoia is about my personal space being breached. My paranoia is about my personal safety and that of my family. My primary fear has always been safety. I remember this fear from my earliest childhood in South Africa. My mother cautioned me to always check the area, lock the gate, lock the steel safety gate at the door, lock the doors, close the windows and lock the car doors. Be aware at all times of your immediate area. I believe that this has protected me from becoming a victim of crime of any kind. Germs on the counter top, the water bottle, or on someone else's eating utensils, did not feature in my frame of reference. I have white blood cells to fight those battles. I have since realized that when one has to be paranoid about basic safety and security, there is no space left for fears relating to other, relatively simple, matters.

When one is in a pure state of survival, then one cannot worry about whether the food is organic, the water is filtered, the roofing is asbestos or the clothing is cotton. One exists in another dimension – a dimension which is entirely separate from the present – and is concerned with greater issues. After all, what is greater than pure survival? At least there is food, water and a roof.

> It took me a while but I became what I would call hyper-vigilant – it's a general kind of disquiet one feels, a certain restlessness or a kind of tension when one has to leave home everyday to encounter who knows what.
> CB - USA

I'd also prefer to eat only organic foods, to drink only filtered water and to live in a solid eco-friendly home with no carcinogens or germs in sight but, if forced to face the unfriendly, environmental dangers, I'll do so and I'll take my safety any day.

If paranoia is inculcated…does it ever subside completely?

In May 2002, when we arrived at our first apartment in Richmond, I found the unbarred sash windows, sliding glass doors opening onto a small patio, and free, unfenced park-like surroundings very alarming. I looked around and immediately felt unsafe. How would I ever sleep without those burglar bars and that safety gate, without that sense of security? Across the open grass area, beyond the verandah and trees, there was a busy road and the apartment block was clearly visible to everyone in the area.

> I cannot describe the feeling I get when I walk along the river bank and don't have to look over my shoulder. Burglar bars are not even sold in the hardware shops and the sound of gunfire is something I may have heard once here!
> LS - New Zealand

Occasionally, at night, I'm the last one downstairs and I have to switch off the lights. I am excruciatingly aware that I can be seen from the road through the big picture windows and I feel naked. As I check the front door to make sure it is locked, suddenly, there it is again, confronting me, that old paranoia surfacing from the depths.

I do not feel safe because there are not enough locks on the door. I can't lock it properly. There's only one Yale lock and no steel security gate, only a glass screen door. Someone could easily break down the door or kick it in. I can't look at it. I begin to have a panic attack and then, soothing the inner child, I have to tell myself that it's fine, we're in America, things like that do not happen in this suburb. We are fine. Now go to bed. And I smile.... Where did that come from?

In our suburb, there are no fences around gardens. Our back yard slopes gently into that of our neighbour's. I do not know anyone who has bars on their windows. I do not know of anyone who has had a burglary. This is not a wealthy suburb. These are average, solid working class people with families. They have lived here for 20 years or more. They have children in public schools. They are paying their taxes and their mortgages, watching their children grow up and saving for college and retirement.

We do not realise the extent of the acute stress disorder we live with in South Africa, until it is no longer around. It was two years before I stopped reacting to people walking too close to me on the sidewalk (innocently, but I was accustomed to being cautious about everyone). It was three years, or longer, before I stopped reacting to every noise at night, and before I stopped sizing up people in parking areas, especially men innocuously standing and talking.

> *How long it took my stress levels to reduce. I think it took about 6 months before I wasn't jumping at every sound. It took me ages to truly believe that the postal service worked, that you weren't in danger every time you left your home.*
>
> SS - USA

I go to the gym, the shop or the library at night and I park far away from the building. I don't worry when I walk back, in the darkness, to my car at 9 or 10 p.m., carrying my gym bag and handbag – or my six grocery bags. Occasionally a surge of 'what if' surfaces. What if feeling so secure makes me a target? I smile about it, and yet I'm still aware, still checking my environment automatically, all those years of ingraining are blanketed under there somewhere.

Paranoia – my heritage of fear – surfaces again and again, years after I think I've overcome this. I've been living in the USA for eight years and recently I walked out of my office building at 7:30 p.m. Being winter, the parking area was lit but dense with darkness, and was mostly empty. I saw a car, a 4-door sedan, and a man who was standing, holding the door open, and fiddling around inside the front passenger side. My immediate survival mode kicked in. Who was he? What was he doing? Why was he there at that time of night? Did I have my keys (weapon)? I sized up the area and the safety of the lighted building. Was anyone else in the vicinity? I formulated a plan of reaction. I was poised and in a state of high tension – mentally I revisited basic self-defence moves, the damage high heels can cause and the hardest bone of the body (the elbow – a great natural weapon). These thoughts flitted instantly through my mind and within 60 seconds I was on 'High Alert'. I walked cautiously to the car and skirted that area of the parking lot.

As I made a wide berth, I watched him, and tried to step unobtrusively into the lighted spaces which led to my car. He turned around, called to me, 'Have a good evening!" I realized it was Maurice, one of the night cleaners of the building and, although I didn't know him personally, I relaxed because I've met him, my co-workers know him well, he's friendly, affable, and it seems he was simply cleaning out debris from inside his car.

> *I found it strange being able to walk around London on my own and not fear for my safety.*
> ML - UK

A part of me laughs at my silliness, a part of me is pleased that I am still streetwise and aware, and a part of me is sad that this fear, this paranoia, is something which will never leave me.

∞ ∞ ∞

*During the day on my travels around the Cape Peninsula I'm all too aware of the dangers of crime all around. I'm constantly looking over my shoulder. When walking on the pavement I look in shop fronts to see who's walking behind. If suspicious, I stop and let them pass. When approaching my car I use the side window as a mirror to see if anyone is following. If so I don't open the door but turn away to prevent a possible hi-jacking.*

VA - South Africa

∞

*Last night I went for a walk around the neighbourhood in which we live and came across a group of children playing in the street with no adult supervision. I remember doing this as a child yet it is something my son has* never experienced in his short life. How many South African children are growing up believing that it is too dangerous to even go outside, never mind play in the streets? How can a country with one of the most advanced and tolerant constitutions in the world survive when their very future is being groomed to be anti-social and intolerant of strangers?

SDT - Australia

∞

I also find the people very narrow-minded, especially with regards to how they raise their children. I find that the little kids here are so tightly controlled – they really can't do anything without a mom or dad cautioning them in some way or another.

The Americans (the ones we've met here at any rate) are so concerned about dirt. So what if Tom's feet are black underneath by the end of the day? Kids are supposed to get dirty, aren't they? Play in the sand, make sticks and stones and leaves into elaborate games, really explore the sensory world around them. A lot of the parents here look at me sitting with Tom outside and disapprove because I'm sitting on the pavement watching my son, scratching around in the dirt. I think it's wonderful. They probably think we don't get plastic for toys in Africa!

CL - USA

∞

Here in Canada, although I count my money openly at the ATM (perhaps foolishly) and walk around the neighbourhood without much thought for security, I insist on the front door being locked, even when we're home – the fear of a home invasion never far from my mind. My boyfriend can't understand why I'm always suspicious of men in the park and why I always check cars going past the house (are they casing the joint?).

KC - Canada

∞

I live in Johannesburg in the north and want to assure you – to correct any ambivalence – that you did the right thing. Last night six gunmen opened fire on friends having a braai at their home in Chartwel. Five are estimated to be dead. A guy was shot and killed in his home in Lonehill. Both happened last night and not one was in the paper or news today. They were all relayed through very traumatized friends.

    I am definitely beginning to feel the stress of our violent environment taking its toll on my health, mental state and lifestyle. As you wrote in your article, it is dreadful having to look 'in front, behind, and side ways' ALL THE TIME! My life focus now is all about security. I have the norm being alarms and security gates as well as pepper spray in my bag, car, kitchen, bedroom AND patio. I even walk the dogs with pepper spray.

NG - South Africa

∞

    I've just read your article (The dangers of South Africa..), following the link from News24. It made me want to cry. I live in Sea Point, I have two young children - the baby is just four months old. I fear my older son at five years old is already experiencing a stress disorder (night terrors, biting nails, "I'll kick the baddies mommy...").

    I can identify totally with the paranoia you feel when you're well aware of your vulnerability with two small children to get in and out of the car as fast as possible. I walk around constantly with backup plans and escape routes in case I get attacked. And I carry my keys the same way you used to.

CD - South Africa

∞

    I often joke that I am so street smart that you can plonk me down in the most dangerous ghetto in New York or thereabouts and I will be fine. You have to be street smart to live here – or you will be a victim.

TM - South Africa

∞

    We're currently 'processing' my best friends being attacked by their ex-gardener. She was raped, knifed and hit over the head with a hammer. He was thrown with a pot of hot oil. The man was drunk, on their liquor, and mad because they dismissed him with only two months severance pay after not pitching for work two out of three days for two weeks. Worse is their reaction to this horrific encounter – she told me she's very thankful that he didn't do anything 'funny' when he raped her and he was grateful that the oil had already cooled.

*It's somewhere between sickening, frightening and laughable – I ca*(n't) *decide which, and still we're not really sure of leaving?!?!!??*

*But I do love my country, and most of my countrymen/women. Sometimes I just lose it a little!*  SD - Switzerlan(d)

∞

*I realise that driving around with SIX children in the car is absolutely frightening – I would NEVER be able to save them all..*

*And I drive almost defensively – never driving too close to the car in front especially when stopping at Stop Streets or Robots so I can get away if need be, I always put the groceries in FIRST and kids in last, I have even told my nine year old daughter what to do in the event of a hi-jacking (unstrap all the kids) so the guys can just (hopefully) throw them out of the car or maybe we can get them out easier. What sort of life is this?*  LW - South Africa

∞

*We used to live with all the blade wire, gates, automatic garage doors, alarms, lights, dog and armed response of which you speak. I never felt safe. I would not let the children play in our own garden by themselves. I felt paranoid always looking for the pair of eyes that might be looking at me from the bushes. I worried about driving by myself at night as a woman and also about my husband locking up the business after dark in a bad part of town. And then I also worried about the bigger political picture and the future of my children educationally and in the work place.*

*I knew that we would have a chance to leave but I didn't think my children would have the same opportunity to leave as educated skilled workers if they received a substandard education by world standards. On the up side we owned our house without a mortgage, the children would have gone to private schools and we had income security.*  SL - Australia

∞

*Every South African is moving from work to their prisons which they call 'home'. We cannot walk in the streets without looking over our shoulder. The situation has become 'normal' for us and I think that is why we survive …. I suppose that is the only way you CAN survive. People are becoming*

sive about the smallest things that upset them and I feel it is
the helplessness we as a country feel to try and stop the crime.
are running our country and a life is worth NOTHING to the
walking around our streets.

LG - South Africa

∞

We have experienced crime ourselves (housebreakings, theft from
, credit card fraud, etc) and have seen its impact on friends and family
y mom was held up at gunpoint, friends have been victims of smash and
rabs, a friend's father was murdered for his cellphone). It's terrible to say,
but I acknowledge that we have perhaps normalised the crime issue and just
accept that it's part of our lives now. So we have spent a lot on security and
are very careful, but not paranoid about it. Ironically, the only major serious
crime to affect a member of our immediate family was the stabbing of my
sister-in-law - which occurred in a London tube station.

PH - South Africa

∞

I was 'popping' home at irregular times during my working day to
check on the house, there was often someone sitting on the verge watching
the neighbourhood. We were not getting a single night's good sleep, I was
getting up to investigate EVERY sound I heard.

MS - UK

∞

A few months after leaving South Africa in 1999 we visited Singapore.
We were walking down the street one night and some poor chap stopped
abruptly and asked me if I had a light for his cigarette. I had him on the
pavement with my fist on its way to his throat before instinct kicked out –
that's what our experiences of crime in our South African city had turned us
into – and that was before the big trouble started down in South Africa. I
apologised to the innocent Singaporean and helped him up but he thought I
was a demented psychopath and ran off. Nowadays I would gladly help him
out with a light if I smoked and would not have that instinctive and defensive
'kill or be killed' reaction. That is what worries me about returning.

Were we paranoid? It would seem so now but after some bad

experiences in one year, one involving an intrusion into our bedroom at 3 a.m. by a known criminal who did not spend more than a few hours in jail, and another where my wife was mugged and they got away with it again, we had to make a decision. The others were having a 4x4 stolen out of a locked driveway, bag-snatching (from my wife again) and making off with passports, credit cards and cash, cell-phone snatched from daughter and a break-in and theft at our house. Were we stupid or unlucky? I don't think so. We had the locks, the dogs, the savvy. I think we were lucky we were not murdered or worse. My wife will not even go back for a holiday. I would eventually have had to take some action that I would have regretted and maybe even been incarcerated for, so it was time to go.

BM - United Arab Emirates

∞

The incessant fear of crime could have sad repercussions and it makes it so much harder to trust people. Here's a really vivid example I remember not long after someone tried to steal my car outside the gates of my house. I was stopped by a guy on the street waiting outside the front gate. He pleaded with me for help. He said he had come about an ad in the paper – a bicycle for sale by my neighbour in the adjoining cottage (another tenant, like me), but our landlady was refusing to open the gate to let him in, and he showed me the ad, too.

My first comment was rude and I brushed him off. He persisted, though, and showed me the ad. I apologized. He sounded sad and tired and he said, it is hard, yes, everyone is so suspicious of everyone, and that no one could trust anyone any more. He said he understood. I helped him after that and went in and went and got my neighbour and the guy was able to look at the bicycle after all.

CB - USA

∞

South Africa is my land and that of my forefathers. It is a country that I am passionate and proud of but CRIME is destroying the very fabric of our society. I had a conversation with a Brazilian friend of mine and we always joke about which country is worst and which city (Sao Paolo vs. Jozi). But I have visited Brazil many times and the reality is this – walk down Ipanema or Sao Conrado in Rio and you are amazed by the Favella's that surround the wealthy neighbourhoods. Yet there is almost an unwritten rule that criminals shall not target these suburbs intentionally, despite drugs and poverty running riot in Brazil.

In South Africa it is the unkown that is most worrying, that the gangs do not respect life, person or area and will do anything to survive.... I sit here in London say to myself, 'Cry My Beloved Country'.

MH - UK

∞

I am rather lucky in that I have not experienced any violent crime here first hand, but I do try stay one step ahead in my personal security. I still think there are a lot of people not taking enough precautions (locking doors, etc) and they eventually get nailed. Thinking outside the box helps – my house now does not have a bell at the gate, just a cell number. That way only someone with a legit reason to visit, who have a cell themselves calls (no bergies, etc), and they can't test to see if I'm home as it is not a landline – works like a charm!

PK - South Africa

∞

We used to live in Pretoria until the 3rd time they broke into our home, so we decided to buy a place out of town because of the safety issues. It seemed to work out well, until they broke in one morning just after 3 a.m. This time they brought guns and they fired three shots, one through the bedroom door, nearly hitting my wife, one into the wall and one while running away with their loot. We ran out the other side of the house and as we were running to the neighbours, the thief standing guard fired several shots at us, but not one bullet hit us. All they made off with was my wife's PC.

This changed my perception on South Africa. I was always a firm believer that crime is just fallout of Apartheid, but to break into someone's home and just start shooting and then stealing things that does not belong to you cannot be blamed on Apartheid. It was done purely to enrich whoever is responsible. I read in the newspaper yesterday that the robbers believe it is their right to steal from the rich because they have money to replace whatever they lost. How do you replace faith in your country and it's government? You also can't replace a human life, which we all know is worth *nothing in this country.*

*The government is also making crime so much easier, they took away the death penalty, sentences for crime is getting lighter and lighter, and the police force we won't even speak about. In the case where they shot at us, the police forensic team only came around five days later to find fingerprints. What a joke. It had rained in the meantime and there were no fingerprints to be found, which means whoever broke in is still free and doing what they do best, steal and kill.*

*There was a case where we phoned the police because we saw people breaking into the neighbour's house. The police only arrived three hours later and the policemen stated that they were not prepared to get shot for someone else's belongings, that's why they didn't respond when we phoned. Then they wanted us to serve them coffee! I just asked them to leave my premise because I was so disgusted. To this day I don't trust any person in a police uniform.*

MN - South Africa

∞ ∞ ∞

# 17

∞

# A Day in the Life

*You either decide to live in an African city or you leave, if you can.*
LOS - South Africa

*T*he daily life of a South African goes something like this: House alarm goes off at 1:00 a.m. in the morning. You and security company can't work out if it was the neighbour's cat or some serial killer/child rapist. You go back to sleep when your heart stops trying to break out of your chest.

Alarm goes off again at 3:00 a.m. This time baby wakes up and it takes two hours to settle her and calm yourself.

Get up at 5:00 a.m. – you're awake anyway (one hour earlier than two years ago – traffic forces this). In garage realise you have a flat due to pot hole you drove through yesterday. Same pothole has been fixed 10 times in last month by incompetent government employees. If it had been done properly the first time, the patch would have lasted. New rim costs R500 to replace.

Leave for work/school an hour late. Stuck in traffic for 1.5 hours. Truck breakdown number 1345276 in the last month. No rail system so roads are overused. Roads are not maintained. While you sit in the queues of traffic, minibus taxis come screaming down the emergency lane, then push in front of you. When you confront the driver, he gets out and damages the roof of your car with a metal tool (this has actually happened to me – I guess

I'm lucky – he didn't kill me).

Watch as a policeman stops the next taxi. Watch a bribe going down. (The going rate for life-threatening offences such as running a red light is R20). Work out that a policeman can make R20 per bribe x 50 bribes per day x 30 days per month = R30 000 tax free monthly. Consider changing your job. You earn a little more than this after studying for seven years and working yourself half to death honestly.

Get to work over two hours late. 'Load shedding'. Our Eskom directors were so busy paying themselves bonuses and 'work-shopping' that they forgot to increase the electricity output capacity. No, sorry, that was not the problem – the problem was the apartheid white directors (vague explanation follows of the convoluted way in which apartheid was to blame).

Leave work normal time. Take half an hour longer than usual to get to the school to pick the baby up due to 'load-shedding' – the traffic lights are off. While you (again) sit in the traffic, you hear on the radio that Jackie Selebi, our NATIONAL police commissioner, has been charged with corruption. You wonder if having a criminal background will actually count in your favour if you were to apply for a government position. Plus you'd get a free Mercedes… with a bought driver's licence if you don't have one.

Hear on the radio that Robert Mugabe, the president of Zimbabwe, has threatened to eliminate every non-supporter. He is shocked that the elections have not gone according to plan – clearly they have been rigged… after all, all of HIS machinations have not pulled off a success. South Africa's president states that it is not yet time to step in. He will use 'quiet diplomacy' to force Mugabe's hand. Very successful strategy – five million illegal Zimbabwean immigrants join the millions of Nigerian drug dealers to overburden South Africa's floundering economy.

I feel guilty for how 'fortunate' I actually am. I feel terribly sorry for the immigrants. I imagine how it must feel to not know where you will sleep, not know if you will ever see your beloved children again, not know when you will next eat, not know when you will be arrested and beaten, sent back to your country where you will be punished for having left.

Then I get smash-and-grabbed and my pity flies out the window, and the hatred swarms in. One thousand Rand excess to replace the window, six months to sort out what was in the wallet (new cards, driver's licence, etc). When I tell family what happened they are horrified that I left the wallet on the front seat. "How could you?" – as if the crime is somehow MY fault.

*Frustration is so deep that by the time I get home I'm shouting at the baby and the husband. Husband has had just as tough a day. His company's phone lines are down as the cables were stolen. His clients are all screaming for generators due to the load shedding. Our stress becomes unmanageable.*

*Husband tells me that Robert McBride, our Chief of the Metropolitan Police and of one of our largest municipalities, has written off his car in a drunk driving accident. McBride claims that the 30 witnesses who all saw that he could not even stand straight, and all told that he reeked of alcohol from five metres away, are ALL lying. (As one of our cartoonists pointed out, he must have been drunk on 'Milk of Amnesia'). The courts believe him, after our taxes of R5 million are used to defend him.*

*I realise that if I become a government employee and I kill a taxi driver in a road rage incident, I will be able to use the 'budget' allocated to my department to talk myself out of it. The job sounds more and more appealing. Plus I only have to work two hours a day at a push. If I'm fortunate enough to get a position at Home Affairs, I will not need to work at all, will be able to blame EVERYTHING on apartheid/the computer system/the other branch.*

*My husband and I, my friends and family, are all coming to the conclusion that there is a common denominator in all of this. Everyone is too afraid to speak up and address what the problem really is. The people in power are too incompetent to run it properly. They have no accountability and always take the easy way out (blame someone else, lie, bribe, steal). They have made a mess of everything that they have had a hand in. So, sadly, and against our upbringing and consciences, many (and I say MANY) have become racists, due to the fear, frustration and hopelessness of the situation.*

*I know that if anyone were to EVER touch one of my children or other close family members, I will retaliate without a doubt. How sad that a God-fearing person is driven to such violent thoughts, knowing that they are 'selling their own souls' in the process.*

*We hear on the news that a driver chased a 12 year old smash-and-grabber after he stole his cellphone. The child dropped the phone, but the driver shot him anyway. OF COURSE this is wrong (what have we become?) but so many of us understand him and why he did it. What police protection? They are all in court defending themselves of their corruption charges.*

The death penalty won't work in South Africa – no electricity for the electric chair, no cables for the hanging. Anyway, by the time the idiots have gotten so far as to actually arrange for the event, the child rapist will have walked out the front door (no security).

Along with the rest of the world, our food prices have shot up and our petrol price is astronomical (far more than other countries, we hear: the government needs to fund the president's new electric fence around his state residence at a cost of R30 million, even though he claims that the crime is no more than in any other country).

After the alarm has gone off at night, I often lie awake and try to put myself in the shoes of poverty stricken world residents. Would I kill for food for my children? What would I do to get myself out of the poverty cycle? I know from the bottom of my heart, that I respect human life too much to kill for something that does not belong to me. I would make a plan, whether it be digging on a rubbish dump or even begging, but I would not resort to crime. So sorry for you, criminals of South Africa, the past/your upbringing/the government are no justification for killing for R10.

We stay because we hope that somehow we will escape anything REALLY bad happening to us, i.e. something worse than a taxi driver assaulting us or our house being emptied out. We cry for our beloved country and we stay because we love our country.

CR - South Africa

∞

Must get back to my job, and remember to call the car-insurers – got that tracker installed, so now with the immobilizer, gear lock, steering lock, car alarm, garage and security guard, maybe they'll give me coverage, at a highly inflated premium, as I am a 'risk' to them, not a paying client...

CH - South Africa

∞

But when we are living at home we miss the freedom, the safety and security of the life which we have in most other countries. Even in 'less developed' countries, you do not need to live behind burglar bars and electric fences, women do not have to clutch their handbags. It is safe to walk to the shops, or stroll on the beach or in a park, even alone. There you can still drive with car windows open, and do not have to carefully inspect the area near the house, before driving into the driveway.

    South Africa is being held hostage by criminals. We can see how it is affecting all areas of life, including the famous ubuntu. It is just not safe to help strangers in trouble. It is getting more difficult to meet new people and every time we get back we find that more and more of our friends have left the country. We are still hoping things will improve and that we will, one day, be able to retire in relative safety.

JG - South Africa

∞

    I even intend getting a wrought iron gate erected in the passage linking lounge and bedrooms as I feel that the many protective measures already adopted are insufficient to protect me and my guests, especially after reading about an incident where access to a home was gained through a lounge window, despite burglar alarm being activated, and the only thing that saved the life of the family was the gate separating living and sleeping areas!

MF - South Africa

∞

    Where to start, crime has become unbearable, little children being raped is an everyday occurrence, raping in general is an everyday occurrence, nobody even knows how many there truly are because it doesn't even reach the news. There are so many farm murders that farming is the most dangerous job in this country, more farmers are killed every year than in any other job, even more than police, it's a hate crime. Hijackings are probably occurring hourly, I don't think there is anybody in this country who doesn't know of at least one person who has been a victim of crime. My girlfriend has been a victim three times already; at least it wasn't too serious (hijacking, theft and smash and grab).

    We don't have enough electricity supply, with load shedding (areas' electricity being cut off for four hour intervals) occurring often, furthermore cable theft is an everyday occurrence, so more power outages. Even if you are so lucky not to be a victim of crime and don't mind sitting in the dark, but you are white then you have no more rights, can't get jobs because of BEE (black economic empowerment) and if you get a job you will be paid half the salary of a black person.

*Please don't think I'm a racist, because I'm not, I hate it that anybody is treated differently because of their skin colour. The country's best policing service (the Scorpions) aren't allowed to exist any more, because they go after high profile criminals (don't want to mention names, but just do a Google search).*

*The list can continue for days, the state of the hospitals, the state of the roads, corruption, etc. I just want to get out of here before the country falls apart or before the rand plummets or before I get killed or my girlfriend gets raped (which is my biggest fear). I used to love South Africa and didn't want to leave, but I've been left with no choice.*

FP - South Africa

∞

*I remember telling someone in London in about 1998 that I thought the country would start becoming 'third world' within 10 years and that the economy would start teetering within 20. I think that it will hold out untill after 2010 and then thereafter things will be very different economically. What is definitely a problem is the crime, exacerbated by the enormous influx of foreigner, legal and illegal, flooding over the borders.*

*Zimbabwe's woes are huge and the fact that Thabo Mbeki still insists, as does Jacob Zuma I gather, that we have to give them support to sort out their problems and that quiet diplomacy is the route to take, makes one realise that the African nations are actually very against white interference or suggestion.*

*My daughter has just handed in her Master's thesis in literature which she did through the Department of African Studies at UCT, and she used two novels about living in Johannesburg written by black authors to analyse the concepts of the individual in the urban environment with reference to the fact that Johannesburg is now an African city with little frightened pockets of white enclosures. And my daughter, who is working on a black television drama, shooting mainly in Soweto, while she waits to register for her doctorate, says that there IS a system in Johannesburg now, but it is of organized anarchy, and you absolutely can't weaken!*

*That said, it doesn't alter the vast difference between the cultures and the very real fear that many have. The only real commonality is the desire for money which is not surprising in the African mind, given the oppression of the past, and the vast 'theft' if you like, of the country's resources by people* not originally of this country. So this must contribute enormously to the corruption that is so endemic here, but which is no different to any of the African countries. So, you either decide to live in an African city or you leave, if you can. We haven't yet.

LOS - South Africa

∞

The country seems to be economically stable, our tourism numbers are up and our country is alive with creativity (Design Indaba and Decorex). People seem to still be investing here in property and businesses. Most of our friends don't seem interested in leaving and people are still optimistic. There is a lot of money to be made here. Schools are still good. Our children are still raised with respect and manners. We don't have the levels of violence that schools in other parts of the world seem to have. We have very few natural disasters. We don't have any real terrorist threat.

And I think all those things combined make everyone here say: "It's a sh#t world out there, if you leave here, where do you go and what will happen to you there? Do you really want to move to the States with the drug and gun culture in schools? And the terror threats?"

Incidentally, we have American friends who say for the first time they're embarrassed about being American. He cannot travel to some destinations for work because as an American he's not allowed access to some countries. We remember when we felt embarrassed about being South African and couldn't get visas for some countries, but we certainly don't live in shame any more.

I think it's easier for people to live in their home country and to understand the local situation than to move somewhere and have to adopt that country's baggage. I don't speak for myself but rather for our large circle of friends. When we lived overseas, we didn't adopt their levels of xenophobia, racism, drug problems, tax problems etc. We simply lived there as lucky expats, with the best the country had to offer us. We didn't read a newspaper or listen to the news, because the problems weren't our problems and we didn't have to get involved.

We do that to a large extent now in South Africa. We live here like expats. We get the best out of the country that we can right now. We go away weekends to places like Stanford, Knysna, Swellendam and Greyton. Our kids are having the time of their lives. We live in a beautiful suburb, we

eat very well, we drive the car we want to drive and we see our families whenever we feel like it. But we have one foot ready to run if we need to. We're lucky as we can get posted to another country at the drop of a hat, so we won't have the costly and traumatic exercise of packing up and saying goodbye forever. And the constant justification of why you're 'giving up and abandoning your country'. For us it would simply be a move to another job. And no-one would ever be the wiser.
LP - South Africa

∞

My mother is 86 years old and is loathe to leave the country at her age but she will have no choice. She is still very active and is driving and working every day in the office of the catholic church she has been a parishioner since birth. Four months ago she was viciously robbed and assaulted when she was leaving the church. Since then she has had to have medical treatment for the injuries and can no longer drive. We are told to consider ourselves lucky that she was not killed. What a wonderful country we live in when we consider a citizen of 80 odd working at a church lucky that she was only viciously assaulted. So she would have no say when the time comes to move on.
LF - South Africa

∞

And although, I'm uncertain of how we'll cope into old age in another country (and I do fear this, together with my husband's possible unhappiness), I know for SURE, that I do not want to grow old here! A little old white lady would be a sitting target... duck!
CK - South Africa

∞

What a wonderful Cape Town welcome for C – an attempted hijacking had just gone awry and the victim, a young lad called Nico, got shot through the femur! M and a nurse attended to the poor kid (while waiting for an ambulance that took 30 minutes to arrive) and I landed up directing traffic as well as the policemen (about five vans arrived!) who were absolutely bloody clueless on what to do!

We eventually got to our meal an hour later and after an initial *discussion regarding the event that had just occurred, carried on the evening as if nothing had happened! Scary to think that we have gotten so blase about crime and that it could have been us....*

M - South Africa

∞

*Do you know that crime has always been a constant in South Africa? The only difference is that pre-Apartheid it did not affect the white people because they were protected by the police who did not care much about the violence in the non-white areas. Most white people had no idea of what was happening on the other side (most just did not care) while they enjoyed a life of leisure in the leafy suburbs around South Africa. During this time I lost more friends and family to violent crime than I have since post-apartheid.*

RP - South Africa

∞ ∞ ∞

# 18

∞

## Letter To My Parents

by BT - South Africa
(used with permission)

I feel so angry at the moment. Here I am, finally enjoying the success of what I have worked for over the last 10 years, with so much potential to grow in my career and myself and now this. I have made many sacrifices (not to mention the sacrifices of my parents) to get to where I am. I am feeling very disillusioned with life in general and the country at the moment. I never really thought I'd get to a stage where I find myself complaining about 'the situation', but well – here it is.

I don't know if the recent developments are signs that I should pack up and go, leave the family I love dearly – to be so far away and only be able to see them once a year with the occasional birthday call. I feel resentful that the selfish senseless illness that plagues our country, makes me have to leave everything I have worked so hard for. I have earned the right to put my roof down on my sports car on a weekend and sit at a trendy sidewalk café and feel safe. I am entitled not to have to worry that when I walk back to my car I won't have some chap remove my possessions from me as he holds a gun to my head – or to have to pay the blackmailing guard who 'watches' my car (even with its state of the art alarm system). I wonder what he would do if a gun wielding man approached him. The smell of that metal is not something you forget easily. Every time I close my eyes I can see the gun.

I have not taken anything away from anyone in getting here. I have not hurt anyone in getting here.

What is there left here for me? A young, white, male South African? If I am to invest in a house in a few years time I will have to buy one with a generator, because the electricity supplier can't keep up with the demand due solely to inherent greed – lovely bonuses those chaps got – I would love to apply that performance appraisal to my firm – I'd be loaded. (Check the Constitution: right to housing etc....)

BEE and Affirmative Action[9] did not fail because of incompetence. It failed because Africa looks after its own. Philanthropy is a foreign notion. You never read in the history books of the Zulu nation making a donation of cattle and grain to the starving Xhosa's during a famine. I cannot recall ever seeing a Bentley-driving, Prada-bedecked African giving anything to the countless beggars at the traffic lights in Johannesburg. It is a society where everyone expects to be given something for nothing. Minimum input – maximum output, *tata ma chance*. I too have suffered in the past. It does not make me expect anything different from the world. Look at the bigger picture...life.

If this was published my comments would not be perceived with the intention with which they were made. Instead I will be branded a bitter, jaded racist. But what makes me, a 4th or 5th generation South African any different from any other African in this country? I have just as much right to be here and to make my contribution.

Despite the cloud hanging over us we continue with our daily routines, only making a few adjustments: running back to make sure the gate was really locked, scanning across the veld when we stop at an off-ramp to ensure no soulless chancer will shoot us for a cell phone, or the R50 in our wallet. Or we hire a guard to stand outside our homes so that we can drive in and out of our garage safely.

I think what I am writing is the same monotonous tune. But what if last night had gone differently? What if I had been shot and paralysed or disfigured? Would we then have made our move? Would I then have

---

[9] BEE or Black Economic Empowerment is an official program in South Africa whereby the ANC government aims to create economic opportunities for previously disadvantaged racial groups.

moved overseas, with even more difficulty? The analogy is like owning a classic car. When the cost of the car and its leaks and incontinence start outweighing the benefits and joys of driving it, you flog it without a thought – or you pay the price.

I look at the Facebook profiles of my friends who have emigrated. They have weekends in Prague, trips to Italy, a carefree environment. Yes they work hard. But no harder than the 180 odd hour month I work here. The only difference is they are free from the truly violent senseless crimes that affect us on a daily basis. Yes society is sick – you get the occasional sick bastard murdering a child in the UK. But then the bastard is hunted down relentlessly. We have neither the resources (nor the inclination I often suspect) to do the same here.

Alan Paton wrote a book a long time ago that addressed the social injustices of this country. A book that opened the eyes of many South Africans of all walks and creeds. The book was entitled *Cry the Beloved Country*. When I watched on TV the news item of the mother of that little girl, standing next to her car and her lifeless daughter in the back, the title came back to me. For what else is there happening now? Is there not just another form of social injustice present here? Is our beloved country still not crying a different wail?

A few of my friends have consoled me for the second very violent incident which I have experienced here – the second for our family this year – "at least he didn't hurt you". What consolation is that? He had no right to do that in the first place. I can almost say with biblical certainty, that if I was hungry and homeless and starving I would steal. But with the same certainty I can say I would never harm anyone. I would steal food and clothes from people's homes when they weren't at home. Yes maybe my cellphone and expensive wallet could be sold for a few Rands and they would be used to buy food, but would it have been worth ending my life for it? If you count the number of times I have actually been a victim of 'crime' you can say a solid 20 or so. Let's do a recap: 16 odd housebreakings when I was a student. Two car break-ins and two gun point events…. I wonder what the average Australian has in a life time – one housebreaking? One pick-pocket?

If one does a minor calculation on the revenue earned by the tax authorities on young professionals like me, and the potential for taxing the daylights out of me for the next 30 odd years of my professional life, it is quite astonishing. Then think about the revenue lost from all the chaps like me who are leaving. That too is astonishing – I wonder if the government considers it. I nearly had a hernia when I heard the CEO of Eskom, Thulani Gabashe, make the statement that South Africa cannot be an island of prosperity in a sea of poverty. I think he was saying we must carry on exporting electricity, even when we don't have enough for ourselves.... Mmmm, *Animal Farm*?

So must we then bring ourselves down to the levels of violence experienced in our neighbouring countries too? I just – really maybe I am thick – don't understand it? Why would I not leave, when the place is falling apart (quite literally)? You should see some of the potholes in Houghton – luckily most families have a 4X4 as a third vehicle, so the Roller is safe from serious damage until the JRA decide to fix it.

I know I am angry but I think what I am saying is that this is the final straw. Maybe I don't have a strong enough constitution to handle this place any more; maybe I am braver than I thought in making this decision. The thing is, it is not just Jo'burg – for heaven's sake, look what happened to 'R' in White River, where we used to sleep with our doors open.

I am sick to my stomach and truly heartbroken that my dream, be it shallow or silly, is truly turning slowly into something worthless. If you take a man's choice away, he will do irrational things. But I think that enough is enough. I need to do something about this for my own sanity. So I am not running away. I am going to search for a better life elsewhere. If I find it, I'll bring you over to join me.

I love you.

∞ ∞ ∞

*South Africa needs to wake up! I tried helping out when I saw a crime, but all that did was uproot me into the witness protection for six months with no contact allowed with loved ones, and therefore I won't do it again.*

LC - South Africa

∞

*We come from large Catholic foreign stock in our family. I have 44 cousins in total. We WERE a large family who all lived in one area. Very, very close. All attending the same schools. We grew up in a safe happy, environment. It is hard for people to imagine how fortunate we were with* aunts, uncles and cousins all in the same area. Today mainly because of crime and the uncertainty of a future in the country they are scattered all over the world and we have lost something that is irreplaceable.   LF - South Africa

∞

Most of my friends and family feel the same – they're happy to stick around when they're single or childless, but as soon as kids come into the equation, they start looking abroad.   EC - Australia

∞

It's now that my wife and I find ourselves in a similar predicament, torn between not wanting to go but feeling that we have no choice. We have two young boys and I feel that I need to remove my family from a situation where they are at a higher risk of becoming victims. We're lucky, we can leave tomorrow, many can't. Every week it seems there is another crime where a child is the victim either directly or indirectly never mind all the other crime.

The collapse of basic services and corruption at all levels of government are further factors pushing us away. I could carry on. So yes we are leaving South Africa with a hope to return one day but not really wanting to leave in the first place, this is our home but alas not for long.
  SM - South Africa

∞

Yes, we would consider leaving South Africa (although we don't want to) because of CRIME! Too nerve racking living here, having to be constantly vigilant. I think 'the closer it (i.e. crime) gets to home' is what would push us to leave. We've been burgled twice, my husband was in an attempted hijacking and had a knife held at his throat and his clothes slashed, he has been mugged six times, I arrived at my friends house when her domestic was being attacked and stabbed, and had to grab the children and rush domestic to hospital and then today my sister-in-law and other mothers were robbed at gunpoint when fetching the children from play school in Constantia. However, no one has been harmed, and I hesitate to say this, YET.

My husband's family has emigrated to New Zealand (brother, sister and their families and his parents). My brother and his family emigrated to America. What keeps us here are my parents and my sister and her husband and we love our country but are fearful living here.

I can put up with corruption, ineptness, inability to run the country effectively but when personal safety is threatened that is the catalyst that would make us leave.

LS - South Africa

∞

Crime in South Africa is a very serious issue at the moment. Criminals are becoming more and more violent with unnecessary deaths and more rapes and child rapes reported on a daily basis. Criminals are becoming less fearful due their use of more force and purely just taking what they want and killing and raping people at will. These actions are forcing the people of South Africa to live like prisoners, which has basically reversed the roles. It was always the criminals behind bars with the innocent and free on the outside, but it is now the innocent and no longer free that are behind bars, with the criminals on the outside doing as they please with very little justice taking its course.

There are more and more police officers taking bribes to earn a better living, leading to less policing of crime. The head of the police in South Africa is being investigated in corruption probes. There are more and more parliamentary officials being questioned regarding corruption and the presidency being contested by a man that is currently also on trial. To combat these officials being taken to justice, the government decides to have the Scorpions disbanded, after they have been the only agency to successfully tackle and bring to justice certain criminal government officials and organized crime within the government of South Africa. This on it's own is becoming the driving factor for people to leave the country. Years ago, all irregularities regarding government, bribery and corruption of/by officials elected by the people, were questioned and made public, but now everyone in government covers it up, sweeps it under the carpet and forgets about it.

The people's voice is no longer heard and we are therefore all living in silence in a corrupt society. There seems to be no follow through for crime and punishment any more, and this is what leads to the next corrupt official being born into a criminal underground, knowing that they will get away with enriching themselves at the expense of others. At least a handful of the *parliamentary officials are still uncorrupted and unwilling to accept this negative change in our society, and are willing to voice their opinion, possibly at the expense of their jobs, but at least we know that it is not all a lost cause.*

*There are still a few positive attributes regarding government in general, but they are far outweighed by the negatives. I believe that if this trend continues, our beautiful country will be raped and pillaged and brought to its knees and may then suffer the same fate as Zimbabwe, which would ultimately impact on everyone's lives, regardless of race, faith or belief, except of course for those that enriched themselves and too fled the sunny shores of South Africa.*

MH - South Africa

∞

*The high level of violent crime is horrific, yes, there is high crime in other countries, but it is the violence that has escalated and appears almost beyond control that is most scary. There is no regard for human life. Having said all the above, I'm still here and really, truly hope to be here until I die – of natural causes! I should add, that my father was British and I hold dual citizenship.*

NA - South Africa

∞

*It is time that everyone here and abroad realized that our diversity is our strength – and that that diversity means individual colours on the rainbow. To try to make our rainbow nation into one homogenous group will simply muddy the waters, resulting in some mediocre, indefinable colour, rather than the vibrant, vital, individual colours which side-by-side form Bishop Desmond Tutu's beautiful rainbow nation.*

*My feelings have always been that when the women of this country, irrespective of race, creed, colour, band together, stand as one, and tell the government that they are TIRED of the violence, crime, etc, and follow this by action – as only women can, then, and only then, will things start happening here, and will we see progress.*

*Currently the cultural thing is enormous. In tribal cultures no matter what the chief says or does, his clan will follow and honour him. This psychology tends, in my view, to spill over into politics and into this whole thing of democratic voting. People can be desperate with conditions, but the* respect and obedience owed to a chief is inbred, and as I have said when the safety of children and women becomes such that the women are no longer prepared to tolerate it, despite whatever loyalties they may have, THEN we will see changes here.

JH - South Africa

∞

I believe that this country is being run into the ground. There is a culture of un(in)accountability and cronyism. When the ANC took over in 1994, the air itself vibrated with positivity. We were all so excited, you could feel the potential in the air, it was something palpable. Fourteen years later, it is a joke; this country is going the same way as every other country on this continent.

Fourteen years ago, there was crime, but not like there is today. The only crime that I have been exposed to, thank God, was when my house was broken into. My father has been mugged, his house burgled three times and his car was stolen - all on separate occasions. My mother-in-law was held up in a bank robbery and my sister-in-law was held up at gunpoint. We live in a secure complex. This means that we have a guard at the gate and two always walking the perimeter. The complex has an electric fence. In our house, we have an alarm and are linked to an armed response company. All our windows and doors have burglar bars. We essentially live in a prison.

I understand that the inequities of the past are coming back to haunt us. I understand that crime is rampant because of poverty. But when the government pockets the money that is supposed to be spent on alleviating poverty (and don't get me wrong – they have done a lot of good work – it is always the few that poison the barrel) and they themselves set the example that crime is tolerated – that is not on. I don't care that most MPs were struggle or liberation heroes. If an MP or minister commits a crime, they should be suspended without pay immediately. Not allowed to go on a fully-paid holiday while the state bumbles along trying to find a reason to not prosecute them.

The Scorpions are the only thing left that could possibly save this country from crime in the upper echelons and of course they are being dismantled because they are so successful. The thing that really bugs me is how stupid the government must think that we are, that we cannot see this for what it is.

Shall I discuss the electricity crisis? If this had happened in any first world country – the government would have been toppled. What do we do here? We pay the executive of Eskom millions more in bonuses on the 31$^{st}$ March 2008 and then they request a 53% increase in electricity tariffs. Alec Erwin defended the bonuses saying that if they did not pay them out, the executive would not be motivated to work. Now, excuse me. I am paid a salary to do a job. If I do it particularly well, I will get given a bonus. It is not a right, it is performance based. The Eskom executive sat around and did nothing for 14 years except occasionally bleat at the government to say that there was going to be a problem. Then they sat back and pocketed their obscene packages. And now, together, they have run the country into the ground.
AS - South Africa

∞

The big trick is simple: Keep the people warm, fed and housed while you EDUCATE the youth. Tax the rich, educate the poor. I consider myself to be a capitalist businessman who believes in a free economy but I'm prepared to make a large tax contribution if it means my great-grandchildren will not have to carry a gun.
BM - United Arab Emirates

∞ ∞ ∞

## 19

∞

## Living in My Kasteel[10]

*Are we leaving or aren't we?*
*That's the question everybody is asking everyone else.*
*And the answer is...we're not leaving today.*
TW - South Africa

The large old farmhouse, with clay brick walls that were 2ft wide, had become my sanctuary. Over seven years of living there, I'd fitted into the space contained in the small village environment. I had never believed that I was a small town girl. I was a big city, metropolitan personality – New York was my ultimate destination – who enjoyed department stores, lights, cinemas, theatres, street cafes and trendy one-off boutiques. I enjoyed being surrounded by the energy and organized chaos of a city. In visiting Paris, New York, London, Hong Kong, Frankfurt, Madrid and Washington, I had felt at home in every place. I was a dedicated city girl.

Suddenly, I found myself in a small village of maybe a thousand people; one café; one hotel; a small post office; a library; a municipal office and a statue of a red ox on the village square apparently erected in 1938 to honour the brave oxen of the Great Trek.

---

[10] 'Kasteel' is the Afrikaans word for castle. It is also part of the name of the village, Riebeek Kasteel, where we lived before our move to the USA.

There were no traffic lights in town. There was no need, for there were never enough cars to be loftily known as 'traffic'. One Saturday night, as we walked down to The Royal Hotel, three cars hurtled down the main road. It was a scene from an avant-garde movie – quiet town, five people walking down the road, moonlit night, absolute stillness and suddenly, loud noise, three cars race by and then ... silence resumes, five people continue walking, moonlit night and absolute stillness.

The bottle store, an adjunct to The Royal Hotel, was named 'Jou Ma Se Likkewaan'. This was not a name that I could understand so, to everyone's amusement, I translated it as 'Your Mother's Liquor Wagon'[11]. Now that was a name that made sense to me. Although I had studied Afrikaans, a required language, at school, I had never used the language in daily speech and it became an interesting exercise in literal translation and learning.

The ordered chaos of our old house's design suited my personality. Made of dense clay bricks, some of the walls slanted slightly, wider at the base and narrowing infinitesimally towards the ceiling. It was unnoticeable to most visitors and you'd have to look closely to see it, but to us it meant that paintings would never hang correctly. Solid wooden doorframes weren't quite square to the ceiling or was it the ceiling that slanted instead? Never mind, it really meant that if you hung anything on the wall, in order to make it look square, you had to skew it a little to left or right.

Something about the house reminded me of Alice in Wonderland. There was no conventional, central passage with rooms leading off. This was a mash of rooms. A lounge lead to a bedroom and a dressing room with a view of the road, which led into another bedroom with another dressing room, which lead into a dining-room which lead into a hallway, or into the lounge or the sunroom – four doors from all directions opening out from the dining-room – the central gathering place of our home. The huge hallway, lodged between the kitchen, dining-room, sunroom and guest bathroom, had intense acoustics that echoed from mounted speakers,

> South Africa is changing from a nation into a group of numerous tiny city states, each the size of one house, armed to the teeth and highly suspicious of the next door neighbours.
> SDT - Australia

---

[11] The correct translation would be "Your Mother's Monitor" or "Your Mother's Large Lizard."

throughout the old house. We danced in that central hallway because it was big enough for a party. An Afrikaans speaking neighbour, visiting us one Sunday, when Anton Goosen's music was raising the roof in the hallway, said "Waar kry julle rooinekke hierdie musiek? Ek het nie geweet...." ("Where do you English get this music? I did not know....")

The kitchen was painted bright, cheerful sunshine yellow with Oregon pine cupboards made by my husband from old floorboards we had lifted from the lounge and dining-room. Fifteen foot wooden ceilings kept the house cool in the summertime as we slept with doors and windows open, under our mosquito nets. I'd painted the dining room a deep avocado green with stencilled stars and moons and bought a huge gilt-framed mirror in Cape Town which opened up the room and reflected the golden stars opposite. This was a room of magic and happiness. Filling the eight-seater table with people, food, laughter, and a couple of bottles of wine from the local winery, was one of the great pleasures of my life. Jerepigo or Hanepoot completed our meals while we ate dessert – my home-made Cassata ice-cream or perhaps candied figs with cheeses made locally in the valley.

A ubiquitous array of local wildlife (creatures not people) patronized the house. Lots of black button spiders and house button spiders (or brown button spiders) delighted in nesting in the highest corners. We relocated as many as we could but sometimes I temporarily silenced my inner Buddhist and sent them on to their next incarnation. I remember finding an adder living in the guest bedroom, frogs that used to take refuge in our dressing room occasionally, a couple of huge rain spiders in the bathtub one night.... From being a big city girl, terrified of 'creatures', I became a magnanimous host to the 'critters'. Our cats, Heneage and Pecan, kept the local bird and mouse population under control. Every afternoon, like clockwork, sitting in the sunroom with the window open, you could hear one of them crunching happily outside through mid-afternoon hors d'oeurves.

> *I miss scenery, and places, but it's the people and the comfort zone I miss. I'd love to go back to the South Africa I remember, sitting on the stoep on a warm night listening to the insects and drinking a glass of wine. Now that would be home.*
> 
> LM - The Netherlands

Our furniture was an eclectic mix of donations from parents and family as well as a couple of new items given to, and purchased by, us. My husband and father-in-law's woodworking business filled our house with unique handiwork. Standing lamps, salad bowls, table lamps, a crib and a dressing table (made by my father-in-law and passed down through the family). Our Pau Marfin (a hard Brazilian yellow wood) bed was made by James when I was pregnant. Up until that point, we had been sleeping on a mattress on the floor. He took pity on me trying to roll over and out of the bed in the morning, top-heavy, like a tortoise flailing on its back. The bed was tall enough for both dogs to sleep comfortably underneath it. Bracken perfected the art of jumping onto the bed to sleep with us, until one night, in a particularly deep sleep, he rolled over and off the bed – clunk! A deep, lengthy sigh emanated from the floor and his snoring resumed.

James wanted the walls painted white which was a non-colour and too insipid for my taste. The gaily painted walls were green in the dining room, yellow in the kitchen, peach in the guest bedroom, animal murals in the children's room, and a deep shade of pink in the hallway.

This eccentric place defined me.

∞ ∞ ∞

*Besides my house looking like the upper grade version of Fort Knox, no wait, let me rephrase that, a high security prison would like to know my secrets! Let's see, I have high walls, electric fencing that has been spiked, armed response, lights all around the house so its daylight 24/7 around my property, four Rottweilers, a 9mm, a shotgun and a magnum, burglar bars and gates all around, and a poodle just in case something happens to the big dogs then he will bark and alert me. If this is what the new South Africa is, if this is freedom, then I would rather be locked up because I'll be safer.*

CVZ - South Africa

∞

*A fundamental love of Africa – my motherland. Also the fact that my personal history is rooted in South Africa. The fabric of my life is woven into that of the places, events and people with whom I have grown up and grown older. Maybe if I could have taken all my friends and family along then I would go... but even so what about the places, the events, the culture?! I do not fear the other country or people, or my ability to make a living there, being given the chance. What I do fear is the difficulty in building up a new 'network' of people with whom one can share a sense of belonging. I also think one will always be an 'outsider', a 'foreigner' in another country. If* things deteriorate in South Africa to the point that it has in some other African countries, e.g. Zimbabwe, then this will not stop me. I think the whole thing is a balance between our fears on the one hand and the hope/expectations we have that things will either not get worse, or will improve. As it is now one can still live with it – just.

PH - South Africa

∞

We have both lived in Johannesburg since we were three, and we're still living in the same 5km radius where we grew up! Our kids are going to the same schools we went to – which is quite significant to us because, since all four of our parents immigrated here, we did not go to the schools they went to. So we like the feeling that we're strengthening our roots. Also, several other parents at these schools, like us, also went to these schools as children. That is quite a community to belong to.

TW - South Africa

∞

My two children and I live alone in the Free State as he (husband) does contract work in Johannesburg. The night that person broke into my house was the most frightening night of my life. Luckily the person could not come into my room, as I would push my bed and my son's cot against the door (because it can't be locked) since the break-in in my car. And I thank God that I did. Things could have turned out so much worse.

All I want to say is that if I could, I would also move out of South Africa. I am so scared these days, of everything. I feel like I am being watched and I feel as though I am more vulnerable now than I was before all of this happened. Things are just getting worse. And the police don't really have sympathy when something like a break in happens. They see it every day. Their words to me were "It won't really help to open up a case."

LJV - South Africa

∞

Here our home has burglar guards, burglar gates, perimeter alarms with armed security and electric fences and would you believe me if I said at night time, when I put my head on my pillow I still do not feel safe. When my husband is away I gather the kids and have them all sleep in my locked bedroom with me. I know it sounds ridiculous but I would far rather seem ridiculous than be pushing up daisies. One of my daughters friends (nine year old) lost her Mum a couple of weeks ago, her parents owned an upmarket guest house (right near our home) and she was murdered in her bed and raped while her child slept in the room next door... And that barely made front page news before being replaced with another horrendous story.

LW - South Africa

∞

(What has stopped you leaving thus far?) The familiarity of my wonderful country... and I suppose, to be 100% honest, the fear of the unknown. (What fears do you have about leaving South Africa and settling in a new country?) Leaving my 'comfort zone' and going somewhere where I know no-one and where I have no family.

LG - South Africa

∞

I sit outside on my patio and don't 'dare' to feel at ease – I now keep my cats with me outside and watch their reactions – a dog would bark and alert any intruder but with a cat you'll know something's amiss before the intruder is even in sight. I discovered this one day when my cat, sitting next to me in my lounge in Woodstock where I used to live, suddenly stood up, poised silently in that alert feline way, eyes fixed on my front door. I was already alerted when I spotted a man trying to sneak oh so silently around the corner from my front door into the house. That was several years ago and the man pretended he was looking for work (this was a sunday morning, and my husband and father were working at the back of the house). I was only lucky - 9 times out of 10, you're not.

Since then, my cats are my best alarm. When I go into my house after work every day I always look for the cats – if they're not happily curled up on the couch or quietly sitting in their usual spot, I won't go into the house. I bet this brings back memories for you.

CD - South Africa

∞

I hear from my brother living in Pretoria about the latest attacks and rapes that are increasing. Neighbourhoods having a single entrance and exit point with security guards to stop attackers coming into the neighbourhood. Cars protected with smash and grab 'strong plastic darkened window foil' as rocks are smashed at cars to grab cell phones and bags at robots. Friends that get home after dark call and pay for an extra security firm to check if their houses are safe before going inside. They lock themselves in their rooms at night and bar their passageways and hope there is never a fire!

KB - Germany

∞

The crime was starting to affect us almost on a daily basis. Our cars were broken into, our neighbour was burgled. They stole one of our cars and a mugging in front of my workplace in broad daylight left a German tourist stabbed and bleeding in our lobby. My house had a two metre high perimeter brick wall with electric wires and broken glass on top of it.

LRK - USA

∞

If you put your head in the sand, as most people do here because they have very little ability of being able to change things, life is good. The schooling, if you can afford the private route is good and is a lot less expensive than overseas private schools. Yes, perhaps the boys will have to go overseas to University but we will cross that bridge when we get to it and make provision in the meantime. Also private medical facilities are very good with leading edge technology and support. We have lots of sunshine and our children are able to grow up in a outdoor/sporty environment.

CR - South Africa

∞

My husband and I did not join the mass exodus when the new regime came into power. Things were going very well for us business-wise, our daughter was doing very well at school, life was good. We had no intentions of leaving then and we constantly had the wool pulled over our eyes by the media mentions of what a great 'rainbow' nation we had become. We laughed at our neighbours who had emigrated to New Zealand, only to return four years later. The return of expats was comforting as it made us believe the grass is not greener, and that we do indeed live in the best country in the world.

When the crime began to increase, we just built our walls higher, added the electric fences and carried on with life. We adapted our social life too, so instead of going out to restaurants where one had to drive for more than 15 minutes at night, we would resort to going to the local steak house a couple of blocks away. And so we became complacent about all the crime in the country.

LK - South Africa

∞

If they reported the actual crime figures we would be terrified for the people we have left behind. It is the one single element that deters us from even visiting there. A mate of mine (ex 1 Parachute Battalion) who turns fifty this year had to use all his training to avoid shots being fired at him by a gang of thugs trying to high-jack his BMW. A while later another bunch scaled his ten foot wall, blanketed the razor wire, fortunately tripped the motion sensor beams running across the garden and could not get through the 25mm burglar bars before armed security arrived. They got away with a Weber BBQ. He reckons he has a lucky angel. I don't need that sort of lucky angel, thanks.

BM - United Arab Emirates

∞ ∞ ∞

# 20

∞

## From A Distance
### Non-South Africans Speak

*Maybe if we had decided to live there for a longer time we could get used to all the stuff (fences, armed response, windows closed at the traffic lights and so on).*
CT - Italy

It's hard to explain to people who haven't lived in a country so crime-ridden what this hyped up feeling is like. I can only say that when you've lived in countries where crime hasn't been such a problem, and then go to one where it is, you may begin to understand. It really feels like, well, for lack of a better word, like a 'war zone' one had to live in and travel in.

I would never go walking after 6 p.m. at night in my northern suburban neighbourhood in Johannesburg – I'd take the car and drive to the café instead or to anywhere. Locking and unlocking rooms, grille doors, doors became second nature, elementary, as did setting alarms. Even in daylight, it was never good to leave an outside door open to a courtyard even behind a front security gate and high walls. (Even in Pretoria, and I always felt safer there). I got into the habit of scoping out everything and everyone whenever I approached or left my car in a public place or went into a bank or a public place and even with other people would be the same. I'd knuckle my keys between my fingers. I became quicker in all my movements too.

I avoided driving in the Johannesburg CBD whenever possible and

NEVER at night – I think I went to the Marketplace Theatre only one time when I lived there the second time. I had a friend in Fordsburg then whom I'd go and visit, but I'd never stay more than two hours or so and never late in the day. When I stopped at robots (traffic intersections) I'd always be looking around me. And I know I got off lightly in only the two years I lived there. And I know most South Africans have had it far, far worse.

In the two years I lived there in Johannesburg, here is what happened to me. Please note, I'm not counting things that happened to my parents. They have their own stories: I house sat with my family for a family friend in Woodmead for a time. One night, some guys stole one of our friends' cars from the garage and broke into the house servant's quarters. Another time, someone grabbed my watch off my wrist outside the OK Bazaar in Braamfontein near where I worked. Someone attempted to steal my wreck of a car outside my house in Parkhurst when I stupidly briefly parked on the street – the demobilizer slowed him down and prevented him from stealing it. The car wasn't worth anything, it was a battered old car.

The house my brother and I rented for a time in Rosebank was broken into in the middle of the night. The police woke my brother in the early hours of the morning to report they had come upon the thieves passing stuff over the garden wall of the house to the street. We discovered that they were trying to unscrew and pry open locked doors to get to the bedroom sections of the house during the night. My brother slept with a gun for weeks in his bedside table and instructed me on how to use it. I never had to and I don't think I could have, anyway.

All of my co-workers had similar experiences of break-ins and my Indian friend in Fordsburg was robbed on several occasions at night. Her children refused to stay in their own beds at night. They were trying to move from the area. This was in the space of two years! CB - USA

∞

My husband and I came to South Africa on June the 16$^{th}$ 1973 and found no one to meet us at Jan Smuts (airport) as it was a public holiday and the company representative had forgotten about us. We also could not raise anyone on the number we had as they were office numbers, so we booked into the Holiday Inn at the airport as we knew we had connecting tickets to Upington at 6:30 a.m. the next day. We caught the flight with much apprehension having no idea where we were going or to what – all we had was a contract for the Sishen Saldhana Railway from the Orange River to Sishen Northern Cape.

As we flew over more and more desolate landscape with windmill pumps and snake dirt roads we got more and more apprehensive as our first impressions had been of flying over neat houses and swimming pools of Kempton Park and it really looked like paradise. The Northern Cape did not look like paradise and we soon learnt that all the contractors on this railway project were foreigners brought in because no South African would go there unless they were really starving or really desperate. The foreigners were out to make money and have an adventure. And we did.

Fortunately we were met by an agent in Upington and put in the Orange Hotel to live which turned out to be for six months since we soon discovered that the house they had rented was on the wrong side of the Orange River at Grobblershoop village and although the contract started on the other side, the nearest crossing was Upington 120kms away. They had bought a generator too as there was no electricity, no transport and actually nothing else either.

Now at that time I was 22 years old and wore mini-skirts and had come from a land with television and all the mod cons. Everyone in this part of South Africa spoke only Afrikaans and wore Crimpolene and lived a very ordered Afrikaans life of Kerk and work. The Sunday Times came on Wednesday and it was the only English newspaper apart from the Goldfields Advertiser from Kimberley. The culture shock was enormous – not only was it very hot but everything about Afrikaans society was alien and also the restrictions and censorship of everyday life. There were times when the attitude to the English speakers was just as restrictive as to the local coloured population since there were no Africans in the Northern Cape then.

We eventually sorted out the accommodation by getting 3-bedroom park homes and renting another farm on the right side of the river and the railway began and lasted for three years. We decided to stay and make a life here. We then moved to various towns and cities in South Africa over the years and I can easily say I have seen more than any South African of their country and had enough adventures to easily fill a book.

We have raised two daughters both of whom have left recently for America and the UK – both very staunch South Africans with strong ties to the country. Both of them had only ever gone abroad to have fun and get experience until this last visit. They had strong urges to come home as they love everything about South Africa and on this last visit in March they both came to the conclusion that this was no longer a sensible choice.

On the positive side the country is still beautiful and the weather is brilliant but they cannot give you a normal life. We never relax at any time of any day and you cannot sleep – you are in fear no matter what you do or where you are. It eats away at the will to stay here because the question everyone asks when will it be me and will I survive. 'Cry the beloved country' indeed, hello Nigeria and I have been there – I know it well.     CD - South Africa

∞

I have a story to tell also. I am actually an American pediatrician. In 2003 I sold my house, my medical practice and all my possessions except for five pieces of luggage and shipped half a container of necessities, mostly books, to Durban. I bought a car in Johannesburg and my daughter and I looked at various places to live work and go to school. I got a South African medical license and a job with the government working in Stanger, KwaZulu-Natal. I was there when the government finally rolled out antiretrovirals for the poor. The rate in my area was about 50%.

I was the only pediatrician. I worked hard. In September 2004 a group of Zulus, under the guise that I was a racist and had called someone a kaffir (a word an American would never use!), came to my ward where I was dealing with dying children, wrestled me to the ground and carried me out of the hospital and dumped me on the street. The media and police were there. There is no doubt that many of the people carried weapons. I was suspended from working and a case was opened against me for assault. I loved my work and my patients. I was actually a scape goat for the 'union' that decided they didn't like the white administrator who was Dutch and who wanted higher wages. (Interestingly, the American Nazi party thought I should have been killed. 'Remember Amy Biehl'.)

I cried a lot, but I did not leave. I joined another union and they brought my case to court and I 'won'. That meant I could work again. Nothing ever happened to the people who instigated the violence and they are working at the hospital still. The good Zulus who work there are afraid they would get killed if they had stood up for me. I noticed one of my HIV workers who I had often given money to for food was up there with a bull horn telling me to go back to America.

After my forced vacation, I worked again in a more rural clinic again with AIDS patients starting them on meds. One day a drunk policeman came to the clinic and said the case was still open and wanted me to come immediately to jail in handcuffs. I talked him out of it but he said, "Just remember, we know where you live." I hired a lawyer, but more importantly, had met a highway policeman who had a lot of influence. He came with me to the police station and talked to the people and I never heard anything again.

Believe me I had my bags packed as I had visions of being in general population, getting raped and ending up with HIV. (By the way, I am now 60 years old!)

I was again fairly happy doing my work, when one day, when the regular nurses were at a meeting, a young nurse from the city came to my office, barred the door, and said, "We don't like you and want you to get out." Not knowing who 'we' were, and having had enough, I packed up and left. I wrote letters to the government, the health department, and the European charity who gave money to this project, and never heard a thing. I left the country soon after.

I loved my work and South Africa. I loved the women and the children. I began to believe that we should not give medication to the men with HIV because all they did was feel better, then rape, rob and murder some more.

KL - USA

∞

I am one of those people who lived in South Africa for a couple of years and have never recovered from it (in a nice way). I'd love to relocate my business there and take my wife and two children and live in my favourite place in the world. We make a good living and could provide endless opportunities for others, but I can't bring myself to expose my family to risks that I was prepared to take when I was a bit younger and single.

JB - UK

∞

It was, I think, 1965 when I arrived in Johannesburg and stayed at the original Carlton Hotel. A couple of days or so later I was en route to Meikle's

Hotel in Salisbury in a well used Ford Zephyr driven by someone named Stan whom I had never previously met. I was Export Manager for a British company and had never before visited Africa. Over a couple of Lion Ales (not Lagers) I asked Stan about the slight smell of smoke as we had travelled, car windows down, into Salisbury from the airport. I will remember forever his words. "John, that was the smell of the bush and having noticed it you will come back to Africa." I did, took my wife and three small children to Johannesburg where we spent 30 years of our life only to return in 2000 due the ill health of mother and mother-in-law. We have still not overcome the culture shock of today's Britain.

JB - UK

∞

My son and daughter-in-law taught for one year in South Africa and unfortunately had to leave after that year. They simply loved Cape Town and the surrounding areas. We spent a month with them in December 2004 and also fell in love with the people of South Africa. Their housekeeper took us to her township where we hung out for a few days. My husband played pool and I played with all of the kids! We stayed at her house, shopped at the market, learned to cook a few dishes, visited her healer, and simply got to know a few people. Living conditions were very primitive, but everyone was very friendly and I was overwhelmed with the warm welcome we got from everyone. At first there were a lot on onlookers because I guess it's not often that 'white' visitors come to stay. Although 'grandma' didn't speak any English we managed to communicate quite well. It certainly was an experience I'll never forget.

BF - USA

∞

I was transferred from the Middle East on business by my non-South African employer. The original employer closed its South African operation so I started my own business and stayed seven years (local legislation pushed me out), 1995 until end of 2001 (Jo'burg, Cape Town, Durban, Port Elizabeth, Kimberley, East London and many other major towns).

I loved the diversity of culture and geography. The dining quality was excellent both food and wine is some of the best in the world. I believe Jo'burg has the BEST climate in the world and my quality of life was good, albeit behind six foot walls and electric fences. I loved my time in South Africa, I met my wife there and I love the people. My belief is that I arrived at the right time for the Rugby World Cup: that was fantastic, I'll never forget the celebrations afterwards. But I am certain that I left at the right time.

I see and hear only bad things about South Africa right now and all my clients and friends are telling the same story. The crime is getting worse, the power cuts are killing businesses and the economy and the school system outside private schools is shot. Most of my clients and friends with young families are either leaving or want to leave which is a sad indictment. Most of my professional clients have already left! After all, when the South African Football Association President is calling for the World Cup to be held elsewhere, it doesn't inspire much confidence. A number of people that I speak to are becoming more worried especially since the issues in Zimbabwe are ever present and seemingly getting worse and there seems to be even less confidence in the government with the forthcoming departure of Mbeki.

AS - USA

∞

I lived there from 1971 to 1974, and then from 1995 to 1997, in Johannesburg. We also visited there several times in the late 1970s and in the 1980s. I remember two rather different South Africas — one from the years of high apartheid, and the other after majority rule succeeded at last. One was mostly good, the other somewhat frustrating, disillusioning.

The South Africa I returned to live and work in for two years in the mid-1990s was different, because I was an adult and so much had happened since 1974. My impression was mixed and more critical. I was proud the country had majority rule. I was proud it had won World Cup rugby. I was proud of how the country was far more open about racism and confronting it with the TRC (Truth and Reconciliation Commission), beyond anything that my home country, the USA did for its own. I still love its beauty and admire the leadership of President Mandela, Cyril Ramaphosa, De Klerk, Sisulu, Tambo, Mbeki (back then, anyway).

It struck me how incredibly patient South Africans were with things and how they tolerated services not running efficiently. Service people were often rude, and, pardon me, just unhelpful. I was astounded at how disrespectful urban South Africans had become of the elderly. On the bus one day, the driver closed the door on an elderly man attempting to enter the bus and started to drive off with him only partly on board. He only stopped when we yelled and screamed to get his attention to stop.

I had to go to South Africa only to discover how much I took for granted in the way of postal, phone, utility services that worked effectively and efficiently. I found the government bureaucracy – Home Affairs and the city/provincial government offices I had to work with – sometimes hard to deal with.

Johannesburg, so much of it – even the northern suburbs – was crime-ridden by the mid 1990s. My family had been living there again since 1990s and they warned me about it and how it was different from the South Africa I had grown up in as a girl. It took me a while but I became what I would call hyper-vigilant – it's a general kind of disquiet one feels, a certain restlessness or a kind of tension when one has to leave home everyday to encounter who knows what.

CB - USA

∞

While, in the UK we could leave our house unlocked when we were out, and left it vacant for the 2½ years we were in the USA, that was more of a function of where we lived – in the countryside. Sitting having coffee at Hard Rock Café on Hyde Park Corner, I had my cell phone stolen. I was also mugged in Liverpool Street Station in Central London, not being alert to my surroundings in rush hour – it's a fact of life – live with it. In other parts of the UK crime (and rising armed crime) is rampant.

MC - UK & USA

∞

I used to feel more optimism, that the new South Africans post 1994 would eventually govern institutions better, that they have to do it their own way. I can tell you this, though. I found it disturbing how over 10 years after majority rule came to South Africa, many white and coloured South Africans and now black South Africans felt like they lost any say in their future, at least, economically and politically. I think the party roll system in the parliament and presidential elections needs to be scrapped. MPs need to be held accountable to a local constituency, not to the senior ANC leadership.

I really do feel that the tragedy of Zimbabwe has somehow changed

South Africa irreversibly – economically and politically and socially. Truly I do. If the country does not step in and actively bear on Mugabe to go, then the abuses in Zim will eventually spread to South Africa. A democratic country has to value democracy both within and without, I believe. My own country, the USA, is being tested over this very issue right now. So is South Africa.

CB - USA

∞

    I've read with a lot of interest your story. Let me introduce myself, my name is C, I live in Italy and I love Africa in a mad way! I've lived for just one month and a half in Johannesburg with my family (my boyfriend and my daughter S). I perfectly understand your feelings and all the things you've written in the web article.

    We have left Italy with the idea of living the rest of our life in South Africa (maybe not Johannesburg, maybe Cape Town). We have felt happy all the time passed over there, we fell in love with people, with our job, with the landscapes and the skies... the only problem was the crime situation... my daughter was 11 months when we arrived and I felt very scared thinking to leave her home all the day with a nanny (a girl from Zimbabwe), about robberies, about rapes and all the stories you heard when you live in South Africa. Lots of people told us "don't believe in what you hear, not everything is truth! Most of the stories all urban legend! Johannesburg is not that bad!" and so on... but we were asking to ourselves, "Is living in fear what we want? If S won't exist we should remain, but with her things change a lot." This is our dream not hers!

    So we decided to come back to Italy (as you made we left a lot of things, furniture, clothes and other things to people met over there), but every single day I think about Africa and if we made the right choice to come back here.

    Now we have a new job offer, to Cape Town. I was trying to understand if the situation there is better than in Johannesburg but seems to be similar... so probably we'll decide not to go....

    Sorry for my poem... I needed to talk with someone who understood my feelings! Thanks for your attention... try to be happy anywhere life will take you and your family! I really understand perfectly your peace of mind now that you live in a country (with all the problems that US have) with a different lifestyle as South Africa.

I have been treated as a racist too from a mate that we met in Johannesburg and that still lives there. He has moved in Alexandra (a black suburb in Johannesburg) where he says people are friendly, everyone is very poor but he's trying to help them to survive. I said I could not take my daughter there because of the danger we could run and he said to me that I'm a racist because I don't know at all all the people who live there and I have never been there (I have just passed by once... it was enough!).

I am not racist, I love Africa, in all the things that it's made of... I met a lot of poor black people there, I tried to help them with money, clothes, furniture, everything we could do, but we're not rich as well and we can't change their life.

If I had not a baby maybe I would have chosen a place way worse than South Africa to live, maybe a place that you can reach only with MSF (Médecins Sans Frontières) or with other human associations. I am a psychologist and I wanted to join MSF to work in Africa... then S was born and our life changed completely (as you perfectly know!).

But the sensation to live in a jail, always to look around you to see if someone is following you home and trying to robber you is very bad. If you have experienced a different life, safer, you can not accept that life.

People born and that have lived only in South Africa told us that we are European and we are too used to comforts and to an easier life here... maybe is true... but it's not a harder life that scares me, it's the probability to put in danger my child that did not make me sleep at night. I can live in a very poor place, in a village in the heart of Africa, without water or electricity, it's not a problem, even with S, but I can not stand the constant fear to be in danger.

Maybe if we had decided to live there for a longer time we could get used to all the stuff (fences, armed response, windows closed at the robot and so on), but, as you have said, maybe we could wait still some months... and if something would have happened to S? What we would have done? In which way we could live?

It's too difficult... our love for South Africa and our love for S... probably we will decide to stay here and if things will change in the future we'll try again to move.

I wish all the best, too, I know it's hard to fit in another country without knowing anyone... you and your family are strong, don't listen to *your president or to people that say you are a racist... you simply love your children and, as all the mothers in the world, if you can choose, you choose the best for them.*

CT - Italy

∞

*I read your story with a lump in my throat and tears in my eyes. I left South Africa three years ago in April after having lived there for ten years. I feel like a South African and not and American! I moved to Johannesburg when I was 25 from NYC. After ten years I had learned sufficient Afrikaans and embraced the culture. I love the people and feel that I understand them more so than Americans. The cultural difference is immense and I found on my return that I no longer related or fit in here.*

*I obviously do not regret my return to the US, as I have secured a much safer place and brighter future for my now 7 & 8 year olds. Your account of daily life filled me with anxiety as it could have been my own.*

NG - USA

∞ ∞ ∞

# Part 4

∞

# Leaving

*I am glad that I have a route out,
and it will break my heart,
but the time to go is now.*

AS - South Africa

# 21

∞

## The Long Goodbye

Introduction by James McIntosh

**D**eciding to leave can take a long time as you weigh up the pros and cons, as you search for 'best' ancestors, as you hope for a country that will welcome you, as you pray for a miracle. Even if you do decide quickly, leaving takes time. Time seems to slow down as you wait for everything to fall into place, as you deal with the pangs of preparation, the reams of red tape and the ghastly goodbyes. On the other hand, even if you are able to grab-and-go, time still drags because once you have made up your mind, you want out. Today. Now!

In looking back, I see what I could not fathom then. Time expands or shrinks according to your commitment. I now understand, from practical experience, what Goethe[12] meant when he wrote that 'until one is committed there is hesitancy, the chance to draw back, always ineffectiveness'. If you just cannot commit, if you keep hesitating, how do you finally tear yourself away from South Africa? Well, it helps if someone else in your life is already committed. Like your spouse. And it helps if this significant other is committed in a way that enables clear and succinct communication of his or

---

[12] Johann Wolfgang von Goethe (1832)

her intention: "We are leaving this godforsaken, #&*!#x@ country!" At least, that's how my wife expressed it to me. I got the message. Loud and clear.

In the next chapter, she will explain how she came to feel the need to express her commitment with so many #&*!#x@ words. But first, we need to consider Goethe's complete statement on commitment:

> *Until one is committed there is hesitancy, the chance to draw back, always ineffectiveness. Concerning all acts of initiative (and creation) there is one elementary truth, the ignorance of which kills countless ideas and splendid plans. That the moment one definitely commits oneself then Providence moves too. All sorts of things occur to help one that would never otherwise have occurred. A whole stream of events issues from the decision, raising in one's favour all manner of unforeseen incidents and meetings and material assistance, which no-one could have dreamt would have come their way. Whatever you can do, or dream you can, begin it. Boldness has genius, power and magic in it. Begin it now.*

When people ask me how we managed to pull this off, how we managed to change continents, then one single act stands out in my mind. Yes, there were many critical steps that had to be taken involving lots of luck along the way, and with every step and bit of luck we had to be ready and willing. We had to, as Goethe pointed out, 'begin it now'. That 'begin it now' was one bold step and Bronwyn was the woman to take it. She sold our house.

Actually, Johann Wolfgang von Goethe was only partly right. Boldness does indeed have genius, power, and magic in it. But it also takes a huge dollop of madness. Enough to get Providence's attention. You see, when Bronwyn sold our house, not only did we have nowhere to move to. We also had not yet started the formal process of applying for a USA work visa. And so I reacted the way any hot blooded South African male would. I shouted, "What the #&*!#x@!" and panicked.

But then Providence moved.

∞ ∞ ∞

# 22

∞

# A Day Forever

*I never would have thought that I would be the one
to say, "I am outta here!"*
TM - South Africa

The 29th of September 2000. This is a day that will forever be indelibly etched on my memory. It was a Friday. How do I remember the date so clearly? I was driving the hour long drive to Cape Town to meet a close friend. It was his birthday and we were having a celebratory lunch at the Waterfront in Cape Town.

It started as one of those ordinary days – a day where everything that is known to you, stays known to you and nothing is likely to change your routine. All things, people and events are in their place and life continues as normal. Little could I guess that nothing would ever seem quite normal again.

Leaving home, my two toddlers were with two maids (my husband had insisted that, on days when I was visiting the city, there be one for each child) and my gardener. This day was to be spent in town, meeting my bank manager, then a birthday lunch with my friend as well as seeing other friends and perhaps going shopping. Nothing was out of place.

The sun seemed unusually vibrant on this crisp clear Spring day, glancing off the farmlands and imbuing them with golden light while a clean blue sky promised that it would later be warm. I was driving along the N7 and, knowing me, probably breaking the speed limit because I loved to drive my red Toyota Camry. I was very proud of the fact that once (just once), I put petrol in my husband's old Opel Rekord at 6:55 p.m. in Sea Point and I arrived in Riebeek Kasteel at 7:35 p.m. – 180km per hour all the way. I wouldn't advise it, usually, but it was a brilliant experience. Obviously there were no traffic officers on duty that evening.

I digress.

I began perusing my thoughts about the forthcoming meeting with my bank manager and trying to decide the best approach to achieve my objective (a lower mortgage rate). My husband was completely disinterested in finance and household matters so it was never much use asking his advice. He left everything to me and, being the control freak that I am, I loved all of it. I pondered calling C to probe her ideas about the best way to approach the problem. C was a staunch friend, my ex-boss and an astute business-woman serving as Financial Director for an international company, with its head office based in Cape Town.

The innocuous call from my cell phone, during a boring drive, would precipitate a series of events that would change my life, and the lives of my family, forever. Besides, I needed to multi-task; I couldn't possibly drive and just appreciate the scenery – the sight of Table Mountain stately in the far distance. I did love the drive from the small country town of Riebeek Kasteel where we lived, through the larger town of Malmesbury and along the N7 towards Cape Town, passing Bokomo wheat trucks, petrol tankers, farm trucks loaded with pigs, cattle and chickens destined, no doubt, for the abattoir in Maitland. Driving sets my thoughts free and I looked forward to the hour on the road. After nearly six years of this route, I had become jaded enough to no longer appreciate the clean white farmhouses, cows grazing alongside the highway and the brilliant spring colours of the winelands and wheatlands.

> The space. We have so much space.
> JW - Japan

In the distance, the quiet mountain cast its shadow over Table Bay, with not a wisp of the famous white 'tablecloth' of clouds or any hint of the Southeaster. This wind was famously known, by locals, as the 'Cape Doctor' since people believed its gusty strength blew illnesses and ill will out of the city and surrounding areas.

As many women working in Cape Town will testify, the gusts of the Cape Doctor also blew all modesty right out of you. After all, when every person in the vicinity has seen your panties (during a particularly violent gust), propriety goes out of the window – it's either hold desperately onto the telephone pole, maintain your balance and lose your modesty or preserve your sense of propriety, take the chance of being (literally) blown off your feet and, no doubt, losing your modesty anyway as you flail wildly trying to keep your balance and at the same time trying to bind your skirt tightly around your knees, while risking life and limb. Newspaper photographs, the day after this wind comes through, generally show ladies caught with embarrassed expressions, skirts wrapped around their chests, thighs and panties exposed to the elements and frantic hand gesticulations.

I dialled C at her office number. "..... Company".
"Can I speak to C, please?" Her gentle tone answered at the first ring....

The children and I were frequent visitors to C's home. Patricia, her nanny, simply absorbed my two young children as though they were extended family. On arrival, her enormous, earthy, unflappable, presence engulfed them and they greatly looked forward to being with her. This freed C and I to spend time talking while the children flocked to the kitchen. Images of many boisterous lunches around their kitchen table filled me. The four children jostling for attention; the two adults trying to keep a rein on the commotion; and Patricia soothing frazzled tempers, passing the tomato sauce and managing to hush a fractious toddler positioned on her hip while eating her own lunch at the same time. I'd only met a handful of these nurturing earth mothers in my lifetime. Caregivers whose presence in a room dominated and calmed the energy of mothers and children alike. There was Lizzie who created the security in the environment of my younger years; Anna and Sophia who cared for my children in Riebeek Kasteel, and solid, grounded, Patricia.

"I haven't spoken to you in ages." There was a silence.
"It hasn't been a good time for us. I've got some bad news."

What? Did something happen to one of her children? Her husband? Are they getting divorced? Did her mom pass away unexpectedly? Or, knowing C, had something happened to one of her animals? It couldn't be her job, I knew that was secure. Wild thoughts threatened to overwhelm me.

> *Pretty negative at the moment (we've just had an armed robbery in our home – five black men, each with a gun!).*
> DB - South Africa

"What? What's happened? Are you OK?"
"No. It's not me. It's Patricia. She's dead. She was murdered."
"Oh my God! What happened?"

Through her gulping sobs, C told the dreadful story of the cold-blooded murder of Patricia and her youngest son. In the early evening of Monday 25th September – a public holiday – they had been sitting in their lounge, at home, watching television. A man walked into the house, shot them with a semi-automatic rifle, and walked out. On arriving home, Patricia's elder son discovered a grisly scene of devastation and death and he immediately called C. Her husband promptly called the police, only to be told that they did not have enough police vans at the station and they couldn't sanction going into the township with only one van. The chances of the call being an ambush were too great and they were not willing to take a chance. Appealing to their humanity, C pleaded with them to think of the young boy sitting at home, faced with the spectre of his dead family.

The policeman refused and suggested that she send her husband to the scene, to assist. In order to secure their survival, the police could not afford to demonstrate any compassion for the teenager. Another day. Another death. Sorry. Wish we could do more.

The police eventually arrived much later that night, after Richard (C's husband) had spent hours at Patricia's home consoling her son. It turned out that Patricia's senseless murder was a 'mistake'. A contract killer, searching for his prey, had simply walked into the wrong house and gunned down the wrong family.

Deviating from my plan to drive directly to the city, I turned the car towards Table View. I marched into my husband's office. The mid-morning sun had not yet penetrated the coolness of the room.

"We're leaving!" I said.

My husband, accustomed to my histrionics and general Type-A personality and behaviour, looked up mildly and said, "Really! Where to? Are we going away for the weekend?" I had developed a habit of, once a month, handing over our children to my parents for a weekend, and booking us 'couple time'.

> *My running partner was killed in a highjacking. My husband walked in the door and told me to get ready to leave.*
> LBM - USA

"No, we are leaving this godforsaken, #&*!#x@ country!", I said.

"Oh! Really? What on earth has happened now?"

I relayed the awful news of my phone conversation and repeated that I had made my decision. After the 1994 change of government, I had spent years trying to persuade my friends not to leave – stay and build the country, be a part of the future, the crime rate will drop, don't desert South Africa.

For the first time, South Africans were free of the international stigma and restrictions that had formerly pervaded our lives, we could breathe deeply of the positive energy exuded by people everywhere. The Truth and Reconciliation Commission had given South Africa a reputation for being a model country, a country which had shown the world that people could forgive and move beyond their differences. There was much to be done here but there was also enormous energy to do it. My husband knew that my decision indicated a great deal more than simply 'leaving' – I was giving up all in which I believed.

I'd simply been worn down. Over the years of my life in South Africa, and ever since I could remember, I'd been cautioned, warned by stories of possible harm, beginning with the petrol bombs of the early '70's. How many 5-year olds are taught to hide under their desks, with hands covering their heads, in the event that a petrol bomb or teargas canister is thrown through their classroom window? Then there were the ongoing burglaries at our home and the ongoing stories of young children being abducted, raped and murdered. Insidiously over time, the stories grew worse and there were more burglaries; more muggings; more rapes and murders; more hijackings and the stories came ever closer. Vague acquaintances (a friend of a friend's family member) became people of acquaintance who became distant family members in other towns. It was when the stories surfaced in our own suburb, a couple of roads away, that the fitful sleeplessness began. I moved into my first flat in Rosebank at the age of 21. The recent stories of girls being raped in their second floor flats, by a supposed cat burglar who scaled the drainpipes, incited me to install safety gates and burglar bars before I'd even slept there for one night.

> I have ongoing debates with friends and family in South Africa about whether leaving is right or wrong, for better or for worse. There is no definitive answer.
>
> AS - USA

"Oh Thank God", we'd say, "it didn't happen to us because we're careful, we know the tricks, we know what to watch out for, and we'll be even more careful from now onwards." Or, when mugged, a family member said, "At least they only mugged me. It could have been worse."

In growing up, I'd learned to adapt and be cautious of every stranger, every

> I have wondered about this a lot and believe that a single incident of violent crime to me or a direct relative or friend, is all needed to pack up. Until then, I simply hope that day never comes...
>
> JG - South Africa

unusual noise and occurrence. The recent story of a gang travelling from Cape Town to Riebeek Kasteel to steal cars had shaken me. I had left Cape Town to escape the constant wariness of life near the city but now the village where I had chosen to raise my children, and make a life, no longer felt safe. The place where I had slept with doors open and sometimes a gate unlocked was also not secure. The old stories of caution and fear surfaced inside me. In order to ensure that my children would reach adulthood safely in South Africa, I would have to create the same climate of fear in their psyche. I felt overwhelmed by a lifetime of anxiety about the possibility of being a victim. Coupled with Patricia's senseless death (just another death in a society permeated with these events), something snapped inside me.

James knows me well enough to know that I'm an erratic creature, given to idiotic whims, and sometimes it's best to leave well enough alone and allow me to sleep with my decisions for a few days. Many of them dissipate like the remnants of a bad dream. He had time, he could wait – he wasn't ready to get onto an air plane and leave that same afternoon.

His parting words as I left his office were: "And how do you intend to arrange for us to leave the country?"

"Don't worry. I'll sort it out. We are leaving!" was my response.

I spent the next 18 months researching every possible opportunity, country and continent. I researched ancestral links and possibilities in various countries all over the globe – we considered Canada, New Zealand, the United Kingdom (my great-grandparents made us too far removed), Australia (adding up points) and even Argentina (James's paternal grandfather was born there). I actually seriously considered Argentina and then bounced the idea off James.

"Argentina?" he asked. "What the hell am I going to do in Argentina? I can't even speak the language." I had no idea, but that wasn't the point was it?

At the same time, friends and family were questioning me. 'Are you really serious?' 'Haven't you changed your mind yet?' 'Do you know what you are giving up?' 'Do you know what it is going to do to your family?'

> *My biggest fear in fact is staying in South Africa.*
> LK - South Africa

Frankly, I'd decided that if nothing else turned up, we'd take the kids and go on an extended tour through Europe and Asia, maybe India or the Himalayas and find some farm or retreat where we could settle peacefully. I weathered all the questions and comments. It took a lot of time and an enormous amount of research. The internet finally came into its own. I discovered I could find British birth and death records – scanned copies – of family members born nearly 100 years ago. I found a website, escapeartist.com, aimed mainly at Americans who wanted to get out of America. (Huh? Escape from America? What's all that about?) The site was a source of enormous wisdom and factual information about almost any country on earth. I was inspired because there were so many opportunities out there. Maybe there are, but having children limits the choices because you can't just pack up and ship out easily.

And then close friends in the USA created a business opportunity.

∞ ∞ ∞

*I never would have thought that I would be the one to say: I am outta here. My husband started saying in 2001 that we should have a 'Plan B' or a 'backdoor' out of South Africa, 'just in case'. I was adamant that we would remain. I was convinced that South Africa was going to be the land of milk and honey. Crime was a problem, as it has been for many years, but I felt that we could all pull together. I have realised that this is not the case. In 2006 I realised that things were not getting better. I could not see the light at the end of the tunnel, or I could, and it was an oncoming train! I don't know what happened – one day I just woke up and heard the most horrific story on the radio about a family that was hi-jacked, raped and murdered in a suburb not far from us and it was the final story that I wanted to hear about with regards to the crime that is literally out of control in South Africa.*

TM - South Africa

∞

*What surprises me is how many of my former die-hard friends committed to South Africa are beginning to look at their options overseas. I find it laughable when people refer to those leaving as cowards. They cannot imagine how much courage it actually takes to leave your family, friends and established life behind. It is far easier to stick with what you know than head for the unknown in a foreign country, no matter how similar the cultures are supposed to be. South Africa is a beautiful country on many levels, and leaving that behind is hard.*

*I don't know that I won't want to come back, but learning from my* family lessons in Zimbabwe I will not return until I hold a foreign passport and bank account. Who wants to work their whole life just to see their money eroded to no value when you're about to retire on it? In any event, what good is money if there is nothing on the shop shelves? It's easier to say "it won't happen to us" than it is to move overseas and buy that insurance policy in the form of a foreign passport. I have no crystal ball and I don't know what South Africa's future writers of laws and the constitution will bring to the country. Mr Mugabe has given us a sound lesson in how easily change can happen.

Incidentally, it is the 'cowards' in my family now established overseas who are helping many of the very friends who attacked them in the first place to relocate.

MF - South Africa

∞

It was time to move. I should perhaps give you a quick history of living in Durban for the previous six years. We had four motor vehicles stolen, one being driven right through my front gates. Our house had been cleaned out twice right down to the beer out of my fridge, in the middle of the day whilst at work. When my gates were smashed after the car was stolen, in the two days it took to get it fixed, I lost my braai, my hose pipe, a pair of running shoes, and my lawn mower.

My factory had been broken into once and my wife had the week's takings stolen out of her office. I personally knew at least 12 people who I worked with or played sport with, who had been shot and killed. This did not faze us in the least. I was untouchable. I had worked with the local population forever and understood what motivated them. Nothing could harm me.

However, one Tuesday morning at about 10.30 whilst in the shower, we had a home invasion. Three Black men forced themselves into our home. I came out of the bathroom with only a towel around me and was confronted by a black man who pointed a gun to my head and told me to keep quite or he would shoot me. I screamed at him to get out my house and he threatened me again as I walked toward him to protect my two year old daughter who was between us. He moved backwards and I hit him, as hard as I could. As I punched him he shot me in the chest. We grappled around on the floor until he broke loose and ran from me. I chased after him and he fired another shot at me which missed me and my daughter, and he fled.

At the same time another two men had forced their way into our front door after shooting two shots through the door at my wife. They had my wife on the floor face down with a gun to her head when the shots went off in the back of the house. They left her and ran down the passage and ran into the bloke who had shot me. They then took off out the back door with me chasing them. I ran to the gate and watched them saunter off up the road.

We had armed response who arrived very quickly and about 15 minutes later the South African Police arrived. It took an ambulance 30 minutes to arrive by which time I was losing consciousness and blood was frothing out of my mouth, and I couldn't breathe very well.

Then the fun started. They loaded me into the ambulance, with my head down and I started to drown. They then argued with the hospital for 10 minutes because I didn't have my medical insurance number. I was still only clad in a towel. Finally, we proceeded to Umhlanga Rocks Hospital slowly so as not to stress me – no siren; stop at all the red lights. When we arrived at the hospital we were refused entry into emergency because we didn't have a permit. So we had to go around the block to a separate entrance and wait while the man from Kings Parking hand-wrote a free entrance ticket.

Before I was seen to a deposit of R10 000,00 was made by my medical insurance company. Finally, an hour after being shot I was seen by a physician who told me I was very lucky and would not die. Intensive care was a joke, another story worth at least five pages. I was discharged on Friday and was too scared to go back to my home. We stayed at a friend's house who was away and that night we had prowlers who stole all our clothes out of the laundry. It was time to move.

CS - Australia

∞

Have I thought about leaving South Africa? Yes, I have. Especially in light of a lot of our friends and family seriously considering emigration or currently leaving the country. But have I decided to go? No, not yet. But I will never say 'never'. Things may happen and my views in this regard may change. I think a very violent crime being committed against any of my close family members or friends may push me to leave, but at the moment I really believe that South Africa can solve its problems and become the country that we are meant to be.

Life here is not perfect, but I don't think it is anywhere else either. Currently all my close family members are all still living in South Africa, and since both my husband and I are blessed with close-knit and very supportive families, this is a big consideration in our decision (so far) to stay in South Africa. We are fairly dependent on our support systems, and although not impossible, it will be difficult to duplicate it elsewhere.

I don't think anything in particular has stopped me from leaving – there has just not been enough reason to leave.

CC - South Africa

∞

Remember the movie Titanic where the boats leave and the balance of the people are left on board to a dismal fate, they were aware of it, but there was nothing they could do. They were helpless and powerless. That's where most of us are at the moment.

JM - South Africa

∞

(One August) sitting in our TV room watching some TV with my family we heard a car's tyres screeching outside followed by what seemed like back firing, but I knew too well what it was. But not to alarm my family I stayed sitting and then looked out the window onto the street to see a commotion outside the house. I went into the garden after seeing the local armed response company appearing on the scene. I found out that our neighbour across the road had been shot at while he tried to get out of a highjacking situation. Thankfully, besides a cut on his face and the emotional damage, he was otherwise okay. On discussing the event it transpired that my wife had decided not to stop at the local petrol station to get some cigarettes. If she had, she would have been driving up the road as the would-be highjackers were shooting down it after our neighbour was trying to get away. My first thought was, "it is time to leave and get my family out".

SOR - UK

∞

Shame on South Africa and the South African government that is forcing families apart and breaking the cycle of life. How many South Africans have been forced to leave their home country in search of a better *life for themselves and their children. Not to say that life cannot or is not good in South Africa – of course it is – but not with the crime! How many mothers – now grandmothers – do not have the pleasure of seeing their children and watching their grand children grow up and to be the grand mother to them?! The sorrow and anguish I have witnessed in my own family and others is shocking to say the very least.*

*When a country and its government fails to provide the most basic and fundamental requirement to its people – which is to keep them safe – there is no alternative but to search out alternatives. People do what they have to do in order to survive and to create a better life if it is possible. Not everybody is lucky enough to have alternatives to consider and for them we should all pressure the South African government to affect change. Oh! How hollow that sounds!*

T - USA

∞ ∞ ∞

# 23

∞

# Leaving Cloud Cuckoo Land

by Anthony Krijger

In the run-up to the elections in 1994 we were concerned about the increased level of violence, but the newspapers reassured their readers that this was politics out of control and that after elections this would cease. The politicians themselves referred to most crimes as 'political' in nature, so while there was a concern, we were sure that someone was telling us the truth and that we had a bright future to look forward to. Nothing could have been further from reality, and in truth we were living in cloud cuckoo land. Our lives came to a crashing standstill on the morning my mother was shot dead in her little cosy home that my sister had made for her.

All of us decided to emigrate as we realized that we had all been hoodwinked into buying into the 'new' South Africa, which in reality was no better than the 'old'. I would guess that one old lady's murder probably cost the South Africa economy around 1000 jobs as the families involved closed down or sold their various businesses.

This is our story.

My mother was born on June 7, 1920, in a small Spanish town called San Sebastian near the French border. Her mom died when she was 15 and she became a trainee nurse in 1936 during the Spanish civil war. Having lost most of her family she somehow endured the horrors of that war and went to live in Paris after the civil war. She got there just in time to endure WWII, at the end of which she became governess to the family of the man subsequently appointed ambassador of France to South Africa. As Europe and Spain were in ruins, she figured this would be a good chance to begin life again in a brand new land.

At more or less the same time, my father found himself in a desperately ravaged Holland at the end of WWII and decided to look for his sister and brother-in-law who were in Indonesia before the war. His sister's husband had been shot down in some remote jungle and she had been interred by the Japanese in one of those women's POW camps either on Java or Sumatra.

After WWII, the Dutch were booted out of Indonesia and my father's sister found herself on a boat to Holland, which stopped for a bit in Durban. I gather this was their meeting point and my father was deterred from travelling further and he stayed in Durban while waiting for a boat back to Holland. This never materialized as he got a job selling Joko Tea as a travelling salesman and liking South Africa, he decided to stay and start a business here.

My mother, having being subjected to a politically oppressed upbringing, always felt empathy with the victims of apartheid and we were never allowed to use derogatory phrases to describe people of other races, neither were we allowed as kids to discriminate in any way. A thick ear was our reward for any transgressions. Curiously my two sisters and I grew up speaking fluent Zulu, as my pint-sized fiery 5ft tall mother made the rule with our maid, Ginger, that she was absolutely forbidden to speak to us in anything but Zulu. My mother had struggled to learn English in those early years and always felt that she missed out on what Zulu employees were trying to convey, so she made it a strict rule that any Zulu speaking employees were only to speak to us kids in their own language – if they were ever caught speaking English, they were threatened with Spanish fire and brimstone, so we grew up speaking a curious baby talk mix of Zulu/Spanish/English, which eventually separated into their own languages when school started.

Speaking Zulu fluently has always been a huge advantage for me and I later went on to take Zulu higher grade as a matric subject. My mother had her own rule that she only spoke to us in Spanish, at least until we went to school, so I was able to simultaneously blot up a few languages when I was small enough to have a sponge for a brain.

Anyway, Ginger was well rewarded for her efforts as when each of us became teenagers, she had a gift more or less of her own choice. When I turned 13, Ginger wanted one of those wind-up gramophones (remember the 'His Master's Voice' instruments that needed constant changing of needles?) My sister Mercedes's 13th elicited furniture of some sort and finally when Teresa turned 13, Ginger asked for and was given a small diamond ring, which she really treasured. Ginger's son David was a constant companion during school holidays but we lost touch when my boarding school hols no longer coincided with his.

We had a very liberal upbringing and I went to Michaelhouse, probably one of the first non-racist schools in South Africa. After school I ended up in the army doing compulsory military service. It was a bone of contention that I had to be a much-taunted English speaker in a largely Afrikaans army. Naturally baiting those that taunted us became a sport which kept us amused during the seemingly endless years of 'camps' spent what I always thought of as fighting someone else's war. I am a fluent Zulu speaker and always had more affiliation and understanding of the Zulu people than I ever did with Afrikaners.

After army I had the opportunity to study in the UK, which I did and also ended up living there for a few more years. I came back to South Africa in 1976, just in time to see the country go through some serious riots. However, there was no sense of fear and plain crime was relatively unknown. One could still walk one's dogs through the neighbourhood and children still rode their bicycles to one another's houses. I worked in Hammarsdale and used to buy all my meat for the month at the Mjambo Family Butchery which was located deep in Mpumalanga Township. The folks were friendly and many of those waving greetings knew me from the big textile mill at which I worked.

I left Hammarsdale in 1978 to work as production manager for Ascot Shirts, an old and well-respected clothing factory in Durban. I left this company a year later to go into business on my own in Durban. I also lived in a flat on Durban's South Beach area, as my first wife was a nursing sister at Addington Hospital, which was a 5-minute walk away.

We never realized that by the end of the 1980's the rot had slowly set in and society as we knew it was in a state of decay. Crime had begun to pick up and my mother who lived alone in a house in Kloof was burgled a couple of times. My mother was persuaded to sell her house at this time as my sister and I thought she'd be safer in a complex and she moved to a 3-bedroom townhouse in Hillcrest. This was convenient for her as she had a little haberdashery shop in Hillcrest. All was well for a short period until the break-ins and attempted robberies started.

In the meantime Mandela had been released from jail, we had all voted to end apartheid in De Klerk's inspired referendum, the year 1994 dawned and we were all looking positively to a refreshing 'New' South Africa as it was optimistically referred to in those heady days. In all the run-up to the forthcoming elections we were concerned about the increased level of violence, but the newspapers reassured their readers that this was politics out of control and that after elections this would cease. The politicians themselves referred to most crimes as 'political' in nature, so while there was a concern, we were sure that someone was telling us the truth and that we had a bright future to look forward to.

As I said, nothing could have been further from reality, and in truth we were living in cloud cuckoo land. Our lives came to a crashing standstill on the morning my mother was shot dead in her little cosy home that my sister had made for her.

It seems that the crime that has beset this country really got a lot worse as the old government took a back seat in preparation for handover to the new. My mother lived alone in a house that she built on land acquired as part of her divorce settlement. It took a couple of burglaries to get us to put pressure on her to move to a cluster type of townhouse. This seemed fine until the local miscreants worked out that this little and by now old lady went to open her shop every day at 8 a.m. and did not return until after dark, so the burglaries began yet again. This prompted my sister and I to put our heads together and the idea she and her husband came up with was to convert old stone stables on her property to a lovely little cottage for my Mom. For just over a year she was happy there.

When she moved there aged 72 she gave up work at her shop and prepared herself for an old age occupied with babysitting my sister's new born child, gardening and generally enjoying sitting in the sun. Sadly the criminals, now ever more brazen, felt the need to shoot her when they broke into this little home and she died aged 74, having had the 'retirement' she was looking forward to, curtailed in the most brutal manner.

We (the family) had this empty vacant feeling that was only replaced by the gnawing pain of intense grief and inexplicable sense of loss. All these raw feelings of intense hurt were exacerbated by the knowledge that the killing was totally deliberate; the victim was a gracious and helpless 74-year-old lady. The act was brutal and the entire family was emotionally gutted. We all decided to emigrate as we realized that we had all been hoodwinked into buying into the 'new' South Africa, which in reality was no better than the 'old'.

This senseless act of barbarism cost many people their jobs as the family between them shutdown quite a few manufacturing enterprises, some sooner, some later. I downsized the transport business that I started in 1987 and then sold what remained to my partner. In mid 1994 my wife and I moved to the UK. My sister and her family moved to Germany. Her in-laws (two couples with children and two elderly folks) also moved to Germany. A brother-in-law, (incidentally a most brilliant neurologist) wife and three kids moved to Kentucky, sister-in-law, husband and two kids also moved to Kentucky.

Basically it took us about two months to dump everything we wanted to and relocate. Not one of the plus/minus 16 of us formally emigrated. We just slid out. This had a knock-on effect as my ex-wife's family also started the emigration trail. Her brother moved permanently to Thailand, sister went to Redding University and then relocated to California where she is married and currently lives. Her other brother relocated to Tasmania and joined a large mining house. He now works in London. Her stepmother recently moved to the UK, as it seems most of her family is there.

I have had loads and loads of friends (plus minus 15 families) who emigrated to Australia and New Zealand. More are still going. On my ex-wife's side of the family, my side of the family and my sister's side of her family, there are close to 50 couples (married and unmarried) that left. I haven't counted the children! If each of those that left employed about four people, that would mean 200 families having to find alternate jobs/income. In my case alone, when we shut down half the business, we retrenched 50 male breadwinners. One of the families' factories that simply shut down retrenched 250 workers. The rest of the businesses must have been somewhere in-between so I would guess that one old lady's murder probably cost the South Africa economy around 1000 jobs. As there are on average 50 murders per day in South Africa, the cost is probably incalculable.

Since my mother was killed we have lost other friends in car hi-jacking, murders, housebreak-ins.... What was shocking to us years ago seems quite commonplace today. The most recent one to die was my good friend Richard Cassels, who was stabbed in his home, in front of the two children he was protecting, so his TV could be stolen. This was about a year ago (in 2009) and he lived two streets away from us in Westville. He was a brilliant man, CEO of a very large advertising company whose skills and contribution to the South African economy have now been lost, just like the other 49 people murdered that day in South Africa.

I never really left South Africa properly. I started a business in the UK when my ex-wife and I left. We also applied for (and received) migration visa's to Australia, so I started another business in Australia. However, the rules and regulations are quite claustrophobic and living in Australia seems to make a frontal lobotomy essential as life is so clinically mundane after the continuous stress and excitement of being a white African in black Africa! So I never could quite settle down to the required frenetic pace of an Australian snail and ended up commuting between South Africa, Europe and North America. A bit like those nomadic Persian carpet salesmen of old I guess. I've just replaced the camel with a cramped economy class airline seat and live on a diet of bad food and good water. This had an effect on my marriage and my wife and I are now divorced. I had a really nice little flat high on Durban's Berea, a veritable haven of peace and tranquillity; probably because it was so high up one felt close to the clouds and far away from the pit of seething criminal humanity down below.

Currently, these circumstances have also changed. I have a girlfriend, 'S' whom I met a few of years ago after my marriage to Susie failed. She has two daughters. They are both teenagers and the constraints of my apartment are an anathema to them, so we find ourselves in a house in Westville. Her daughters' safety and future are a continuous source of worry to 'S'. They don't have the EU passport that I have, so relocation for them must be a long-term plan to a decent country. I recently bought a business in Canada. This will allow 'S's daughters to live in Canada in the long term. The eldest matriculated last year. She wanted to go to the USA or Canada and spend a year as an au pair. This would have suited her as she has an affinity with small children, and they don't give her the rash they give me. However, she was thwarted by the global recession and her au pair family cancelled as their circumstances had changed and they could not afford an au pair. She has started a BSc and hopes to specialise in child psychology. The youngest hopes to join me in business. We all know that their future cannot be in South Africa. Lifestyle has deteriorated and we all live like parrots in a paradise of gilded cages.

My mother's murder 14 years ago has had this odd effect on me during the last year or two, a sense of relief that I have one less worry, one less person that can be raped and tortured before a lonely and terrifying death. Life in South Africa has taught us that sooner or later we WILL become a statistic as we have had so many friends and family become victims of crime. The housebreakings are endless, some ended in tragedy, some with relief that they were allowed to live.

'S' (my girlfriend) has not been spared either. They are tough Rhodesians who came to South Africa in the early 80's with nothing but the clothes on their backs, an old car and a positive attitude to life. Her Aunt was murdered on their smallholding in Ficksburg. This didn't satisfy the bloodlust of locals who then murdered her Uncle a year or so later on the same farm. She is under no delusions about safety and security in South Africa, but after enduring an uphill toil from humble beginnings, it seems too late for her parents to start all over again somewhere else as they are now of retirement age. 'S' herself feels that she will stay until her parents have departed this mortal coil and meanwhile she will persuade her daughters to make their start to life in a place more worth the effort than Africa. Hopefully my Canadian and Australian business will eventually be able to sustain us in retirement to a 'pondok' in the south of Spain.

So as you can see, perhaps I've managed to emigrate financially, but whether I've done so emotionally is an unanswered question. Basically, I've been able to make the grade financially in Australia, Europe and North America. However, the chasms of culture are hard to bridge. The South African mentality, sense of humour and camaraderie are quite unique. My friends in Australia were immediately networked by South Africans who didn't even know them. To make Aussie friends in Australia or American friends in America is not easy. We lived in England for two years in the 90's and never made a single English friend. We made many acquaintances, but no friends. So in the pubs and restaurants we met lots of people who would chat about the weather and any other frivolous conversation, but they would never think of inviting us to a braai or dinner and get to know us better. We would not even get "return invites" unless it was to meet at a pub or rugby game.

I could give people loads of advice before they emigrate or even think about it. I've lived in or spent a lot of time in the UK, Australia, Canada, the USA, Thailand, Spain, France and Bali, Indonesia. However I would temper the advice according to the type or person I'd be speaking to, but there are some things I'd say to everyone thinking about emigrating: It isn't easy, it will affect your family, it will make you closer as a family, financially you will struggle, some people may never recover financially, doing business in South Africa is totally different to anywhere else, generally speaking schooling is better, kids adapt quicker than adults, you will miss things South African, planning to leave South Africa and planning arrival elsewhere is paramount. Medical care is expensive in America and Canada and it is important to have a good scheme. When applying for a job, especially in the USA, do ask about their medical scheme and their retirement scheme. These vary hugely from job to job and sometimes it is better to earn less but have a better medical scheme. Australia and New Zealand have good social health schemes so one's own medical insurance is not as important. The UK had a good national health service, paid for by taxpayers, but it has now become limited and private insurance is worth looking at.

Having emigrated and gone through the anguish of leaving loved ones, friends, family and job security behind, it can be very easy to become despondent, particularly if you think you have made the wrong decision. *Positive thinking is an absolute must.* South Africans not of African descent have become socially displaced people, which have caused them to become the new nomads of the world, modern day carpetbaggers perhaps. This in itself is depressing, hence the necessity for positive thought!

One of the most definitive positives that will compensate for all the stress and uncertainty of emigration is the security of your new society. Kids can play in the street – cars are their worry, not criminals. Burglar alarms are not the norm, they seem to be an expensive toy when people have them. When they do have them, they don't connect to any armed response – they simply make a noise and irritate the neighbours. Usually there are no fences or little picket fences designed to keep pets in, not people out. Kids can WALK to friends' houses without fear. You can go to an ATM machine without the notion that someone is waiting to grab your money or card. You can drive with the AC off and enjoy having the window down without the thought that someone will smash & grab your cellphone or handbag. In general the majority of people are honest and aren't continually trying to steal or con you out of your possessions. Most of all you can learn to walk again! It is so nice to be able to walk home at night from the local pub or restaurant without fear of criminals wanting to rape or steal from you.

The crime and mayhem criminals create is totally out of control in South Africa. In most countries South Africans find themselves in, there still is an element of crime, but it is small. When it occurs, it is properly investigated and criminals are brought to book, tried prosecuted and jailed. No crime is too small to be taken seriously in the USA, UK, Canada, Australia and New Zealand. Police are happy to take statements, even if it is only for bag snatching or a lost wallet. I left a wallet with a little money in it in a motorway café in the UK. Police found my business card and wrote a letter to me in South Africa advising me that my lost wallet had been handed in to them and asked for further instructions. I asked them to donate the money (it was all there) to a good charity and post the wallet back to me in Canada, which they happily did!

Curiously, I never was able to establish myself properly in a new country, so I'm still commuting. However, I don't think of my stay in South Africa as permanent, nor do I think I will retire here, probably because I don't see 'retirement' as a goal or situation I want to attain! It will just be a period where I kind of work less, or work when it's fun. And now I fear I have rambled on too much. I really hope you, the reader, can make use of this information.

∞ ∞ ∞

*I have caught criminals breaking into my parent's house, know friends that have been raped and hijacked and family who survived because during an attempted robbery the gun got jammed while pointed at point-blank range! You drive around Jozi (Johannesburg) and in the wealthy suburbs residents have taken the law into their own hands – hiring private security companies who look like a military force – simply to cope with the firepower that they face from criminals!*

*When President Mbeki or any other person shouts 'traitor' or 'racist' when we complain, I simply laugh because it is a pathetic attempt and they don't have a real answer. They sit behind their closed walls and protection units and I always say "until they have stared death in the face and understood what that feels like", they will NEVER, EVER comprehend or sympathise.*

*I can also narrate a story whereby family friends of ours who emigrated to Canada many years ago, headed Mbeki's call to return and invest in the country and what happened? Not even two months upon their return they were firstly hijacked and then burgled in one of Cape Town's most wealthy suburbs! There is no price for life and they subsequently returned to Canada.*

MH - UK

∞

*I love South Africa and I will always love it. But I cannot continue to turn a blind eye to what is happening around me and while commending some government departments for some very good work that they have* done, I am tired of the corruption, unaccountability, nepotism and sheer incompetence. I am glad that I have a route out, and it will break my heart, but the time to go is now.

    I am degreed, with a post-graduate certification. I am a highly skilled resource. So is my husband. But until the government of this country does something to fix the problems instead of blaming them on the apartheid government – it doesn't matter how much Mbeki complains  – we are going to leave, and we are going to leave in droves.

AS - South Africa

∞

    My wife and I need to complete a thought process to ensure that our reasons for considering leaving are valid, to ensure that we are making the right decision for both ourselves and our children, to ensure that we truly understand what it practically means to be emigrating and lastly to ensure that we have given the necessary consideration to alternatives.

    I guess this is the problem with white South Africans – we tolerate and put up with so much and always look for our own solutions instead of taking the government to task on the issues. We are however a minority and are realistic about the situation. So we rather contract our own armed response company, pay extremely high medical aid premiums for private healthcare and bankrupt ourselves to put our children through private schooling.

AJVN - South Africa

∞

    At the moment it is very emotional in South Africa – many families from the school (whose parents went to that school) are leaving – it is like a deluge. And those of us staying say things to them going like "Oh, what a big decision you've made. What an adventure it will be." and in the meantime we, who are staying, have also made a big decision and we are also having a big "adventure"; the fragility of our future in South Africa is as nerve wracking as making new roots in another country.

    When I imagine my friends living in another country, I see them crying just as much as I am crying now. I literally mean I am crying. I am sobbing, my face drenched in tears, six or seven used tissues on the table in front of me, weeping about everything to do with South Africa. The life-threatening decisions that we make everyday (to stay or go, to raise my front wall by 12 brick courses, to say hello to strangers on the street as I walk my dog, etc.) are not unique to South Africans, but perhaps they are more stressful to us because we worry about the effect they will have on us staying alive. We are digging deep into our survival instincts that people in safer countries don't have to do as frequently or as deeply.

As soon as our parents have passed on we will reconsider our options very seriously again and we are thinking of retiring in another country. We believe South Africa is a fool's paradise, and being in the minority is not a safe place to be. We are already very sad that our children's children probably won't go to the same school as they did and we have acknowledged that roots are a luxury in the modern world.

TW - South Africa

∞

In the early 1990's I advised governments in Central Europe, and Russia, and western companies wishing to invest there. The core issue which predominately all of these countries subscribed to was the tripartite commitment to the rule of law with the concomitant independence of the judiciary, the exercise of inalienable property rights and the independence of the media. Without these the near century of communism would not have been wiped away so successfully. Most governments in the region realized that these were axiomatic to ensure that tyranny would not return and the hoped for freedoms would be sustainable.

When I moved back to South Africa in the late 1990's, I also believed that these prime institutional requirements had become enshrined into the constitution and the government's psyche. I was optimistic that this would form the bedrock to propel South Africa out of a centrist dominated, command side economy which would not follow the ineptitude, corruption and despotism so often exemplified throughout sub Saharan Africa.

It is with sadness that I have had to change my opinion on the development of South Africa's evolution along this path. Each of these three cornerstones has been eroded; they are not gone, but the poison of suspicion is doing its evil work well. Compound this with the deliberate de-motivation of the country's greatest asset, its people, by the implementation of BEE which as a system has been, just as communism was shown to be, a failure and suspicions start to turn into resolutions.

Add to this the government's incessant and extraordinarily

incompetent intervention in the economy and business, the lack of electricity being an example, and resolutions turn into convictions. Now add the extraordinary level of savage crime and convictions turn into actions: All that is required to move is the right pull from overseas, whether it be relatives, job offers or just the desire to have a broader, less myopic instead of an increasingly isolated and alienated world perspective.

EVW - South Africa

∞

I always maintain that those who leave South Africa are braver than those who stay behind. From my numerous discussions with people about the political situation in South Africa, I am convinced that the following are the most important reasons why people choose to stay rather than to leave: lack of guts to take the risk of leaving; lack of skills; 'easefulness' (gemaksugtigheid); fear of failure; lack of appreciation for the political risks that lie ahead in 20 years time.

WVB - South Africa

∞

The dream and hopes when the country changed over was not evidenced by behaviours that I experienced. Freedom in name whilst crime is largely out of control cannot be freedom. First world charters and bills of rights where people cannot visibly feel safe are in fact empty vessels. Perhaps the most defining moment was when smoking in public was banned and it just became plain stupid that we had this new law that was just not going to be applied. Let alone people smoking in public we had people being murdered and in fact urinating in public. It just brought home to me that first world countries were influencing the leadership and that we would have all these wonderful laws yet in reality no-one obeys them and no-one polices them. So I left because I no longer believed in the leadership or its ability to understand freedom in its widest sense. The symptoms of that were crime, violence, alcohol and drug abuse, woman abuse, hatred and mistrust.

JW - Australia

∞

I am one of a growing number of South Africans who will be leaving South Africa this year. I've made quite a lot of effort in getting involved in *the registration and running of a Residents Association in my area. My thinking was to participate in creating a safer environment. Thabo Mbeki's advice on doing just that was definitely not the motivating factor. In fact it angered me that the responsibility for safety was shoved so unceremoniously onto the shoulders of the public. All I can say is that this was an interesting exercise in the study of human behaviour and an eye-opener as to the real facts on crime in my area.*

GP - South Africa

∞ ∞ ∞

# 24

∞

## Prelude to Leaving

*It's too difficult... our love for South Africa
and our love for our daughter.*
CT - Italy

**N**ovember 2000. It is early evening, and I am standing at the kitchen counter. The light is soft and the air comfortably warm with the late afternoon breeze shearing off the mountain and through the house. James has arrived home from work, eager to show me the CD he's taking to a friend in the States. He's busy packing for his 2-week 'LSD' trip. (I've recently discovered this colloquialism online which, to South Africans, means he is taking a 'Look See Decide' journey.)

For me that moment remains unforgettable. I'm familiar with the music of Laurika Rauch though I've not been an enthusiastic fan – but this track which I'd never heard before, converted me. We're standing in the kitchen. James forwards to track 14 and says emphatically, "Listen!"

Haunting strains of *Stuur Groete Aan Mannetjies Roux* fill our kitchen. The words and the heaviness of the dirge fill my heart and, as if I can no longer bear its weight, I clutch the counter. At last the sombre tones die away and, wiping my tears, I say, "If you play that too often to me, I'll never leave this country."

The evocative words conjured images of the hills around Riebeek Kasteel and farmhouses dotting the landscape, joined by enormous patchwork squares in shades of brown, green and grey. An old bakkie making its way slowly along a dirt road, 'hoor jy nog sy motor met sy klap-klap-klap'.

I'd never thought myself a country girl; growing up in the Southern Suburbs of Cape Town, I had no desire to live further away than that. After five years in Riebeek Kasteel, the landscape had changed me. The colours of the valley and the scent on the air changed seasonally. A dry, musty smell seemed to permeate the valley during the harvesting of the wheat, and a tartness filled the air when the grapes were being picked. A tartness which was echoed in the dryness of the grape skins after you'd really chewed the grape. Only skins were left rolling between your teeth, but still, there remained a flavour.

> I love my country deeply but I think I must leave.
> WF - South Africa

I knew those images. I recognized them in my daily life in the village. The song bundled all my emotional attachments and hit me hard in my solar plexus. Already then I knew, and could clearly see and feel what it would be like to be an immigrant in a foreign land. I could feel the pain, and recognize the trauma, in advance.

Turning to James, I said, "You know, we'll be like those immigrants after the war, building a life in a strange country, listening to 'our' music, to words that no-one else can understand, knowing that no-one else will ever really, deeply understand us and where we come from, again, and longing for home, longing for a life we had somewhere else, far away." It didn't stop me, nothing much does once I've made up my mind.

Re-reading this paragraph brings a rush of emotion back to me; the feelings of things and places that I seem to have forgotten and then something happens and I am shunted suddenly back there, that kicked-in-my-guts, gasping sensation that almost stops my breathing. And I realize that I don't belong here, I carry a closet[13] full of life and experiences and memories that no-one whom I've met in the last eight years will ever understand about me. A whole past that has just been closed away, shut down somewhere inside, like a precious trunk full of mementos. I will always feel like an immigrant. And I do. I play my Afrikaans CDs loudly, sometimes I cry and sometimes I sing.

---

[13] I no longer refer to a cupboard, or a wardrobe, because Americans understand closet and it's easier to make myself quickly understood when I use American English.

And despite knowing about the sadness we'd feel, despite realizing the enormity of what we'd leave behind, despite the overwhelming heaviness in heart and mind, we did it anyway. We walked away into an uncertain future in an unknown land.

∞ ∞ ∞

*I am definitely TORN…. Being one of those remaining in this wonderful land, but seeing everyone and everything near and dear being eroded or leaving…. Yet, trying to see the silver lining and glimmer of hope somewhere?*
AG - South Africa

∞

*Congratulations on a piece well written, it summarizes the feelings of stress and anguish most of us feel living here. My wife and I live in Johannesburg (moved from Pretoria last year) and leave for Brisbane, Australia this weekend for job interviews. We have also started the formal process of applying for permanent residency in Australia and can't wait to leave South Africa permanently. I don't know when you wrote the piece, but I can say that today the level of violent crime is probably three to four times what it was even a year ago. There is total anarchy in all major cities.*

*Don't regret for a moment what you've done. I believe the good things in life usually require sacrifices – it's almost always worth it! Three thousand families a month are now formally leaving the country.*
GS - South Africa

∞

*Prior to our decision to emigrate, our home was burgled four times. On the last occasion, our older daughter entered the ransacked house, stood in the doorway of her room in the passageway and said tearfully, 'Daddy, look what they've done to my room!' She was four years old when that took place. That's when my wife and I decided that she would not go through another experience like that again.*

*Some of our church congregation left for New Zealand at that time, after witnessing a failed car hijacking in which the driver of a BMW was shot* and killed before her son, who was a passenger in the vehicle. The family were still shaking when they arrived at church that morning.  ANJ - Australia

∞

The only self questioning aspect remaining which needs to be satisfied is the certainty that one is not just being hysterical about the decision, but that if one were to stay behind then all one would be doing is procrastinating. It is this final tipping point where Kofi Anan's insight on the lack of good governance and endemic corruption ("…a pernicious, self-destructive form of racism that unites citizens to rise up and expel tyrannical rulers who are white, but to excuse tyrannical rulers who are black.") provides the nail in the coffin to the frightened leaver.  EVW - South Africa

∞

Immegrasie is die moeilikste ding wat ek nog ooit aangepak het. Daar is soveel wat ons nie weet nie, gaan ons aanpas, gaan ons kind aanpas, gaan ons werk kry, ens, ens. Ons voorsate het ook sekerlik die wind van voor gekry van vriende en familie toe hulle besluit het om hul besittings te verkoop, hul ossewaens te pak en weg te trek van die onderdrukking van die regering van die dag. Selfs Jesus se ouers het land-uit gevlug toe koning Herodes Hom wou vermoor. Ek belowe ek sal aanhou om vir my land en my volk te bid. Hopelik sal ons met tyd die slegte dinge, die haat en die geweld vergeet en net die mooi onthou. Ons gaan maar oë toeknyp en hierdie maak werk. Ons gaan Aussieland toe.  D - South Africa

∞

Its been incredibly hard, in fact far harder than my first divorce which was a very acrimonious bloody affair. I think for the first time in my life I experienced pure depression and had to face my own demons.  JW - Australia

∞

It is all so unknown and scary.... Will we get good work? The time taken to find good jobs and re-establish business connections. Will we have as comfortable standard of living there. I am currently a stay-at-home mum,

*I suppose, sadly, this would need to change. Will we be able to afford a nice home as we have here. The change in domestic lifestyle with housework and gardeners. Leaving the support system and friends we have here (we live with no family in the Province so friends become important). Moving to a cold climate. My husband's reluctance. These reasons will not stop us from leaving.*

RW - South Africa

∞

*We've been considering emigration to the USA and then my husband was hijacked two weeks back. Emigration is no longer a consideration for us. We have to do something to protect our family before anything worse happens. We have two small girls of two years and 16 weeks – I just couldn't bear for anything untoward to happen to them. Our reasons for leaving have been many besides the crime, but as a mother, this is foremost on my list. It just breaks my heart though to leave my parents and my sister as we're a close family. I am hoping that they will follow us.*

LS - South Africa

∞

*We're tending towards the leave option. It is such a big decision that frankly I wish we did not have to make. The pain of leaving family and a known lifestyle is a difficult. However, there is no longer the question 'when will crime hit us'. The question is 'What crime hit you that finally made you leave?'!*

PS - South Africa

∞

*I am a South African artist. I lived in London between 1995 and 2004. I am now back in South Africa running a theatre company. But I am feeling poised to leave once more.*

*Fear is curiously not a motivating factor. I am not frightened of the threat of crime or violence. Well, at least not enough to make me leave my home and family, my sea and sky. I was mugged five times in London, and have never been attacked in South Africa.*

*No, the reason I came home was the feeling I had every time I got into the plane to fly back to London after holidays in Durban – that my heart* had been nailed to the runway, and as the plane took off the wrenching, soul shaking pain was too much to bear.

Now, after for years back here, I am ready to risk that same agony again. Because of the corruption and lack of accountability pervading every aspect of our infrastructures on a macro and micro level. The general degeneration and decay, the pollution and destruction of our natural heritage, all these things have given rise in me to a constant low-level rage that is poisoning my life.

If this destruction was the result of some equalising action, if poor people were somehow empowered and their quality of life was improved in some way by our sacrifices, I would be able to live with the compromises. But there is no visible improvement in the lot of the poor. It is just getting harder for them to live at all while a small group of elite, absurdly over-paid civil servants enrich themselves at the country's expense and completely neglect their responsibilities.

This is not why we voted and motivated for change in this oh so beautiful country.

SS - South Africa

∞

Crime was the reason my daughters and families had to leave South Africa. My close friend was raped at age 48, her husband tied up by a teenage intruder. I went through months of watching her and her family deal with this, counselling, HIV/Aids treatment in case she had been infected with this deadly virus. Almost every friend I know has been touched in some way by crime ie assault, hijacking, robbery, murder... At one time while living there, the daily sensational headlines in the paper were faceless people, but, over time, those statistics were including people I knew personally... then you know it's time to move on.

KLB - Ireland

∞

We are in the throes of making 'the decision', having three small children, but feeling completely and utterly torn – to the point of being distraught and traumatised. I feel that we have already started to go down 'that road' (selling our house etc) and already I feel I am not the same person, nor will I ever be. I have shed tears and lost sleep already – I shudder to think what I may be like on the other side.

What an individual journey it is for each of us! I have friends who could not wait to leave and have had no problem settling. I am in the category of 'least likely to adapt happily' as my roots go so deep here and I am passionate about this country. My mother had a genuine love for African people and this rubbed off on her children and gave us an understanding of the other side of the coin of living under apartheid.
JW - South Africa

∞

Leaving has become my focal point. I have nothing in South Africa except worry and fear. The fear (of unknown) factor has stopped me.
LG - South Africa

∞

I was conscripted for South African Army – one year in Walvis Bay – only English speaker in a battalion of Afrikaners – I was going to die in Walvis Bay. It took me 48 hours to plan. I got a seven-day pass, hitched home to Jo'burg, bought a plane ticket and legged it to the UK. It was not difficult to leave – my uncle was banned, I was being bullied in the army, I simply did not look back for a second. Suddenly I confronted terrifying loneliness arriving at Heathrow with no-one to meet me and nowhere to stay.
PC - UK

∞

It's difficult when one emigrates. I read once that emigration is like a marriage that doesn't work. A failure of partnership.
RS - Australia

∞

I am sitting here reading this article of yours on my last night in South Africa. We are leaving for Australia tomorrow night and as I sit here I cannot think why I am doing this. As you said the stuff is easy. My dogs and family are a different thing. We also don't know if this is going to work and we certainly don't see Australia as the land of milk and honey. Only that we will be able to find work and be able to send our kids to school and not live behind bars and fences.

Yes I do agree. I feel sorry for those who have even less and that makes it even more difficult to leave because don't we have to stay and try and make South Africa a better place? I don't know. On the other hand it takes lots of guts to go and it is much easier not to go and endure life as it is here.

EG - South Africa

∞

I have lived in Johannesburg for seven years after returning from abroad to support the hopes, ideals and goals of the New South Africa. After experiencing having friends hijacked, robbed, kidnapped, raped, murdered, paralysed by bullet wounds, as well as experiencing various crime first hand, I have become completely paranoid. My wife and I started mentioning the possibility of emigrating and were overwhelmed by the response of those around us. It was as if everybody had been waiting for the topic to be brought up. We now are a group of five couples (possibly more) who are wanting to start a new life overseas – probably in Australia or New Zealand.

NL - South Africa

∞

Numerous friends have left in the past 2-3 years, most of them for Australia. This has left a huge hole in our lives. It is quite something to start planning your birthday party and realize that literally half the guest list is no longer here.

PH - South Africa

∞ ∞ ∞

## 25

∞

## Time To Say Goodbye

*I want to go out at night,*
*I want to walk in the park and know I am safe,*
*I want to sleep at night with both eyes shut!*
*I want to leave my window open when its hot,*
*I want to get out this prison I live in.*
SCVZ - Australia

A whole year of my experiences, and my life, was neatly wrapped into one song. My 'Time to Say Goodbye' consumed 2001.

It was a year filled with saying goodbye to places and people. I made my choice to leave a country, the only one I had ever known. This meant leaving behind beloved animals and people and family. During that year, I sang the song loudly as I raced into town along the highways.

I decided to learn to speak Italian so that I could sing along with Andrea Boccelli in his own language. I sang it softly as I drove over the mountain, arriving home to the valley. The beautiful quilt of colours - yellows, browns, greens, oranges, greys, lavenders - laid out below always astounded me. And then, I would stop singing because the catch in my throat prevented the words. Was I really leaving this? Was I really saying goodbye? Did I know what I was doing?

I spent a precious two weeks in London in July 2001. This was my first time away from my two-year-old and my four-year-old. For my birthday, my sister treated me to a seat at an open-air Andrea Boccelli concert at Hyde Park. At the end of July, sitting under a summer night sky, I watched the jets circling as they waited to land at Heathrow. I shivered in the coolness of the air as I once again heard 'my song'. The real-life, raw experience of hearing the song made me wonder about all the goodbyes that I had willingly chosen to embark upon. I remember the night, I remember the song, I remember the jets overhead and I remember being almost overwhelmed by the cold. I don't think anything else about the concert imprinted itself on my memory – I was emotionally exhausted from a long flight with little sleep the previous evening. I was running on adrenaline.

Three months later I would be sitting beside my father's hospital bed trying to say another goodbye with another catch in my throat. I had said to friends, a couple of months prior, that I didn't think he would survive the year because he had given up on life. I didn't really believe it and I hardly listened to the intuitive part of myself that said it. After all, he wasn't sick, was he? I didn't know where that statement had come from – another bit of my melodramatic nature – so I ignored it.

> Having to wait for 24 hours before being with my mother, after my brother's death, was a special kind of torture.... This is a big price....
>
> DM - Australia

Sitting at his bedside, I looked out again at the stars and Lion's Head looming over the old hospital building. The silhouette of the mountain against the early night sky was eerily beautiful through the enormous picture windows of City Park Medical Centre. It was as though we should be sitting in a restaurant laughing, and joking, over a glass of red wine or whisky. The setting was perfect, the situation was awful.

The irony was that he wanted the song *Time to Say Goodbye* played at his funeral and to honour his wish, I had to bring another dimension to 'my song'. This was a dimension that I hadn't anticipated when singing it madly while driving. I stood upstairs in the nave as I played the song from my CD and my CD player. I leaned my hot forehead against the coolness of the wall. As I fought tears and bit my lip, I couldn't believe that the song had taken over another significant event in the same year. This wasn't a planned goodbye.

I still listen to the song. I love the depth and intensity of the words and the rich tones of Boccelli. I still sing softly along with the words, and I cry madly inside and out. I cry quietly if I am with others and, if I am alone, I cry loudly and I cry long.

*Time to Say Goodbye* represents an entire period of my life where all I did was say farewell to everyone and everything I loved, every place, every moment, every memory I had ever experienced or created. All my partings wrapped up into one evocative piece of music.

> Ultimately I think I am just biding time. I know I'll leave.
> RDP - South Africa

Saying goodbye will never be quite as hard again. I've immunized myself against the pain. Andrea Boccelli helped me come to terms with it. Next time my goodbyes will be shorter and sweeter and I will not look back as I walk away.

∞ ∞ ∞

*I'm sure there is nothing new to you in what I write. What I would like you to get from my letter is that in my opinion you have done the right thing by leaving South Africa. Yes, we have all been traumatized by having at least one sad farewell at the airport. As big as what I am, I cry every time I get to the airport and remember all the goodbyes. But, hey, they're safe where they are now....*

PD - South Africa

∞

*For the past few years I am waking up (sometimes very early) every morning hoping I will not have to take this step. I (more than my wife) am dragging my feet, using a number of both good and bad excuses, in order to try and convince myself to stay in South Africa. But this eternal see-saw / yes-no scenario has to come to a conclusion, this self made torture has to stop! Rather sooner than later.*

JVD - South Africa

∞

*My sister had left for New Zealand two years earlier, but we did not really consider following in her footsteps. Then my husband decided to take voluntary retrenchment at work in the gold mine, because they told him that he will not advance in his job because of affirmative action, despite completing his studies. In August 2005 a colleague of mine was brutally raped and murdered in her house in Klerksdorp. The very next day I was on* the internet to find out about obtaining permanent residence in New Zealand.

We were tired of living like prisoners behind bars with five security gates in our home. We were getting older and the fact is that you have to start all over again. If we wanted to leave, then it was time to do so. The fact that my sister was already in New Zealand made it easier, although we do not live on the same island. The week after my friend was murdered, we started applying for passports and birth certificate. I applied on-line for residence in January 2006 and we received our passports back in November 2006. My husband booked our flight and we left South Africa in December.

We packed our bags, got on the plane, decided on a map where we think we wanted to go and live and that was it. We did not have any job offers beforehand.

AB - New Zealand

∞

I think the most difficult person to leave behind was my father. This because I knew that he was facing the death of my mother who had been bedridden for over three years. It was very difficult leaving him knowing that he would have to deal with this without my support. Another difficulty was leaving behind my very best girlfriend and her family. They had been a very big part of our life for at least six years before we left. It's not often that such a true friend is found and her absence leaves a big gap in my life.

AW - Australia

∞

I feel almost like we're running out of time, to leave the country of our birth, our home, our family... OUR LIVES! I have many friends, family members and patients who have left to live in UK, New Zealand, Australia and Canada, struggled emotionally, moved on, accepted citizenship, and will NEVER return, to a country spiralling downhill, with hideous crime levels and breakdown in human values and social systems. Sad, but true, and I believe that too.

CK - South Africa

∞

The only reason I am leaving is because I want to live! I want to go out at night, I want to walk in the park and know I am safe, I want to sleep at night with both eyes shut! I want to leave my window open when it's hot, I want to get out this prison I live in. The kids even suffer under this, they can't be children, they go out and my nerves are shot as every second goes by.

SCVZ - Australia

∞

I feel that the longer I'm away, the less I miss it. I still miss the great food, wine, drives in the country and Sunday afternoon walks along the beach. While living there, I was happy, led a charmed life and crime always happened to other people. Then one day it cruelly touched my life. I just couldn't live there any more and six months later I was gone. On 1 July, 2000, my fiancé was murdered at his (own) company.

NVD - Germany

∞

I am a fourth generation South African, who is currently facing the dilemma of upping and leaving. I have a deep gut feel of 'now or never' and it is actually one of the most disturbing and disconcerting feelings I have ever experienced. The strange thing is I am not averse to taking risks. But when you are faced with making the decision – and risk being a person with a foot on both continents, it makes you sit back a bit. If I go it's forever. I don't think I can mentally handle that situation.

BT - South Africa

∞

It is not one factor that would induce me to leave. In fact, I would prefer to have made a decision about leaving before anything happens to me or my family personally that will cause us to leave. There are however a number of 'external' factors which do or will impact me or my family now or in the future, and include the following:

(1) the level and nature of crime; (2) the inability of the current ruling party/government to govern; (3) the deterioration of public infrastructure (electricity, clean water); (4) the lack of sufficient public healthcare facilities; (5) the unsustainable and damaging practice of affirmative action; (6) the joke of a public education system; (7) an uncertain future for my children's ability to be employed and earn a living when the finish their schooling; (8) the fact that I, along with my other mostly white compatriots, are the goose

*that keeps laying the golden egg.*

*The collective goose is being abused and is gradually leaving for an environment where their contributions are appreciated and where they get something tangible in return.*

AJVN - South Africa

∞

*Most of my colleagues had been burgled at least once, with increasing violence. Two had been murdered, one had lost her brother in an armed robbery. My partner and I had lost four cars to theft already, not including several unsuccessful attempts. The government closed the very busy hospital where I was working, for some stupid reason. More than half of my patients were HIV-positive, unable to get effective treatment – hopeless. It was too sad to watch the decline of the universities I had attended during my studies (UNISA, Wits and RAU). So, with young kids, we just decided to leave before anything really bad happened to us.*

AD - Australia

∞

*Then I wrote a third list: How crime has affected us or our friends. These are people WE KNOW, not what we have read in the paper or heard on the news. At the moment, this list has 32 events. Of these 32, 12 are dead. Others have been raped, hijacked, beaten up, robbed, shot. This list grows weekly. Every time we speak to someone, they have a story. I don't always write them down. So, that is how we got to be investigating a move to New Zealand.*

BM - South Africa

∞

*I am a devastated man. I am extremely grieved and broken that I am 'forced' to leave my beloved country. I am devastated that I am no longer welcome here. It breaks my heart in a million pieces. I have not been directly influenced by today's crime. Thank God for that. However, strange as it sounds, I have been affected indirectly in that, amongst others, I cannot sleep at night.*

*I sometimes think that I am the only one that hears the gun shots at night. I don't talk about it any more as people get sick of this kind of chatter.*

*Ten to fifteen gun shots 2 a.m. in the morning has become the norm. Or a bomb blast when they blow up an ATM machine. Crazy stuff!*

*I was conscripted onto the old SADF in 1987 to 1988. That was supposed to be a war. Yea right! Let me tell you, the latter was a walk in the park compared to a gunfight between cops and robbers at Boksburg Mall with mothers and babies taking cover while daddy is at work. We've become like frogs in a pot. We are exposed to extreme danger as the water heats up; we just sit there and take it. Not good.*  RVR - South Africa

∞

*I tried all I could for two years to get to USA, it cost me more than I could afford and I'm still here. The woman who I love with all my heart is there but I remain here. The only way we can be together would be for her to return to South Africa. How could I ever ask someone to risk their life for me? So, yet another sad farewell at an airport. A relationship reduced to emails, SMS and the occasional phone call. I guess I have learnt my personal interpretation of 'Cry the Beloved Country'.*  PD - South Africa

∞

*No. We do not want to go, have no intention of going, and although we understand why many of our friends have gone, we can't stand it when they urge us to join them or preach at us about how terrible it is in South Africa. We respect their decision to go, but we find several of them do not respect our decision to stay.*  PH - South Africa

∞

*My children have never dared venture out of our property unassisted in all the years that they have been alive. They have grown up surrounded by razor wire, electric fences atop ten foot high walls, alarms with panic buttons, security gates on every entrance or exit into the house and the threat of violence against them, as a norm. They have never walked to the store or to school; they don't know what it's like to visit a neighbourhood friend on their own. Being left alone at home with a baby sitter is a scary situation and not fun as it should be, and staying up past bed time, eating more ice-cream than* is normally allowed, is poor compensation! I gladly say farewell to all of that and will endure whatever hardships might lie in wait in the new country we are moving to.

PP - USA

∞

A pivotal event that affected me, and made me realize that I could no longer do business in South Africa, was when I was asked for a huge bribe by a board member of a large parastatal, for a contract I had legitimately bid on.

DS - USA

∞

I'm one of those that refuse to leave... my husband calls me an ostrich, but I insist, this is my country, I have a right to be here. I myself have been touched by crime, having interrupted a burglary, tied up and gagged with a knife to my throat... I don't know what to say, just that I don't want to leave.

TH - South Africa

∞

My youngest son had a motor bike accident and, as we could not afford private medical aid, was taken to the local Frere Hospital (in East London). While waiting to be attended to in A&E (Accident and Emergency), my husband and I noticed dried blood on the floor, instruments and metal frame above the gurney where he was lying. After he had been treated, we made our way back out through the busy reception area, and to our horror had to 'step over' a dead man! He had not been lying in the 'doorway' when we arrived and no-one in the waiting room seemed the least bit perturbed by this. I then realized that this could be any one of my family members being treated in this horrific way and, looking back, I think this was the 'cherry on the cake'.

SK - Ireland

∞

I always said that I never want to leave this beautiful country of my birth, that I don't want to give up and be a deserter and leave my family and friends behind to face an uncertain future... but one of these days I think it

*will not be a choice, it will be absolutely necessary to leave. Just the thought of leaving makes me want to cry. I won't be able to take everyone with me, I'd feel like I'm leaving them to be victims of this country while saving myself.*
YP - South Africa

∞

*I am torn between leaving the country that I love, and my friends and family that will not leave... and myself not wanting to leave but torn between my life ahead and that of the children that I will one day wish to have... it sure is not the same country that I was brought up in as a child and loved so much.*
MM - South Africa

∞

*Our hijacking and armed robbery with child in backyard and wife being dragged to the bushes was not the final straw, the perpetrators being out on R100 bail in my driveway, waving at my five year old daughter was.*
DJK - Ireland

∞

*Having been sent from Zimbabwe to stay with South African family when I was 10 years old I find it very worrying how the state of affairs in South Africa is tracking those of Zimbabwe in its early independence years. It made it easier for me to decide to leave knowing that by the time he died my father's Zimbabwe pension was literally worth nothing, and had he not died he would have been living off handouts from his South African family. Being as proud and independent as he was this would have broken him.*
MF - South Africa

∞ ∞ ∞

# 26

∞

# To Those Who Aren't Concerned[14]

by Alison Wolfson
(at the time of writing: South Africa)

**O**K – I give up. Finally, today, I have had enough. I have today consciously made the decision that I am selling my farm which I built over the past seven years from a piece of bare wheatfield and I am leaving this country. I am giving up my South African citizenship and I am moving on.

I apologise to all other people who have left this country earlier who I have criticized. I apologise to myself for wasting my energy and emotion on a land that is unable to afford me any rights whatsoever, despite the fact that I have always stayed within the limits of the law and obeyed the laws of this land.

Law abiding citizens of this country are being held hostage by a very small minority of people who are using the mechanisms contained in our various laws for the protection of indigent and ignorant people to their own advantage. This handful of people who have no morals or values are able to manipulate and corrupt the law for their own benefit and advantage to the destruction of the concept of justice and equality for all. The property which

---

[14] Originally published as a letter in the *Landbou Weekblad*. 29 September 2005. Used with permission. Shortened, not edited, by James McIntosh.

I have practically single-handedly built (with the aid of our diligent and brilliant local labour force) for my family and their families to come no longer has any meaning for me.

Those within the law have no constitutional rights whatsoever. I beg you to look closely at this. Please don't let this go unchanged. Make the changes that are necessary so that law-abiding citizens do have protection, or by the time your grandchildren's children are grown, not much will be left of this country.

And understand me well, this is not a racial issue, the issue that has caused my extreme unhappiness and discomfort and has torn the African from my soul stems from an incident with an ex-farm manager of mine who has the same skin colour as I have.

Until today, I was full of fight for my country of birth, but the discussion with the Labour Department has made me realize that, truly, this is the reality we live in. This bridge is just too far. How can anyone expect me to feel pride for a country that treats its own citizens in this manner?

I have no rights.

I have no protection.

I have no country.

∞ ∞ ∞

*I am angry at having to make this decision, but I am fortunate to have options – thousands of others do not. Will I become someone who will shed tears when listening to the 'Scatterlings of Africa', and will those be tears of sorrow or happiness or both?* AJVN - South Africa

∞

*What factor/event would induce me to leave? When our neighbour was robbed of his car, phone and wallet at gunpoint in front of his house in broad daylight? When three attempts to burgle our house (whilst we were at home) were unsuccessful? When I came home late one night from the airport from having visited my children in Europe and narrowly escaped being* robbed of my luggage, and/or worse? But it also goes beyond mere personal interests, i.e. the fact that in general the poor in South Africa are probably worse off than 15 years ago.

JVD - South Africa

∞

I simply got tired of living behind bars and fences with a security system and armed guards ready to come and rescue me if the need arose. What kind of life is that – and what kind of message does it send to our children? So we came to a country so similar to ours in many ways and yet so alien in others that it might as well be on another planet.

The homesickness and uncertainty are constant niggles at the back of your mind along with the constant fear – what about those that you care about but which you left behind? What will become of them?  SDT - Australia

∞

I left that area because I was sick and tired of the new South Africa. I was sick of living behind 8 ft walls, security gates, infrared alarms and such. I was sick of having to tell competent and qualified white candidates that I could not employ them in my division at (the bank) because they were not black. I was sick of being forced by racist legislation to hire incompetent people because they were not white, and then have to see declining standards at work, and watch the competent people leave because they could not carry the workload for the incompetent co-workers.

I was sick of having to take a gun everywhere I went, even to fetch the mail at the end of my garden, behind my 8ft wall, in the evenings. I was sick of seeing declining standards everywhere I looked, and being filled with fear at hearing a noise in the middle of the night. I was tired of being afraid for my daughters when they went to school, to the movies, to after school sports activities, and even when they slept in their beds at night.  AS - USA

∞

In my group of 11 friends, all qualified engineers, only two will remain in South Africa from December 2008. I don't think it can get any worse in fact. It is very difficult to identify and say something positive,

therefore this response is very negative and does not reflect the type of person that I am. I am always positive, always smile and always see the positive side. I cannot do it any longer.
JE - South Africa

∞

We still think of the people that remain – do they think differently or are they willing to accept the horrors that occur. Have they become so used to the dysfunctional ways or do they have more 'guts'? Why can they stay and we fear to? Can I become like them?
AMS - USA

∞

I used to love South Africa and didn't want to leave, but I've been left with no choice.
FP - South Africa

∞

Life is a journey, why waste it, living in fear of your safety? Why waste your life because governments do not think of the consequences of their actions/laws? People who feel obliged to leave a country for safer locations cannot be blamed for having a strong desire to survive in better conditions – this motivates most immigrants.

For many, the horror of the apartheid system has come to roost, and the consequences are part of the evolution of the new South Africa. Africa, a beautiful continent, seems plagued by corruption, has been raped by many, and could be the next emerging world market, but not in my lifetime. The South Africa story has been played over in history many times over. Most recently, in Zimbabwe, an abomination which continues, unchecked, without intervention from any. Shame on you South Africa.
AMS - USA

∞

I love this country, I love the people who live in this country and in my field South Africa is the world leader but unfortunately I become very reluctant when considering to start a family. I feel that a country so high in crime is not suitable to raise children in. It is not fair on them. I did not study six years to be forced to physically fight for basic needs like safety and security for my family. I have been accused of being a coward when voicing my opinions but this is a basic human right that the government in our constitution has agreed to supply.

AV - South Africa

∞

What makes it even more painful is that I was one of those who fought for and supported the change. I supported an end to Apartheid and eagerly voted 'yes' in the referendum. We wanted a society where people were free and equal, but the rampant crime has turned our hopes and dreams into a nightmare. Instead of the paradise it could very easily have been, it is hell on earth.

EN - Arizona

∞

Job availability in the public Sector. Initially I was not "white enough" being of Indian origin, then I was perceived as not being "black enough", so any job applied for in the public sector I was turned down. So I elected to relocate.

NG - Qatar

∞

As the white population decreases over the next 10 to 15 years South Africa will slide very swiftly into the same dilemma as Zimbabwe. Most of my colleagues and friends say I'm far too optimistic. They put the collapse at just a few years.

The big danger here is that the ruling Blacks in government and those in business (who were put there under affirmative action and given millions of Rands in shares) have grabbed all the wealth and the millions of Black citizens, refugees and illegal immigrants are being totally ignored. The majority are living in squalor and without the basic necessities, such as food. They are fed up and their only option is crime. This will lead to a second revolution which will destroy the land. Unfortunately the rest of the populace will be plundered and much blood will flow.

Am I being alarmist? Not at all. This scenario will be denied by government and many white liberals but speak to the businessmen and the middle class citizen as well as the moderate Blacks and you will find the daily conversation and conviction of the above events that they all believe will take place here. It's the talk on buses, in coffee shops, at the golf club and in the work place.

I was once a proud and optimistic South African. Even when we were being hammered by sanctions being imposed on us by overseas countries I never doubted my country's ability to excel in the face of adversity. Today I'm disappointed and frustrated at the willful destruction of my beautiful country.   VA - South Africa

∞

On Christmas Day in 2007, my whole family spent the day together at our house, as we always do, and when I look back now, I remember how at that point not one of us was seriously considering emigrating. We would always say 'one day, we'll have to get out of here', and the conversation would turn into discussing all the bad things that were happening in our country. But that's as far as it went.

Yet who knew that just two months later, the wheels of the country would literally start falling off? My daughter had started her new job in Sandton that fateful week the power cuts first started. It arrived without warning and was absolute chaos! She spent two and a half hours driving to Sandton – leaving at 5.30 a.m., to get there at 8.00 a.m. – a trip that would usually take 20 minutes. The robots (traffic lights) were all out and there were as usual no pointsmen around to assist with the traffic. Driving back was just as bad, arriving home after dark.

On top of that we had weeks and weeks of torrential rains in Johannesburg, so the whole city was grey and gloomy, and so were the people. The radio stations adopted a habit of playing a song by Mika "Relax, Take it Easy" just to calm people down in the traffic.   LK - South Africa

∞ ∞ ∞

## 27

∞

# Saying Goodbye to Bracken on the Mountain

Sadly my dog had to be put down in South Africa a few weeks ago.
I kept hoping we may be able to bring him here someday.
HVG - USA

28 December 2001 – a quiet day after the rush of emotion over Christmas. In the wake of my father's passing on 31 October, it could not be considered to be revelry. It was a simple day, relaxing around in the rented house while the children, satiated by Christmas, calmly played with their gifts. We were still packing and sorting, I remember nothing of actual gifts which James and I shared – an empty anticipation of the year that lay before us.

We went to sleep early, only to be awakened around 10:30 p.m. by loud 'popping' sounds. Being conditioned to life in South Africa, I hurtled out of bed thinking that there was a shootout in the street. The road was in darkness but I could still hear a staccato of extremely loud 'bang' sounds, which appeared to be in our immediate vicinity. A derelict double-storey school building, only two doors down, had caught alight and the blaze was already 30 feet high. The sounds that woke us, were window panes exploding from the heat. Although there was no luxury of a 911 number, within 10 minutes the village was mobilized and people appeared, bakkies appeared and, miraculously, water appeared too.

I remember us standing on the verandah and watching the flames. It was near midnight, the summer weather coupled with the heat from the flames made the night intensely hot. The myriad of tall trees in the area, with dry foliage, made me fearful of the fire leaping across the road and consuming the houses.

"Should I wake the children? Should I pack anything?"

I smiled. What was there to pack anyway? We had condensed our lives into so little. For months, I'd been saying to friends that I had reduced the clutter and stuff in my life to such an extent that, if I was told to leave the country immediately, I could fit my essentials into a backpack and be out within 2 hours. I wondered if this was the Universe's way of testing my statements, a last laugh on me, as it were.

James, being the calmer personality, said, "No. It will be fine. Let's just wait and see."

I had never been that close to such a big blaze before so I was inclined to be far more apprehensive about the situation. Eventually, they did bring the fire under control, the shouting died down, and the clusters of villagers, who had collected in the road, dissipated into the night. We went back to bed sometime after midnight.

The next morning, James woke me with the news that the dogs had gone missing. During the commotion and clamour of the previous evening, it appeared that they had broken through the fencing at the back of the property – strands of thick black fur were left clinging to the wire.

I spent Saturday morning driving around Riebeek Kasteel and Riebeek West to place 'Lost' posters in prominent positions at various cafés, village shops, police stations, hotels or any other public area that was willing to take them. I posted a substantial reward since, in a poor farming community, that was the most likely factor that would cause the posters, and the dogs, to be noticed. I was distraught but the more I fussed, the more James told me to calm myself, someone would find them.

After lunch, I commenced driving on every tarred and dirt road – calling, whistling through the open windows (causing much amusement for the villagers 'kuier-ing' on their verandahs) – around both villages. My lips were dry and cracked by mid-afternoon when James called to say that Rebecca was home but the person would not accept the reward. It seemed that no-one had seen Bracken.

I was sure that my brilliant idea – to take Rebecca for a walk to pick up her brother's scent – would lead me to him. It was immediately apparent that she thought this was an exciting field trip. She led me in a multitude of crazy directions, with no focus on the task, no matter how many times I said, "Bracken. Find Bracken."

Ha! Party time! Bushes! Telephone poles! Fields! She dragged me from left to right across the roads. I quickly realized that she was not going to be of any assistance.

Later, I resumed driving and as I drove, I made ever-increasing and widening circles around the villages onto farm roads and byways. My erratic heartbeat was interrupted by every black speck in my peripheral vision – but nothing. After dinner, again, I was driving around until darkness had enveloped the valley and there was absolutely no chance of finding, or seeing, a black dog.

Dejected, I finally went home and fell into bed, exhausted, at 10:30 p.m. It was almost 24 hours later and there was no sign of him. I lay awake, thinking, wondering, where could he be? Why was he not responding? Our connection was so strong – where was he? Was he hurt, somewhere, alone? I had to find him. Taking deep breaths, I closed my eyes and imagined the terror he must have felt with the noise of the fire and people so close, I imagined how that fear would have driven him away from the source of the commotion.

If I was Bracken, where would I go? I would run away from the noise, as far away as possible. I am irrational with fear. OK. I've broken through the back fence and there's a road directly in front of me. I'm not going left because that will lead to the fire and the noise, I turn right. And now? I run hastily towards the next corner, bordered by a house on the left and the open school fields. I doubt I would turn right again because that would take me down to the next road – close to the source of the excitement, the people and the loud sounds. I'm running as fast as I can so in my haste, I take the route of least resistance and I head across the open fields of the school towards the vineyards, and the mountainside beyond. The land is open and the fields are clear; it is night time and no-one sees me; I run as fast as I can until the land runs out and I can no longer hear the noise.

"It's OK, boy. Stay calm. I'm coming to fetch you, I'll find you, it's OK. I'll be with you. Just be still and be there. Stay there." A silent sense of having made a connection overwhelmed me and I fell asleep.

6:30 a.m. found me dressed and out in my car. The first stop was at the school fields. Although I had been there a multitude of times on Saturday, I clung to a hope that my connection with him the previous evening meant that, this time, I would find him somewhere nearby. I parked the car and walked around the school buildings, calling, whistling, over and over again, but nothing – no answering response. I gave up, climbed into the car and drove towards Moorreesburg, onto the farming lands – hoping that I wouldn't incur the Sunday morning wrath of a farmer finding a stranger, in a strange car, driving his dirt roads. Two hours later, and I was sure I had exhausted all possibilities in that direction. He had to be somewhere on this side of the village.

At 8:30am, I decided to return home for breakfast. We had friends arriving late morning for lunch – although I was in no mood to spend time visiting with anyone, I was tired, dejected and irritable. But, first, just in case, I thought I'd stop at the vineyards beside the school fields – one more time – to admit I'd tried everything.

I stood next to my car, and whistled once, twice, three times. An answering high pitched series of yapping barks filled the air. Bracken? No, probably the baboons (they had been spotted on the lower reaches of the mountain on Friday). The barking continued. Frantically, I grabbed my cellphone, called Jonathan (Bracken's soon-to-be new owner in the village) and said, "Listen! Listen!" and held the phone up to the air, facing it toward the mountain.

"Is that a dog, or is that a baboon?"

"It's a dog."

"Are you sure?"

"Yes."

"That's my dog and I'm going up the mountain to find him. I'm not coming down without him."

"Bronwyn, wait. Just wait there. I'm coming up with the Land Rover. Where are you?"

I gave him details of the area and waited. I called and whistled but no more sounds, no answering from the mountainside. What if that was his last? What if he summoned up his last strength to answer me? It had been 40°C (104°F) the previous day. How could he have survived without water? And now, how will I find him?

Well, I was going up the mountain and whether I had to find a live dog, or bring a dead dog back down with me, I was staying up there until I found him. I didn't consider that the day was predicted to be 40°C again. I didn't consider that I hadn't worn sunblock, that I didn't have the appropriate takkies on or that I hadn't brought water. I was climbing that mountain!

I remember Richard arriving – Jonathan sent Richard because his Land Rover was being used by a neighbour. I remember calling James to tell him that we were going up the mountain. He came to meet us, after dropping the kids off with Jonathan and his wife, my friend Gill. We agreed to split the mountain, James climbed up the left side, I went up the centre and Richard toward the right. I hoped we could maintain cellphone contact and, whistling as I went, the three of us called each other a number of times. Nothing! There were no more answering barks. I saw large birds circling high overhead and wondered, again, if they were watching his body.

An ongoing motivational chatter in my head kept me going – "I can do this, I've survived more than this, I know I can do this, I know I can find him, this heat doesn't matter, the sun doesn't matter, I have to find him. I can't leave him. I can't leave South Africa without finding him. I have to know what happened to him." The knowledge that in one short week he would be leaving us to live with his new owners was part of my desperation. The closure was for me. I had to find him, in order to hand him safely to them and know that I had done my best for him. And if he was dead, I had to know that too.

Unbeknown to me, Richard (who had climbed the Kasteelberg frequently and knew it well) had mentally divided the mountain into a grid. He was planning to solicit help from all the animal lovers in the village and, should we not find Bracken now, the group would comb the area later. Two hours later, 10.30am, and the sun was rapidly climbing towards its zenith; I wasn't quite halfway up – I couldn't see anything above me and there certainly was no dog in the panorama below. My phone rang. It was Richard.

"I've found him."

"Oh, God, is he still alive."

"Yes. Very much so and obviously relieved to see me."

"Just hold on, I'm coming, where are you?"

"No. Bronwyn. I'm bringing him down. I'll meet you at the dam near the vineyards".

I called James. "Well, thank God. I was about to tell you that we need to give this up till it cools down later."

I made it down in double-quick time, slipping and sliding, and lucky not to break an ankle. When I reached the dam, Richard and Bracken had still not arrived; I had to contain my patience and wait. As they rounded the corner, Bracken saw me, made a running leap, and being such an enormous dog, his paws easily reached my shoulders, and with his thick black fur coat, it felt as though I was being enfolded by a large black bear. Not that I cared! He climbed into the water to soothe his raw, cut, paws. We believe that after running across the fields and making it to the mountain, he was chased by a pack of baboons. This would explain why when Richard was climbing, and bypassing a large rock overhang, Bracken remained absolutely still.

Richard said, "I almost walked right by him. He was so quiet. Then I thought I might as well check around the rock, just in case. And there he was, sheltering in the shade – totally silent."

We took him home. I was elated. I'd found him! He was alive, he was fine and he was still my baby. The umbilical cord between us felt stronger than ever. I had found him and I had the closure I sought but I wept at the thought that soon he would leave me to go to his new owners.

James joked to our friends that he felt entirely comfortable going to the USA because 'should I go missing, Bronwyn will find me.'[15]

A week later, Bracken and Rebecca moved on to their new home. Strangely, the separation, and loss was made easier because the incident on the mountain had proved that this village would care for my babies, in the way I would have wanted. The dogs would be living in a home with a larger garden. They would be with children who already knew them well. They would be treated by the same veterinarian who had known them since puppy-hood and, as they would be together, we could not have asked for a better situation.

About four months later, shortly prior to my leaving for the USA, we visited their home for a last luncheon with our friends. Bracken and Rebecca were on the verandah visiting with the guests and playing with the children. Although they greeted me, I was not singled out for special attention or loving. And, in the interests of a healthy separation and acceptance, that is, I suppose, as it should have been.

On our arrival in Richmond, I looked around our clinically luxurious apartment with white walls and cream carpeting and I realized that we had made the best choice for Bracken and Rebecca. We couldn't have brought them to the United States. The instability of our new life was barely manageable for us but having to live in quarantine and being separated from their family would have killed them. How would two large dogs fit into a small apartment with no yard or fence outdoors to contain their energy? I fantasised about buying a house and bringing them across to live with us

---

[15] Note by James: Not many weeks later Bronwyn spoilt it somewhat for me by whispering sweetly in my ear just before I left, that if I failed to contact her on my arrival in the USA, "I will hunt you down!"

again but I knew I could never uproot them from their new family and the second chance they now had. It was a one of those small survival mechanisms; a person must be able to dream.

Bracken was diagnosed with stomach cancer in 2003. He was no longer able to eat solids and he lost weight daily. During the course of my daily correspondence and discussion with Gill and Jonathan we decided that it would be better for him if he was euthanased. I wanted to fly back to South Africa to spend time with him during those last precious few days but James persuaded me not to be capricious – we didn't have money for the airfare and our situation was tenuous without compromising it by leaving. On the day of the procedure, I awoke at the time set for the vet's visit. Mid-afternoon in South Africa was early morning in the USA. As I lay in my bed in the USA far away from my baby, I closed my eyes and for the last time I made my emotional connection with him – spirit to kindred spirit – and let him go.[16]

My only consolation was that it was 'his' vet. It took place at Gill and Jonathan's home with the family present so he was in his own safe space and not some cold, clinical, office. He went to sleep quietly, restfully and peacefully. And, it broke my heart. Eight years later, I cried when I wrote this story and I cry whenever I read it, again and again.

∞ ∞ ∞

*The worst part was having to put my dog to sleep.*     SP - New Zealand

∞

*My cat who was like my child. At nine years of age and facing nine months of quarantine I could not justify taking him with me.*     MJ - South Africa

∞

*I walk my dogs on my own in the forest every day I am in awe that one can walk in nature in safety, something you cannot do at home. I*

---

[16] Even in death, Bracken was treated in the same loving manner in which he had lived. He was buried under a newly planted olive tree in the garden of his adopted home.

brought my dogs with me and they served 6 months in quarantine. It was expensive but I felt I owed it to them for protecting me when I needed them (I would never have emotionally survived as long as I did without my dogs) and didn't want to abandon them.
SVB - UK

∞

My dog – he was a good old mutt but too old to put in quarantine. He died in friendly arms but sadly, four months after we left. We scattered his ashes in the Arabian Gulf. He had protected and probably saved my family's life twice.
BM - UAE

∞

The thought I had, or picture, whatever you want to call it, was this: I was standing still. This fire was coming at me. It started over there, far away. It got closer and closer. Bigger and bigger. I could almost feel the heat. By now it was a HUGE fire, burning out of control. I was the only one there. And I just stood, watching this fire. I did not move.

Since we decided to move to New Zealand I have not had that picture, or thought again! When I think about this country, it is like the fire. We have had it, unless we move out of the way. We are too small to stop it. We must get out of the way of the fire.
BM - South Africa

∞ ∞ ∞

## 28

∞

## You Have To Stay, Ben[17]

by Kate Richards

      Soaring thousands of feet above the ground, all I can think about is Ben, sitting in a box in the hold. I should have remembered to put cotton wool in his ears. I smile as I think about how Ben taught me a lesson in holding one's head high even when wishing the ground would open up and swallow me whole. He did his business in the outdoor restaurant and I had to nonchalantly clear it up with big wads of toilet paper and dispose of it in the loo. Walking back and forth past the dining businessmen, with smelly wads aloft, was not my idea of a dignified moment. Now, gazing down at Midmar and the rolling hills below, I don't care; I am processing my goodbyes.

      We leave for New Zealand in December. As if that sentence isn't heartbreaking enough for us and for the loved ones we are leaving behind; we have to say goodbye to our faithful dogs, one at a time. I am flying Ben to Oliver Thambo airport where I will meet my friend Bev. We will head out to Middelburg, to hand Ben over to my friend's mother, who has kindly agreed to adopt him. I had run out of possibilities in Maritzburg when an intuitive moment led me to asking Mrs. Bradley who agreed without

---

[17] *You Have To Stay, Ben* was first published in *The Witness* (a South African newspaper) on 9 November 2009.

hesitation.

I have been showing Ben images of Mrs. Bradley in my mind's eye, and saying, "Mrs. Bradley is going to be your new mum." I showed him mental pictures of her patting him and feeding him, and wondered if he was receiving them. Ever since he was a highly strung pup I have talked to Ben, because he was my 'child' before I had my human children. He has an awesome vocabulary, for a dog. He knows – "Go and do your wees and poos" at bed time (and preferably not at airports), and "sit" and "water" and "You have to stay; I will see you later," said in a drawling coo. This time I know I will have to omit the see you later bit.

I have been teaching Ben the words 'Mrs. Bradley'. After an afternoon and a night in Middelburg, Ben and Mrs Bradley are starting to bond. We are in the warm kitchen and Ben is sitting gazing into my eyes with his big brown knowing pools and I say to him, "Ben, where's Mrs. Bradley?" He turns his head to look at her over his shoulder, his body still facing me.

My friend Bev charges in from the passage. "Hey wait, I overheard that; do it again," she says. Ben is gazing at me again. I repeat the question and once again he looks over his shoulder at her.

I knew it. I just knew that this dog is incredibly intelligent. I hope his intelligence helps him to understand that kind Mrs. Bradley is going to be his new mum. He will never understand why I am leaving him. We have been best friends for ten years; the best ten years of my life. I met my husband and had two wonderful children in those years, and he was always there to share in the love, the joy, the fleas and the fun.

The day arrives when I have to say goodbye. I am a snivelling wreck, my handbag full of soggy tissues. I hug him and walk to the car. He follows. I say, "Ben, you have to stay," and I close the car door, the floodgates opening.

Mrs. Bradley calls him and he walks to her side and sits serenely next to her as she pats him. We drive down the driveway and he doesn't run after the car. I am incredibly grateful for the home she is giving him; it couldn't be more perfect; but that doesn't stop my heart from breaking.

I thought I would see him through his old age.

∞ ∞ ∞

*Saying goodbye to pets, whether they are old ones that need to go to heaven or younger ones that need re-homing is tough. We decided not to go the SPCA route as we felt that it was imperative to meet the family who adopted our dogs, as well as see their new home. For that reason a personal advert was important so that we could elicit the correct response from an equally dog-loving family. We was able to re-home three of our four dogs. We were lucky that all the new owners resided in the area where we lived.*

*Our fourth dog was 13 years old. Gypsy, an adorable Staffy, had severe arthritis and was developing senile dementia. It was terribly hard for my husband, who took her to the vet and wept as Gypsy quietly went limp. I didn't even have the courage to go with him and just held her that morning feeling the lovely soft textured fur under her neck and front. We sat on the veranda and it was a poignant moment that I won't easily forget. I chatted softly to her and thanked her for being the most loyal pet we had ever had and for being our son's best friend for many years when he was growing up.*[18]

EH - New Zealand

∞

*I do miss my dogs. Rather than put them through seven months of quarantine, I found them a stunning new life on a farm – do miss them though.*

SDT - Australia

∞

*Our family pet dog – I knew I would never see him again.*

NVR - The Netherlands

∞

*Looking back over the last five months after arriving in the UK the biggest thing we had to deal with is the animals that we left behind and our*

---

[18] This piece was adapted, with permission, from an interview with Eve Hemming, written by Mellissa Douman, which was originally published in *The Witness* (a South African newspaper) on 13 November 2008. Eve Hemming also wrote *Out of Love* (Chapter 8).

families. We found home for all our animals except for one. Our oldest dog was 13 years old and she was too old to re-home and she had developed growths that the vet feared where cancerous but due to the dog's age she could not operate on her. It was the hardest thing I have had to do in my life. I had to decide to put her to sleep or to plead with some of my family to look after her until she passed on. I eventually had to put her to sleep as I thought it would be the best.

SOR - UK

∞

Sadly my dog had to be put down in South Africa a few weeks ago. I kept hoping we may be able to bring him here someday. It's not to be and my eyes are starting to resemble 'normal' eyes after all the crying about my dog. . . maybe not only about my dog, maybe about all I have left behind there and the people I miss. Now that we've got our green cards at last, I believe that reality is sinking in: we are never going back there!

HVG - USA

∞ ∞ ∞

# 29

∞

## On the Move

*Basically it took us about two months to dump everything
we wanted to and relocate.*
AK - South Africa

After my dad's death, I couldn't examine things too closely, wouldn't allow myself to form too many bonds with people and places any longer. There were too many ties to break, or to break me. And yet, my garden continued through the seasons, as though I'd already left. I watched the lemon trees as they bowed under the bushels of lemons I harvested for lemon syrup, lemon marmalade and for all the friends from Cape Town who craved the blessing of our regular supply.

Manie (my gardener) harvested the olives, I bottled them, wondering why I'd bother to do that when they wouldn't fill my pantry shelves any more – I gave them away because it was too difficult to see my reflection in the glassy rows stacked above my counter. The olywe (olives) always ripened around March and April and for a few weeks all our efforts were concentrated on harvesting our four trees – black calamata olives, my favourite. Manie would bring them in by the bucketful. Anna and I would duly sit and slash each one once with a razor blade, then pop them into buckets filled with salt water brine, to cure. The salt water had to be changed every day or the olives would not cure properly. The salt water drew out the bitterness and after a three week processing, they were ready for bottling. I would bottle them in olive oil added to some balsamic or red wine vinegar for flavour, a few garlic cloves and sprigs of dried herbs.

The garden was my mainstay and my joy – to trudge through it during the rainy wintertime when your boots would sink below ankle height, to explore it after winter and see the excited peeking of the new green shoots reaching through the earth. Sometimes it surprised me with an occasional new plant that had never shown itself before. I was sure that the sprite in charge of our garden took great delight in tantalizing me with each new season.

The Ficus tree would talk with me as I wandered through, happily lost in my thoughts in my secret garden, or while watering its roots, it would pause, breathe and laugh at my tickling of its 'feet', yet towering protectively over me, its enormous rubbery leaves serving as a protection from heat and rain at all times of the year.

We ate, and we ate. The figs came into season, and I candied them, pairing with local cheeses to end the gaiety of meals with friends and family on our back verandah. The mountain hovered protectively over the bounteous back garden – bags and bags and bags of soft shelled almonds – I shelled them until my fingers blistered. I made almond pesto, we ate and ate, and we gave them away. I couldn't stop myself channelling the bounty of the seasons into our beings; I couldn't stop harvesting and squirrelling away the blessings from the garden – granadillas eaten directly from the vine, their contents heated by the sun, strawberries, pomegranates, red figs, green figs, plums, apricots, apples, lemons, prickly pears and some quinces – wonderful sliced and bottled in vanilla syrup.

> I find it laughable when people refer to those leaving as cowards. They cannot imagine how much courage it actually takes to leave your family, friends and established life behind.
> MF - South Africa

The amazing array of vegetables – tomatoes (jars of apple and tomato chutney secure in their own tart sweetness, no sugar needed), aubergines grilled and bottled with garlic and herbs in olive oil, spring peas, spinach, carrots – no poisons – my son pulled and ate direct from the garden. I braided the onions together and hung them outside underneath the verandah roof, pulling off one whenever I needed it. Sometimes, the mountain glowered over me while I stood alone, absorbed, outdoors.

The tables groaned, I wept, and threw my being into doing as much as I could, relishing the sounds of laughter emanating from the verandah as everyone enjoyed the fruits of my labour. I cried quietly, internally, in the kitchen, knowing that nothing would ever be the same as this magical time and space in my life.

The house went on the market during the winter of 2001. It sold at the end of September. The new owners told us that they were going to tear down the almond trees, sub-divide the property and build another house. I survived the moving process by detaching myself emotionally from the property. Cold bloodedly, I removed everything from the garden that had been planted or cultivated by me. No-one was going to bulldoze the plants I had cared for and loved over the years. Friends brought their bakkie and we filled it with plants. I dug up the love and the energy I had expended into that peaty earth and I cauterized my wounds by sharing with friends.

James gave away his woodworking equipment to Camphill Village in Kalbaskraal and to a school in Atlantis. Many of the tools and jigs were older than him. He had begun woodworking with his father as soon as he was old enough to be deemed responsible. These donations were the end of an era for us. The end of a family tradition. We knew that this was the best home for the equipment. It would be cared for and used in a manner that would enrich the lives of others. James made his peace with the decision. Since that day, he has never picked up another woodworking tool.

My father died in October, a month after the house was sold. By that time I was numbed to much of what was taking place in my life. From afar I watched myself going through the motions of my daily life, mourning equally the loss of my sanctuary and of my father (who had always been a dynamic force). I breathed. I walked. I ate. I packed. I wept and slept my way through a month and awoke to find us living in a rented house on the mountainside in Riebeek West.

> *Leaving South Africa is NOT the answer because it leaves an unfillable void in your heart and soul.*
> AMS - USA

Another old house but not a home filled with energy and love. It was just us, some oddments of furniture; beds; bedding; toys and rugs. Lost souls echoing hollowly in the rooms of a house that wasn't our home. As friends and family visited, I asked them if they wanted any of our possessions. If they did, we gave them away – wedding gifts; family heirlooms; lamps; chairs; ornaments; kitchenware, and everything else.

Travelling light became our mantra. I joked with everyone that if I was told to leave the country within two hours, I could fit all I needed into a backpack. I honed my life to a fine edge and although the pain of loss was a needle piercing my being, it could never reach the core that I'd bound so tightly. I had a very high pain threshold during those days. As I watched my life being slowly decimated, layers peeled away one by one, I wondered if I would ever replace them. When the layers of skin are gone, do they ever grow back? Or does the scar, the gaping hole in the body, remind you of the pain forever?

What would I have put into that backpack? My rings, my purse, my documents, a change of clothes and some walking shoes – perhaps I'd wear a warm jacket, a couple of small toys and snacks for the children. Life can be so simple if we allow it.

After a month in Riebeek West, we found out via an 'unauthorized' source that the bank had foreclosed on our landlord and the rented house. We had one more month before moving on. This time it was easier, our possessions were less, our attachment was non-existent and we had no further options. In mid-January 2002, we moved into my mother's apartment in the Southern Suburbs of Cape Town. This was a second move in as many months. Our lives were now condensed into two rooms and half of the space in a garage.

The tensions of that time were nearly unbearable. My mother was alternating between mourning and silent anger; James and I were constantly bickering because the visa process was unresolved and slow; and the children developed a malingering respiratory flu. Our lives in Africa were winding down and we were more wound up than ever before. Any mixed feelings we had about our actions and our decision had to be suppressed. We had made it irrevocable.

> What advice do you wish you had known before you left South Africa? That is was going to be the hardest thing I had ever undertaken in my life.
> DS - USA

On the 27$^{th}$ February 2002 we watched James board a plane for the USA. I was relieved to see him go because this meant that finally our process was underway. The journey had truly begun. I couldn't sleep that night because I kept wondering if he had just entered into a void and, if so, how would I ever find him. I had no idea where he was to stay. I had one telephone number and, if he didn't call me, I had no other way of reaching him. I was caught in a nightmare and I couldn't relax until the phone rang 30 hours later. At 3:30 a.m. on the 1$^{st}$ of March, I heard his voice say that he was safely on the other side of the world.

That same day saw the arrival of Biddulph's Shipping. They packed one room and the half space in the garage into 19 boxes. I signed the packing slip and tried to assign a value to the innocuous contents which were useless and meaningless to anyone else.

The next day we moved out of the apartment and into a house with my sister-in-law, and nephew, in Durbanville. Jenny's husband was away from home so it was 'women and children first' most of the time. The days were strangely surreal. Jenny was a teacher; her son was at school; my children were at pre-school and I was rattling around like a loose bolt. Many mornings found me in Claremont, biding time, at an internet cafe sending and receiving emails from James. I drank tea, ate lunch, and spent time with friends. The days blurred interminably. I didn't know what to do with myself. The children and I shared the guest room in Jenny's house. I slept in the double bed, one child slept with me and one slept on the floor. They alternated nightly. Our lives had narrowed again. This time we, and our clothing, were contained in one room.

We had our visas; we had our papers; our possessions had been shipped and there was nothing left for us in South Africa. At the end of April, while packing our suitcases (again), I found myself wanting to cry over the myriad of miscellaneous items that were important to me. Would Customs understand if they opened our bags? What would they say about my small, brown, glass, homeopathic bottles and tubes labelled with strangely exotic Latin names? Was I likely to be arrested for drug smuggling? Of what use were my father's business cards, his empty Parker pen, and his broken watch? Why was I carrying torn magazine pages with articles about exercise? My sister-in-law had laminated them for me. I

> I left South Africa almost 11 years ago, arrived in Canada...two adults, a son of 16 and a son of 12, two suitcases, very little money and nothing else to our name.
> 
> GS - Canada

packed my make-up collection and found a multitude of eye and lip pencils, sharpened down to a barely useable length, in colours that I wanted to keep – but were they worth packing? Jenny gave me a miniature Tupperware container for storing the pencils.

My cellphone – useless. My hairdryer – useless. CD's and cassettes, secured between children's softcover books, slid between the layers of clothes. A box of Rooibos teabags was flattened and forced down the side of the case. Baby bottles; a collection of pebbles from the beach; an address book filled with names; precious photos taken at tearful goodbyes; costume jewellery; stones from Scratch Patch; artwork from pre-school; good wishes and farewell cards; and my lace underwear scrunched and pressed between everything.

Gloves, hats, towels, facecloths and blankets were small items I'd kept in order to create some familiarity, some continuity, for the children. There was not enough space so I released my attachment again and donated whatever I could in order to retain the most precious mementos. Gloves, hats, towels and facecloths are replaceable items but photos, pebbles, cards, seashells and artworks are not.

We were on the move again for what I hoped was the last time.

∞ ∞ ∞

*I must admit that at the time there was little heartbreak at leaving – the whole experience was such an adventure and I was caught up in that. It took me years to start missing anything about home (other than family of course).*

RW - UK

∞

*I had a few friends tell us that we are chickens and running away from problems, well I finally got to realize that they are truly not my friends and they are people who just do not have enough points to move away from all the problems. I know for a fact that if they got half the chance to leave they would.*

NH - Australia

∞

*We were fortunate to have only a few minor break-ins but some of our neighbours were not so lucky. Our house in the beautiful suburb of Northcliff was situated on a corner stand, so we were surrounded by five other massive houses. The one house was burgled ten times in a period of just twelve months, despite there being CCTV cameras and laser beams. The other neighbour was hijacked in her driveway after collecting her kids from school one afternoon, and yet another neighbour was burgled by ten armed men carrying AK47s who broke into her house at 2 p.m., in broad daylight. I guess it was the next story that made me begin to panic. A young teenage boy, a couple of blocks away from us, was shot dead in his lounge while watching TV one afternoon, and all that was taken was his cellphone.*

*At that time, my daughter was going to university and had just* obtained her drivers license. Every day when she returned home from college, I would be waiting for her in the driveway, petrified that she would be attacked or hijacked while the electric gate was opening or closing. We forbade her to go out at night, so she lost out on best years of her life, those of the university social life.

Soon we sold our house and moved into a secure golf estate. It was beautiful – no walls, fences, burglar bars; kids riding bikes in the streets; couples walking their dogs late at night. It was how life is supposed to be. We've been here for just over a year, and while there have been some armed robberies within the estate, there has been no injuries or loss of life. We called this place our Resort... our Last Resort!

But organized crime has developed so that gated communities and secure estates are now being targeted. Just yesterday, the front headlines were of a family, also living on a golf estate, who was woken in the middle of the night by burglars. They tied up the husband and two small children, and then proceeded to rape the woman in front of her six year old son. They took nothing from the upstairs bedrooms. They could have taken all they wanted from downstairs and left without waking up the family, but no, they had to go wake them up and terrorize them. This is what the crime has developed into. There are awful rumours of the whites being targeted, and this is evident in the amount of violent crime and deaths that is happening all over the country, not just in Johannesburg, and for petty thefts such as cellphones.

So yes, we are now forced to emigrate. I tell people that I'm not going where the grass is greener, because I truly believe there is no country more beautiful than South Africa. But I'm going where I can feel safe and where my grandchildren can be born. I'm also going so that once I'm there, I can hopefully help to bring other family members across – those who cannot emigrate on their own.

LK - South Africa

∞

Are we going to live much worse off financially than we are now? For example, I live in a beautiful home, but I know for the same price I will get a very mediocre, middle class house overseas. Will our new business in another country succeed? Will we be able to start over at our age (my husband turns 50 soon) and have the energy to get through the first five years of a new business and are we going to be able to retire one day or will all our money be swallowed up in the emigration process? Is my family going to be able to remain here safely until they are able to join us? Will they join us or will I spend the rest of my life seeing them only every few years, instead of every week? Are our three beloved golden retrievers going to handle the quarantine and flight? Is the government going to put restrictions on any of the whites leaving (as they did in Zimbabwe)? There are so many fears one has....like they say 'emigrating is not for sissies'.

LK - South Africa

∞

The uncertainty involved. Was very difficult for my wife. I remember her crying on the plane as we left Jan Smuts (as it was then named).

HH - Uganda

∞

I've heard the first two years are like mourning for a lost loved one and I've also heard after a death it's the most stressful thing to go through, but at the end of the day I'm willing to go through that if it means a better and safer life.

KK - South Africa

∞

I will take the pain now, so that my children can grow up in a place where they are safe and free.

CJ - South Africa

∞

I am in the process of leaving South Africa now. There is no one single event that decided this for me, rather a culmination of years of exposure to stories of violent crimes, house-breakings, rapes, murders, abuse of children, hijackings, theft, police corruption and brutality, government corruption, service deterioration, government incompetence down to being unable to get ID books (essential for daily life) for years!

We sold our property (a 10 hectare plot we were hoping to build on) after the theft of our building materials, a full wooden house including bathroom from the property lifted onto the back of a truck, and even the security fence and gates!

My fears are that my sister and parents will still be here; will we be able to find work in our new country; how much of a 'knock' our lifestyle will take; I worry that we will be able to fit into the new culture; that we will not have any friends; that simply finding a babysitter to look after the children when we want to go out for an evening will be problematic; that I will have to start my career at the bottom of the ladder again.

None of this will stop me from leaving – I will take on all the 'dragons' of migration if it means I can guarantee that my children will not experience living in fear, being attacked, or god-forbid, rape and murder.

Many friends have already left the country, and several family members are in the emigration process. I can only find two high-school classmates who are still here other than myself. Five of my previous classmates are confirmed dead due to violent crimes. Others have left for the same reasons as me – fear for my family, myself and our beautiful, sad country's future.

CH - South Africa

∞

I have just read your article 'Torn in the New SA' and could not agree with it more. We have decided to leave to country – not a decision that is easily made. My parents immigrated to South Africa when I was a baby and I have lived here, loving the country for over 30 years but now the time has come to decide with my head and not my heart.

GR - South Africa

∞

The million dollar (Rand) question is: Am I a coward because I left South Africa? Certainly NOT. I am just a sensible human being, who is not willing to live with his family in a country which has developed a culture of violent crime, I am not willing to be a 'statistic', and I certainly don't want my wife or children to be statistics of crime, either.

I must admit that whilst in South Africa I was lucky/privileged, in that my family and I had the chance to move to another country without need for green cards, etc. I also admit that having the right (at the time) coloured skin, enabled me to get a better education, to own a decent house, and generally to enjoy a better standard of living than the majority of the population.

*However, that in itself did not make me feel ashamed that I left South Africa. This is not about a duty to fight for my country, I am not deserting an obligation of any sort. It is, in a nutshell a decision, which I believe I took sensibly, 15 years ago, to move to a 'safer and quieter neighbourhood'.*

MC - Cyprus

∞

*We have never seriously considered (leaving), despite quite a bit of pressure from friends and family already living overseas – we always say that we will be the last ones left to turn the lights off and close the door as the country shuts down. Nowadays of course we have to amend that and just say shut the door, seeing as the lights will already be off.*

PH - South Africa

∞

*I came here with my husband in 1962. We arrived, from Denmark, with a young baby of eight months and were welcomed by the Nationalist Government of the day who were trying to recruit young white couples. We both loved Africa and it was an adventure for us. I am now 68. I still have a Danish passport but none of my five children were able to obtain Danish citizenship as Denmark was very strict at the time, especially with regards to the Apartheid government of the time, so they all have South African citizenship.*

*I fully agree with your article. Two of my five children emigrated to Australia and now have Australian citizenship. It was heart rending when they left as we had always been a very close family – especially the three sisters. We who are left here love this country but we are feeling very negative with all that is happening and wonder what the future holds for us.*

*To emigrate is a very difficult decision to make. I am now 68 and a widow of three years, with a pension. My three children here are all divorced and do not have the degrees needed to emigrate to Australia. They do not speak Danish and do not have Danish nationality, so cannot live in Denmark, which is where their father came from.*

*They love this country but on the other hand have to think of the future of their children. I think your article was so true and many people here think the same, but for some there is no decision to make as it is economically impossible for them to pack up and leave, for others it is a question of family* ties which they are reluctant to break. You are lucky that you were able to make the decision to leave when you did, and though it must have been extremely difficult at the time, for the sake of your family's future, you made the right one.

    I lived in Africa all my life as my parents were pioneers as early as 1934, so have Africa in my blood. It is a sad state of affairs but think that those young enough to make the move must do it. The old Africa is gone but I still have some wonderful memories.

LI - South Africa

∞

    I have been feeling I should go for pre-immigration counselling but I think an internet chat room for expat South Africans would be more beneficial!

JW - South Africa

∞ ∞ ∞

# Part 5

∞

# Learning

*One of the saddest questions my daughter asked me once was
"How do I know it is any better anywhere else?"*

MH - UK

# 30

∞

# Paper or Plastic?

Introduction by James McIntosh

**M**y first time alone (meaning without adult American supervision) at a Wal-Mart store here in the US of A, well, how can I ever forget that? The cashier asked, "Paper or plastic?" Proudly, I held up my American credit card. She looked unimpressed and repeated, "Paper or plastic?" That's when the packer, obviously an alien from south of the border who understood me at a glance, smiled and held up a paper bag in one hand and a plastic bag in the other. (I have since learned to say "Porcelain, not paper" in a coffee shop, else I would be handed a paper cup. For Pete's sake! I am not a kiddie at a birthday party!)

I left Wal-Mart still smarting and packed the plastic, not paper (because South Africa has few trees), bags in the boot, (not trunk, because where I come from elephants have trunks). And then I opened the car door to find that someone had stolen the steering wheel. Why was I not surprised! When I realized that the steering wheel was still there on the other side of the car, the left hand side, I felt so embarrassed that I acted as if I had planned to open the 'wrong' door all along. Just in case someone was watching me.

In those early days I found myself 'acting cool' quite often, because in my fear and uncertainty I imagined that all the little incidents of not getting it, of not fitting in, would add up to disqualify me from earning the fabled green card.

There were many moments when the curtain between my two worlds, the back-then and the now-here, would part and I would feel quite dizzy with a 'where the hell am I?' confusion. Why are there so many types of bread? Why can't I make sense of this money? Why can't I understand this cashier's English? (Is she actually speaking English?) Why did I look right first instead of left before crossing the road? Why did that driver stop without hooting and cursing at me when I stepped off the pavement (sidewalk!) looking the wrong way? (Come to think of it, why did he slow down and not accelerate? What sort of place is this?)

This was a painfully funny period. Painful because all the jokes were on me; funny peculiar, not always 'ha, ha'.

One thing I learned early on is that we should not judge a country by the movies and television programs that it exports. What we see on the outside looking in is not necessarily what we will find once we pass through the arrivals gate. I found a much more conservative America. For example, imagine my surprise when I realized how love scenes and explicit language were removed from the American versions of familiar programs. Except for the on-screen violence. That's when I realized that there were violent scenes that I never saw in South Africa. Here, cinematic violence is not only tolerated. It seems to be celebrated.

But then, one day, it dawned on me. If I must put up with violence, what would I choose, on-screen or on-street?

∞ ∞ ∞

# 31

∞

# The Ring Of Safety

*I went on a wing and a prayer: faith in myself and the future.*
KW - USA

2 May 2002. I am wearing black trousers, a black top and 7" black platform sandals. One of my useless virtues is that I clearly remember what I wore for momentous occasions in my life, even if they occurred 20 years ago. At this one, I think I look suitably elegant. Atlanta International Airport is overwhelming because the sheer size and layout of the buildings necessitates taking a train from one terminal to another. After a 17 hour flight with two toddlers, all of us bleary-eyed, the train was a treat – something out of the ordinary – which spiced up our early morning exhaustion. Each child was wearing a kiddie size backpack with cartoon scrawl to differentiate them and I of course had a black carry-on bag. I felt nauseated from such extraordinary tiredness. I wasn't even sure we were on the correct train. Never mind. At least we were back on solid land. Each of us was sustained by the thought that soon we would see James again.

After picking up our luggage, we had six suitcases to manoeuvre through Customs. There we were, a 3-year old, a 5-year-old and a mother with six suitcases. I realized that I hadn't thought of how I would manage to clear six cases through Customs when I would be the only adult. This was another confirmation of my general lack of sensibility. Two weary children, with backpacks, each pulling two smaller wheeled suitcases and I, teetering precariously on those shoes, was pulling two larger versions, with my carry on bag tucked under one arm.

A well-mannered Customs dog, deciding that we were obviously the choicest passengers in a lack-lustre bunch, materialized beside me, and showed a distinct interest in my carry-on bag. It was shortly followed by two female Homeland Security Officials. I explained that, yes, we had taken biltong onto the 'plane but, since we knew we could not bring it into the USA, had left it onboard. Their obvious sympathy for me, after a 17-hour international flight with young children, overrode thoughts that I could harbour terrorist inclinations – after all, it was obvious I hadn't a smattering of common sense, (Platform sandals! Toddlers! Six Suitcases!) and I was inadvertently drawing an enormous amount of attention. Still, there were those shoes...! Nevertheless, they escorted me ahead of, and around, a queue of people waiting to disrobe and remove shoes prior to being x-rayed.

A long, tedious and impatient queue later, we cleared immigration and were free to meet James almost two hours after our flight had landed. His second-hand car, a Dodge Intrepid, was a source of wonder and pride. Oh yes. We said, of course, 'we are Intrepid adventurers'. This is a new land and a new life. How appropriate. We hadn't seen cup holders before and there were two new car seats for the children. They found so many exciting experiences compacted into a very short space of time, not least of all seeing Dada again.

James had made arrangements for us to shower at his hotel, prior to our long drive back to Virginia. I don't remember much. James was the only thing in sharp focus. After removing my rings and my clothes, I saturated myself in a hot shower and washed away the residue of a long, tiring journey that had begun 18 months before. The sense of relief lightened my spirits and my only thought was 'now we can begin the next phase. Thank God. Here begins the real Grand Adventure.'

> While moving continents and hemispheres is hugely traumatic, at the same time it is also an adventure and a looking forward with expectation to what lies ahead.
> 
> SK - Ireland

We were an hour outside Atlanta (making good time, according to James) when I looked down at my hands and realized that my rings were lying on a bedside table at the hotel. Those two rings were my most precious material possessions. Although I am not sentimental and cultivate an attitude of non-attachment, the emotions and sentiments attached to the rings over many years had made them priceless. I was in a new country, I'd left everything behind in my homeland, only kept my essentials, my nearest and dearest, and my first experience is to lose one of those precious items. For a few seconds, I mused whether to let it go, not worry about it and not mention it to James.

We were in a new land, living a new life, and perhaps losing them was just a symbolic break with my old life and experiences. But I couldn't do that, without at least trying to retrieve them. Mentally, I reconciled myself to their loss and my being OK with that. I had divested myself of so many material possessions in recent months, that this would simply be the zenith to my lack of attachment. Yes, I love my rings. Yes, I want them back. But we are here, we are all finally here, safely, with loads of life and opportunity ahead. They are just rings, there will be others. When it is time to go, it is time.

We stopped the car because we had no cellphone in the early days, and called the hotel to report the loss. They said, yes, indeed, the room service assistant had found them on the table and handed them in at the front desk. They could not mail them to us in Virginia, we would have to collect them personally.

Usually, if I did something inane, James would complain about it. He was obviously delighted and relieved to have me back and didn't breathe a word about my transgression. For a short while, during the return drive, I wondered if there were any other inanities for which I could find absolution, in those early powerful days.

> *It has been an utter relief to adopt the new culture. There are many differences, but it's easy when you know that your family is safe and secure.*
> AW - Australia

The process of the rings being easily returned to me was symbolic of my expectations of this new country. My possessions were safe, we were safe, I was safe.

∞ ∞ ∞

*I had no fears about leaving – I went on a wing and a prayer: faith in myself and the future – somehow it was going to work out and it did. I did hope for more support from my family in New Jersey, but they were immersed in their own lives and had no idea what an emigration meant – could not help. It's both much harder than one imagines, and in a strange way also easier once one is fully committed to it.*  KW - USA

∞

*I don't think you can compare the two at all. Everything works here in the US. You can leave dry cleaning on your front door for pick up and it doesn't get stolen. Mail gets delivered.*  SS - USA

∞

*Being bombarded by so many different world views was extremely challenging. I am living in a very multi cultural community. These new ideas challenged mine to the extreme. Being surrounded by so much 'otherness' was uncomfortable and I yearned for home and those who thought the way I did.*  JW - Japan

∞

*Most surprising thing about relocating? Few sirens; no action-man stunts required; able to travel on business and know the wife could leave the windows open and the door unlocked and be safe.*  BM - UAE

∞

*Emigrating has been incredibly hard, in fact far harder than my first divorce which was a very acrimonious bloody affair. I think for the first time in my life I experienced pure depression and had to face my own demons.*  JW - Australia

∞

*We have made lovely friends and appreciate the lack of obvious crime and mayhem, and the way our children can walk down our street without us*

*being paranoid. The differences in lifestyle are that I no longer have help in the home, and although it is a huge adjustment, it is one that I have had to adjust to, understanding at a deep level that it's actually a small price to pay for peace of mind. We have never even put our alarm system on!*

DM - Australia

∞

*Most surprising thing about relocating? Feeling physically safe and being able to walk around late at night alone as a woman.*

IM - Australia

∞ ∞ ∞

# 32

∞

## Learning A New Land

*At my first job I kept waiting for someone to haul me out of my seat and accuse me of being an imposter.*
AP - UK

**I** remember a long drive from Atlanta to Richmond. Two days broken up by a night at a motel. The impressions from the drive along I-95 are miles and miles of billboards – mostly advertising fireworks, motels, cheap tickets to Disney World, cheap cigarettes, tattoos, and restaurants. The billboards changed as we crossed state lines – Georgia, South Carolina, North Carolina and finally Virginia. Of course there were also billboards drawing attention to the usual asinine statements of local and state politicians.

I remember admiring the huge American bakkies and SUV's as they passed us by, some of them driving at the speed of light. Or so it seemed. I had never seen such large cars and, looking at their tires out of my passenger window, I felt dwarfed in our sedan. The constant presence of police cars along the road. State troopers appeared to be casually parked in the median strip of trees which formed a central barrier between the opposite strips of highway. A strange introduction to the United States.

Finally, we arrived in Richmond which was a usual city, highways, buildings, urban sprawl and lots of mini-malls or 'strip plazas' as they as known. (I understand the name but it also conjures an interesting mental picture...) James said, "Just remember Broad Street. If you are ever lost, find Broad Street because it runs through the city from one end to the other, and you'll always be able to find your way back on Broad."

Arriving at the apartment on a Friday afternoon, it felt strange to be carrying suitcases filled with my South African life, past people who were obviously going through the daily motions of their American existence. We were conspicuous exceptions. I don't think anyone really noticed but I felt as if we wore a huge sign that said, "I am new. I am lost. Please be gentle."

> *What really hit me most of all was the word alien you used because that is what I was known as. When applying for a National Insurance Number my nationality was put down as alien.*
> DW - Ireland

The apartment looked brand new with white walls and thick, lush, cream, carpeting. Filled with rented furniture, it was stylish but empty, devoid of the life that fills places when people have been in them for a while. We must be on vacation. Are we really going to live here?

The first six months felt like an eternal holiday. The enormous apartment complex had a lake, a clubhouse and a swimming pool. It was summertime, the apartment pool was open so, lacking anything else to do, we spent our empty afternoons there. I lay on a recliner and read my library books, or taught the children to swim. James arrived at 5:00 p.m. and we would stay there until 7:00 p.m. Then we would meander home and decide what to make for supper. There was none of the busy-ness I had associated with my previous life in South Africa, everything was dictated by human schedule and need – sleep, wake, make breakfast, eat breakfast, clean up after breakfast, read a book, decide what to make for lunch, make lunch, clean up after lunch, go to pool, come home, make supper, eat supper, clean up after supper, read book, go to bed. Living in this void meant that the days slid by and unless James took me to the library or the bank or the grocery store, there was no differentiation in any of them. The sound of the Southern accent jangled my auditory senses. I went to bed at night with a dull twangy ringing in my ears. A sound I'd experienced similarly when trying to sleep after attending a noisy party or disco.

In the early stages we clung to each other at night like two frightened rats on a sinking ship. We didn't fight at all. We were stoic and just held fast. At night, once the children were asleep, we sat with our mugs of Rooibos tea, and looked at each other, speechless. Is this it? Is this all there is? Have we made a mistake? Can we go back? The answer was "No". We had given up everything to be here and we had nothing to go back to. We were caught between two lives and we belonged to neither. Our choices had defined our path; there was no alternative. We had to appreciate the strengths and weaknesses of each other. We could not afford to lose our focus so we rode a constant wave of emotions – one day James was up and the next it was me, and ultimately we stabilized ourselves. We learned to respect one other because we had to share a tough time.

After the children began school in September James and I had six hours free on weekdays. I spent two or three hours at the ladies gym (yes, interesting experience to find that there are gyms that are *only* for ladies) while James stayed home to work. It was very vacant, very worrying, but also very free. While the children were at school, I found myself clattering around in the apartment, with odd appliances I didn't know how to use and a measuring system I couldn't understand. I had always loved to cook and used my recipe books for inspiration. I relied on my books because I have always been chronically unable to remember recipe amounts needed. My culinary creativity beckoned so, having bought the necessary ingredients, I opened the books ... to find that the ingredients were measured in quarts, pints, gallons, ounces and pounds. These were mythical terms that I had not ever used or understood. My books were written for a Metric System and I had no idea how to convert grams, kilograms, millilitres and litres into the Imperial Measuring System.[19]

I managed to solve the problem, partly, the children had brought their baby bottles because they were comforted by drinking Rooibos tea with honey from the bottles. Ah ha! The bottles had measurements for ounces and millilitres so I used them as my measuring jugs. Figuring out that 250ml = 8oz = 1 cup helped. I played around with the measurements, as I made rusks, and made a leap that if 8oz = 1 cup then 16oz = 2 cups = 1lb. I had discovered the 16oz = 1lb link when I picked up a package of cherry tomatoes that showed both the Imperial and the Decimal weight of the contents. Jumping a few more obscure mental leaps, I decided that 250ml must equal 250g which meant that 250ml = 8oz = 250g hence 500ml = 16oz = 1lb = ½ kg. Not quite right but close enough, I wouldn't level off the measure and figured the extra would even it out. Math was never one of my

---

[19] Why is Bronwyn going on about measurement systems? Well, in the year 2010 only three countries (Burma/Myanmar, Liberia and the United States) have yet to adopt the metric system. It seems that progress can indeed be slow.

strengths. I did not have access to a computer and hence the freedom to look up measurement comparison charts online. My mother sent recipes from 'Your Family' and 'You' magazines and photocopied Metric/Imperial comparison charts and mailed them to me.

The oddest thing (was he an appliance?) of all was called an 'In-Sink-Erator". That's what the label said. Basically it meant that you stuffed fruit and vegetable peels down the sink, pressed a button and voila – a grinding, churning, scary noise as the creature that lived in the sink would eat everything and then try to get out. I was sure that someone, somewhere, outside had access to all the smushed peelings and was making, and selling, unbelievable compost. I asked people about it and they smiled at my childlike interest. I considered starting a business myself. It seemed such a waste to stuff it all down the sink. I remembered, in South Africa, Manie visiting the kitchen in the late afternoon to fetch the bucket filled with our household compost in order to dig it into the soil in the vegetable garden.

Occasionally a teaspoon would accidentally fall down into this 'Thing' and you could hear the grind of metal against metal while feeding the creature. This would necessitate switching it off and then putting your hand down into the plughole to get it out. James's hands are bigger than mine so it would always be me retrieving the cutlery. It was my scariest moment, putting my hand into the hole, feeling around for the utensil and hoping that the creature didn't have a life of its own. Visions of my fingers and my hand being mauled into mush, and leaving only a stump behind, danced in my head.

> What advice do you wish you had known before you left South Africa? Nothing. Like life, it was a journey of discovery and its very difficult to discover something you already know.
> 
> BM - UAE

There were amusing events, not the least of which was having a dishwasher (in South Africa we called her Anna – we all adored her) which scared me in the beginning. I was sure I would cause it to overflow, or melt something during the heated drying cycle, if I didn't pack it perfectly and properly. Oh, and a tumble dryer. I confess that I don't do laundry – I have no idea how a washing machine or a tumble dryer work. I couldn't use one if you paid me. No more clothes dried in the sunshine on an outdoor line. Clothes smell different when they've been dried by a machine. They smell more synthetic. There isn't the crispness and the warmth and freshness of sheets imbued with African sunshine. James, the laundry man, would ask me to buy 'dryer sheets'. What on earth is a dryer sheet?

I wasted many hours in grocery stores, clutching a list tightly, wandering up and down aisles looking for items and not really being sure what I was looking for. As I am also an inveterate reader of labels, shopping for 10 items can take me an hour. I'm in a new country, I don't know what their bread contains – it all tastes too sweet – and I don't like sugar in my peanut butter or too much added to my jams – I'm buying fruit jam not sugar jam. I make my own preserves so I am fussy about those made by others. An American friend calls me a 'food snob'. I'm also chronically unable to ask for help or directions. I would rather wander aimlessly using my powers of deduction, or a process of elimination, to find what I need. I used up a lot of time in Winn-Dixie during those first years.

> *I missed the silly things, the Pronutro, the fishpaste and Table Mountain and hearing the Xhosa and Afrikaans and English spoken like only South Africans can.*
>
> LW - South Africa

I read the newspapers, checked the grocery sales (how would I know if they were really good prices?). And I did the mental math calculations, converting dollars to rands – horrified at the cost of food. I knew 2.2lbs = 1 kg so I would do the acrobatics of taking the American prices of $5/1lb and multiply $5 x 2.2 to get the price for 1kg and then convert it to Rands with the currency exchange rate (around $1 : R11 in those days). Can you tell I was bored?

The first time I tried tipping an elderly gentleman who brought my groceries to car, he was horrified and literally recoiled at the money. I pressed him to take it and he told me that if he did so, he could lose his job. I was embarrassed and so was he. I found this bizarre and to this day, always take my own groceries to the car or, to the horror of shop assistants, take the grocery bags – up to 6 of them – out of the trolley and carry them myself.

I did not yet have my American driver's license and was not sure how long an American policeman would accept my International Driver's License so, in trying to find something to do each day without needing to drive, I would aimlessly waste more time walking down to the lake and watching the ducks, swans and geese cluster, seeking food. A toddler again, cast adrift in an unknown adult world, I was not sure of anything any more. I couldn't suggest we visit places because I had no bearings, I had no idea of distance or where we were in relation to anything else. We only had one car and most of the time I could use it. I had plenty of free time but I didn't know anyone and had nowhere to go. I was bored but I didn't know what to do.

I found myself in a foreign land which, although people spoke

English, was about as foreign as anywhere could be. No friends, no family, no idea of where to find groceries, doctors, dentists, hospitals, no idea how anything worked. I didn't know about 911. I didn't know it was a free service and I should call them in an emergency. When my son had a croup attack late one night, I rushed him to the emergency room myself.

Every time I opened my mouth the novelty of my origin drew unwanted attention. I became tired of correcting people, "No, not the UK, South Africa." "Yes, South Africa, you know at the very base of Africa, next-door to Zimbabwe." Most people seemed to know about Zimbabwe. "Why did we come here?" "What are we doing here?" "Are we staying here?" "Why Richmond? What do we like about Richmond?" Or "Yes, I know Africa, I once visited a game 'preserve' in Kenya." Or "We had an exchange student from Africa in our school last year and she was telling us about the huts they live in, and they walk to school barefoot and have no roads." Yes, yes, yes, this is all Africa but it is not <u>all</u> Africa and no, I've seen that but I didn't live it that way.

And no (to those who thought I was simply a racist), I didn't leave to escape anyone of any other colour. After a while I wasn't sure why I left any more – the answers and the stories seemed to meld into a haze of words. I was tired of answering the same vacuous questions over and over again. I tried not to be rude when everyone asked the same things. I thought perhaps I should capture the basics in a double sided laminate sheet and, when the questions inevitably began, I could hand over the sheet for them to read. I knew that no matter how I said it, or described it, they would not ever understand, or feel it.

> I thought I was racially prejudiced, but in fact found out that I was socially prejudiced! There were values that I upheld and if I discriminated between people it was more because of their lack of refinement or courtesy than because of language or colour.
> 
> JH - Australia

After a year or two, I caught myself always highlighting the negatives about Richmond. "What do you like about Richmond?" they asked, and I heard my refrain about not liking the weather, not liking the scenery, the houses, the roads and such. Making a conscious effort to answer in a positive manner brought my awareness back to the 'why' we were here. I taught myself to talk about all the things that made life in Richmond a positive experience. Through my conversation about 'positives', I found that many Americans were unaware of how bountiful their lives were. I found that South Africans were more Euro-centric than Ameri-centric and, on more than one occasion, wondered if I should have tried harder to find a European country for our relocation.

Thousands of tall trees filled the suburban areas, everything was green, everywhere I went. Unless I was at a mall or strip plaza, all I could see were trees. There was no variation to this, no scenery or colours to fill my psyche, no garden – just rows of white two-storey apartment buildings, or monotone strip malls, which were so dull after the intense colours of Africa.

I found the lack of vagrants disturbing, and I found the lack of pedestrians disturbing. There are no pavements (sidewalks as they are known here) in many of the suburbs, so people – those who like to take an evening walk – have to walk on the road (just to confuse you, known as a pavement here).

I had days where the tenuousness of our situation, and the enormous gamble we had taken, threatened to overwhelm me and then I went to the library. The library was my one consolation – I knew this place or something like it, I understood it, I knew how these things worked, and I devoured their books – I was almost disbelieving of the enormity of their supply. They had books that were only published three months prior, recent DVD's, children's books on tape or CD, magazines, daily newspapers, reading tables overlooking a lake, free children's activities and adult learning courses. This was a place of peace.

Imagine my wonderment, the giddy breathless discovery that here I could take out up to 50 items at a time. FIFTY ITEMS. In South Africa, I was allowed to check out three items at one time. I never questioned this rule. For months, I only took three at each visit. One day, a librarian was checking out my books and I realized I had inadvertently taken four, I apologized and offered to put one back. She then enlightened me about the rules. When the going gets tough, the tough go to the library.[20]

---

[20] I must confess that I now also have a library card for the county next to ours, so technically I can take out 100 items altogether. I haven't yet allowed myself to gorge to that extent, though I have been known to take out 50 items at one time. I would arrive at the library with 3 canvas bags bulging with books and dvds. I met few people who appreciated my comments about their remarkable libraries. I found that many of them didn't have a membership card and never went to a library. Our local library has 120 computers – including the children's area – and these can be accessed for 2 hours by any member. They are all connected to the internet. A library card means that you could self-educate yourself because of the magnitude of the knowledge available as well as the capacity to use the internet for further research.

People have since said to me, "Gosh! You're so brave. I don't think I could do that." My reply is simple – a realization I've had over the years. Bravery and stupidity are closely related, sometimes different sides of the same coin. I admired my bravery and I admired my response, especially when they admitted they had too much 'stuff' accumulated over the years from family, friends, and from life. They could not transport this with them and hence they could not leave. The 'stuff' had trapped them, sometimes in a life they didn't like or want. Again, I was thankful for my process of divesting myself of attachments, of things that, in the scheme of things, are irrelevant. I asked myself over and over again what I would really, really want to keep, if forced to choose the minimum. The answers were again so simple – my family, my rings, my documents, a pair of jeans and a couple of sensible changes of clothing.

> *Stuff is just stuff.*
> PB - Ireland

And, probably a decent pair of walking shoes. I am not known for choosing sensible shoes. I have a couple of friends, in the US, who still laugh about the day I went on a hike with a pair of chunky, heeled, designer sandals. An action that speaks volumes about who I am ....!

In those heady, early days of 2002, filled with learning and discoveries about this new land, our visa expiration at end 2004 seemed a long way off and didn't concern me.

∞ ∞ ∞

*Don't be scared to have a go, change is good, it wakes you up, it makes you think about what you have and compare things. I should have done it five years earlier. Advice, you are a visitor in other countries (and sometimes I feel the same in South Africa) so, you have to make the first move in anything you want done, even if it's only a "hello" to a neighbour.*
PVDR - Australia

∞

*I didn't realize that I had become so South African! For the first year, I felt like an asylum seeker – and admit that at times, I barely could understand what Irish people were actually saying! A huge culture shock, but as I left Ireland at 17, and came 'home' at 57, forty years is a lifetime, so I shouldn't have been as surprised as I was.*

*To add insult to injury, I was retrenched from a job due to downturn in economy. I was devastated and finding it hard to deal with, but I had to go into the social services office to register for unemployment. After waiting in queue (with loads of drop-outs!) when I got to the counter, the clerk asked if I had a work permit to work in Ireland! She thought by my accent I was South African. I promptly burst into tears!*  KLB - Ireland

∞

*It has been difficult to establish ourselves, on many levels. The exchange rate was 5:1 when we came, so taking your life earnings and dividing them by five is a very sobering experience. Then, finding a spot to call your new home, new school, doctor, dentist, gynae, new roads to navigate, and friends to make, new network of business contacts for my husband to make.... the list goes on and on.*  DM - Australia

∞

*The most surprising thing for us was just how advanced 'third world' South Africa really is. The joy and happiness in the midst of trouble, as opposed to the sad, unsmiling faces of the new land. How lucky and wealthy South Africans really are, despite the difficulties. The indomitable spirit of our people – the soft living, almost depressed state of our new countrymen. An almost unfair trade of community, family, friends, natural beauty, rainbow nation, for safety and security of the land of the long white cloud. I never ever intended to live 'under a cloud!'*  ANJ - New Zealand

∞

*The police are everywhere here on the East Coast – it's a very heavily policed society, law-ridden, in which you can't get away with anything – the easy-going South African style, in which you could get by and charm your way through, simply arouses the darkest suspicions here. On the other hand, people love the English-sounding accent and it gives one immediate cachet.*

*Everyone is impossibly busy, so it's hard to form friendships AND to keep them up: schedules conflict, the children always have priority, and*

women are on the run, seeing to their children's needs every moment they are not at work. Not much domestic life, not much unscheduled time, few people read much, lots of eating out, and lots of bad food in the suburbs. It's not at all a relaxed society, and people don't really seem to know how to simply enjoy an evening together in the old South African style unless they are with family – in fact, most people seem to live in a cocoon of family and friends who date from their childhood and university days and which they carry with them throughout their lives; there is often very little room for newcomers beyond a sincere but passing warm friendliness.

The counter-culture and the 60's lifestyle are definitely dead, a focus of nostalgia – always a death-knell for a phenomenon. But I love the emphasis on a few core public holidays – in no particular order, the Fourth of July, Memorial Day, Labor Day, Thanksgiving, Halloween, Christmas, New Year, Easter, Spring Break – each with its traditions and rituals, and each an excuse to have a huge meal and bring everyone one knows together; everyone mixes in, no one is left out, and the family is at the heart of it all.

What else? Too much anxiety about strangers; the children have far too little physical freedom and there's too much medicating going on; all sorts of strange fears (of germs, etc.) bedevil women's lives. I do like the fact that teenagers can and do hold down jobs; an excellent preparation for adult life, but among the less well-off a bit of a prison as youngsters struggle to meet rent and car insurance and food bills.

With STDs and AIDS very much around, though mostly hidden, sex seems quite a quiet affair here, despite the excesses of the media. This is surprisingly a very sexist society as well – South Africa is more militant about women's equality – just take a look at how Hillary Clinton has been treated in this current campaign.

People stay indoors: not much outdoor life, in New Jersey at least, though everyone here seems to love the Jersey shore (which I find depressingly ugly and boring). And of course I should mention the boundless ignorance of the young about absolutely everything not in their very limited teen and youth culture – for one, they don't read at all, which leaves minds unfurnished to a startling degree. A car culture; huge amounts of time spent on commuting, too much reliance on air-conditioning and central air – when the weather is nice, people hardly notice, they're so used to indoor climate control.

Finally, mine is the typical immigrant experience, I suppose. People

have no idea where one is coming from, and are too polite or too uninterested to want to pry. So connections beyond the superficial can be problematic.
KW - USA

∞

    We came over without jobs and like many South Africans I know have found the job market tough. We also found it difficult to be renters rather than home owners. It is a truly humbling experience to come from a country where you have financial security, a network of contacts and family support to one where you battle to have your application accepted for the most basic credit card with a conservative limit. We have worked harder and worried more than ever before in our lives but I would do it again in a heartbeat. It is not the easy things in life that make us stronger.

    Despite the battle to become re-established I thank God often for the country and the community we live in. My children are getting an excellent education paid for by the State. They are involved in more sports and cultural activities than I can count on my two hands. They took the school bus home from kindergarten.

    I never lock my car doors, even at night when I'm driving. My front door is open or at least unlocked when I am home. When my husband travels for business I rest easy knowing the children are safe at night. These things are priceless and I have come to realize that quality of life goes way beyond financial means.

    Little by little we rebuild our life here enjoying all the benefits it has to offer. We become ever more familiar with our environment, increase our friendship circle and rebuild our financial security. It takes longer than I would have imagined but I know it's well worth the effort.
SL - Australia

∞

    It is a give-and-take scenario when you leave South Africa. Yes, I am also an alien in Australia like you in America and probably not the only South African feeling like that. Having said that, I am most thankful that I have at least found a country willing to accept me and offer me a future and a safe environment. It pains me to think about South Africa – what we had and the fact that nothing will ever be the same again. I miss my friends and the *similar thinking that became part of me. I still need lots of time to understand the Australian culture, their walk and talk. So I guess I will take it day by day and not look backwards too much.*     RS - Australia

∞

*Actually perhaps it would have been good to know that my skills where worth a lot more in the UK than I thought. At my first job I kept waiting for someone to haul me out of my seat and accuse me of being an imposter and far too expensive. After a few months I realised I was selling my services on the cheap.*     AP - UK

∞

*I have changed countries three times now, and admittedly it gets a bit harder making these shifts each time, but generally adapting is easy provided you are prepared to accept the society you live in. Too many South Africans have an arrogant and condescending attitude toward the countries/peoples they find themselves amongst and I believe firmly that this is 90% of the reason they don't settle.*     RW - UK

∞ ∞ ∞

# 33

∞

## Waste Not. Want Not

*It was a wonderful exercise in figuring out what 'stuff'
is truly important in one's life.*
RS - USA

**I**nitially, the most extraordinary cultural difference I found in the USA was the wastrel mentality. I would have lunch with my children at school and watch as other children opened lunch bags – healthy foods – to find a yoghurt, an apple, a homemade sandwich, perhaps a cheese stick and a bag of chips or a health bar.

And then, to witness the ungrateful, uncaring behaviour of those same children, would fill me with horror. A bite, or two, or three – avoid the crust – of the sandwich, perhaps a bite of the apple and the cheese. Nonchalantly, they left the lunch table and, on their way out of the cafeteria, they would toss the unopened yoghurt, barely touched apple, cheese stick and sandwich into the trash can.

My childhood was filled with recollections of encounters with homeless bergies and hungry vagrants. Those childish interactions had given me insight into the effects of hunger and poverty on a community. They fluttered through my mind as I watched the children throwing away perfectly good food – probably food that was not available to families living at, or below, the poverty level.

Unused to wasted food, because I had counted many vagrants among my collection of acquaintances in South Africa, I wanted to find a way to channel this surfeit to those who would be appreciative. I suggested to the school that we place a box at the end of each of the long cafeteria tables. The children could then put their untouched, unopened food into the boxes. We could sort it and take it to a homeless shelter each day. I would take responsibility for the initiative. Naturally, I believed that the suggestion would be gratefully received and the school would be delighted to make a small, yet positive, contribution to society. How naïve. The school's reaction was deeply disturbing and the litigious nature of American culture hit me squarely between the eyes. "No, we can't do that or even allow you to do that. If someone eats food from our donations, and develops a stomach infection, we could be sued. Sorry, but we won't take the chance."

I felt nauseated. I could have fed every single vagrant in our village with the food discarded by those children each day. The idiocy of the rules extended to children being told not to share their lunches with anyone else at table. So… if I wanted to eat your apple, and you didn't, you would be compelled to throw it away as opposed to giving it away. As I said, complete idiocy.

I have fond memories of school lunches spent sitting, with friends, outside in the quadrangle. Seated in a circle, Gillian would offer everyone a bite of her apple. Taking the first bite, she would pass it around for those who wanted some. This was an innocuous, friendly interaction which never caused us a moment's concern – germs, huh? – although we did sometimes complain that her braces had mauled the apple before she passed it to us. It never stopped each of us from taking a bite.

Being foreign here has always had distinct advantages, I told my son and daughter that they were *never* to throw away anything they had not eaten and to be sure to bring it back home. Their argument was that the cafeteria monitors told the children to empty their unwanted food into the trash cans. My response was that my authority outweighed everyone else's and that if they did toss food away, under orders, I would simply go and speak to the principal. I'd ask her if her mother ever told her about the children who are starving in Africa. Obviously not.

My eccentricities about wastage were smiled at, but I could truly find a use for everything – bread crusts for the ducks and geese at the lake; apples for chutney; leftover energy bars would be eaten by us or crumbled and added to muesli; a bag of chips to return in their lunch bag tomorrow; and cheese would be grated and used at suppertime. Most of this food could also be shared with the birds and squirrels we found foraging around the apartments. One of the benefits of being a foreigner is that people tolerate idiosyncrasies that would not be acceptable in a fellow citizen.

If the USA could export all the food, clothing and other materials that are discarded on a daily basis, they could feed, clothe and house the entire planet. In our house, winter clothes are recycled – sleeves are cut to summer lengths and pants cut into shorts. I use my sewing machine to hem the edges. As the children have grown older, they smile at my silliness but tolerate it, nevertheless. I do not think I would have been as enterprising in South Africa because there would always have been someone who would be grateful for the hand-me-downs. I don't want us to be wastrels and I try hard to teach my children never to waste. Sadly we have not met many children here who understand that concept.

I have always been a lover of burrowing around in thrift and second-hand charity stores, occasionally finding something of real value – sentimental, aesthetic or economic. In the summertime, community yard sales are a big event. The newspaper has a special 'Community Yard Sales' column on Friday and Saturday mornings. The sales usually start around 7.30 a.m. or 8 a.m. but the hard-core shoppers sometimes arrive around 7 a.m. or 7.30 a.m. Those people generally pick up a newspaper in the early morning, sit with a pen marking the sales they want to attend and then plan the choicest route. Hard-core! I rest my case.

Advertisements read something like this: "23229 (area postal code – known as a 'zip') – Children's clothing; household appliances; books; toys; baby items; costume jewellery; collectibles. Rain or shine. Everything must go. Sale starts 7.30 a.m. – no early birds." Churches, community centres, retirement villages and often a couple of neighbours in the same road will advertise their event as "HUGE Community Yard Sale". You are equally encouraged to have your own, lone, sale which opens you up to the nosy neighbours who like to know your favourite brand of junk.

I walked the hard-core line for a while but it became a little boring after a month. I'm not an early riser especially if I am not assured of a bargain. Aimless wandering around the city, and cruising slowly down the road to check out the wares – set out on the front lawn – before bothering to find a parking space, eventually became rather irritating. All said though we did find some wonderful items that we still own. You can take $20 to a yard sale and return with a trash bag full of items. A $3 VCR bought at a sale in 2002 is still in perfect working condition.

I also discovered 'yard sale snobbery' where some shoppers will only attend sales in certain zip codes because 'one can be assured of quality'. Ah yes, yard sales take place in all areas, whether your house cost $50,000 or $500,000. To participate in the Saturday morning yard sale exercise is to experience a free education in human nature.

We began to accumulate 'new' household items via our forays into the world of yard sales. This was another adventure for the children, too. At three and five years old, they became intrepid little bargain hunters. And then there was Goodwill, and then there was the Salvation Army and then there were any number of other little thrift stores (some up- and some down-market) dotted all over Richmond. And then there was Freecycle©, which leads me into the story of a real gem I found in Richmond.

While searching the internet for information about recycling clothing, I stumbled upon a Yahoo group known as Freecycle©. The group is international, and is a non-profit group. Many cities have a local Freecycle© group. 'One man's trash is another man's treasure' is the gist of the organization's purpose. This raison d'etre resonated loudly for me and I discovered that there was a Richmond Freecycle© group. Excitedly, I joined.

Freecycle© opened up a whole new world. A dedicated group of people, 14000 at last count, who are unwilling to toss out items that could be of any possible use to others. This is a group that wants to prevent wastage and to conserve resources. In other words, these are my kind of people. After posting an email 'Offer', which is sent to the group of 14000 Freecyclers (as we are fondly known), the responses from those who are interested stream in, "pick me, pick me, I really want/need/can use this."

I've been through a learning curve as Freecycle© taught me about human nature. Some people do not bother to pick up items (despite their email saying that they 'desperately' want the item); some people are not willing to write a properly punctuated and capitalized sentence (they're immediately out of the running); some people live too far away and want you to bring the items to them (what a cheek); I've learned not to give the items to the first responder – wait for a civilized email. I've learned to say, in my posting, that responses without a date and time of pickup will not be considered. I've learned not to bother to respond to those who've let me down before. I've learned to keep a list of the Freecyclers upon whom I can rely, and to offer them, privately, first. I've learned that people who live within a couple of miles can generally be relied upon much more than those who live 20 miles away.

As you can post 'Wants' as well as 'Offers', I've found many generous people who are willing to take something out of their attic, and dust it off, if they think it could be put to good use. I've been able to participate in charitable initiatives and I've been able to encourage my children to give away toys (which would otherwise have gathered dust). I've made new friends and I've furnished my entire home with Freecycled furniture – lounge suites, coffee tables, bedside tables, house plants, media centres, rugs, CD players, pots and pans, desks, books, dry-erase boards, bookshelves, lamps, a free piano, dining room table and chairs and any number of vintage armchairs. Garden plants; an old birdcage; board games; wool; free bread; cheap eggs; kombucha starters; beanie babies; DVDs; oil paints; art canvas; gravel; clothes; shoes; mulched garden leaves[21] and on and on it goes. James complains with each new item of furniture but I've quashed those by passing something on with my next 'Offer' posting.

> Was also surprised at how much 'freer' Australians were, as they weren't paranoid about their houses or cars or bags being stolen.
> DM - Australia

Oh, let me not forget dearest Grayson, the Freecycled cat, an acquisition which took some serious explanation and negotiation with James. On a whim, one Friday morning, I saw the Freecycle© posting for Grayson and decided to adopt him into our two cat family. As it so happened, he belonged to an, until then, unknown neighbour who lived practically across the road – and so, another new friend via Freecycle©.

Such are the joys of a thrifty lifestyle.

∞ ∞ ∞

*The most surprising thing about relocating was the total lack of interest shown by people over here in who you are, and what forced us to*

---

[21] In this particular instance, I posted a want for a DVD (Fantasia) and a want for garden leaves to use as mulch. A Freecycler offered me the DVD – she lived about 20 miles away – and said she had as many leaves as I wanted. Picture the scene! There I was scooping by hand her mulched, wet, leaves into black garbage bags. As logic is not one of my virtues, I hadn't thought to ask my neighbours if they had leaves I could use, so instead I carted a boot full of leaves from 20 miles away, twice! I didn't give the incident a moment's thought until, at a neighborhood party later that year, they fell about laughing at my Freecycle© leaf story.

*leave our country. People over here are only interested in 'bling', celebrity culture, and money. I am English and I have lived all over the world, but never have I known such a mercenary lot.* DH - UK

∞

*When I left, I took only two suitcases – one with clothing and one with books and music CDs. It was a wonderful exercise in figuring out what 'stuff' is truly important in one's life. I have subsequently become something of a minimalist, trying hard to acquire only the bare necessities. That is difficult to do here in America – land of useless crap – and I have caved somewhat now that my long-term girlfriend is living with me ('we need a couch… and a TV… and a dresser…').* RS - USA

∞ ∞ ∞

## 34

∞

# Arguing With a Vagrant

*We were walking down the street one night (in Singapore) and some poor chap stopped abruptly and asked me if I had a light for his cigarette. I had him on the pavement with my fist on its way to his throat before instinct kicked out – that's what our experiences of crime in our South African city had turned us into.*
BM - United Arab Emirates

**6**:00 p.m. Dusk is settling around me and I'm pushing a cart full of groceries to the car. As usual, despite the activity, my head is on another plane. An unkempt, grizzly, tanned man on a bicycle stops next to my car trunk as I'm unloading the bags.

"'Scuse me, Ma'am, but you wouldn't happen to have any change for me to buy some supper?"

"No, I'm sorry, I don't ever have much cash on me."

I'm scratching through my purse, feeling a little uncomfortable, although his energy is unthreatening – he's still on his bike. "I'm trying to save for my daughter's birthday in a couple of weeks time."

"That's great. How old is she?"

"Ten. She'll be ten."

"Oh, my kids are all grown up already. My daughter's 23 and my son's 21."

"That's nice."

I am still scrabbling in my purse to see what is there and noting that he doesn't get off the bike and offer to help unpack the bags of groceries. I smile because, based on past experience in South Africa, I automatically anticipated that he would help with the groceries in order to earn the cash.

Success! I find a dollar bill. "Here, here you go, $1 and a couple of coins." I open my purse wide and show him that it's completely empty.

"No, Ma'am. I don't want to take your last money. You keep that. It's fine."

"I insist. It's not a problem, really, take it." Never in my life have I had to argue with a vagrant to take money.

"No, you need that for your daughter's birthday."

"No, it's fine. Really. You can have it."

"Ok, thank you. Well, have a great evening and I hope your daughter enjoys her birthday. Bye." And he rides off into the sunset.

Memories flood through me and I remember Jeffrey, the vagrant at the traffic lights, religious in his attendance every day. During the minutes of waiting for the lights to change, he'd fill me in on the latest news of his life, his family and his community. Eventually, learning that he did not have breakfast prior to assuming his position at the lights, I'd make a breakfast sandwich and bring it to him with coffee or a bottle of juice. Not being shy, he'd say, "Nay, Medem, ek drinkie koffie nie, ek kannit nee hanteer, my nurves issie sterkie." (No, Madam, I don't drink Coffee, I cannot handle it, my nerves aren't strong.) Next time, I'd remember to bring juice or milk or something else. We inadvertently found ourselves in a relationship – my reliance on him to keep me grounded and his reliance on me because he was assured that he would not stand all morning with hunger gnawing at his insides.

A couple of times a year, he'd disappear for a few weeks and I would hope that he hadn't been consumed by the poverty and the crime in his community. Pondering if there was some way to find out, I realized that I didn't know his surname, I didn't actually know where he lived, and I would not know where to begin such a search.

And then he'd reappear, a familiar toothless grin each morning as he knocked on my car window.

"Hey, Geoffrey, where've you been?"

"Ney, Medem, I gotta job working in 'con-struc-shin.'" This last word enunciated very carefully and clearly.

"And now, what happened?"

"Ney, Medem, jus' part time. Dis klaar, nou." (It's finished now.)

And the next day we'd resume our morning routine.

In the USA, the gentleman on the bicycle caught me unawares because, in my eight years of living here, I haven't spoken to more than six vagrants. I imagine that it is also a reflection on the area in which we live. I know that in the downtown area and the older houses close to the city, there are far more street people. The environment seems very controlled as compared to South Africa where, on a daily basis, you are confronted with destitute people hovering on the fringes of life. Those daily encounters are not limited to urban areas or suburbs; in South Africa, the desolation is everywhere.

As a teenager, walking along the Main Road in Wynberg always meant fending off 'bergies', wrapped in fumes, with their dolorous tales of life. Each 'bergie' was unique in face and weathered features, their stories, and their manner. Some of them followed me, despite my refusal to interact, and kept up a running conversation as they walked behind me. Others argued and swore at me, sometimes one would thank me for listening, one apologized for bothering me and, occasionally, one would simply say 'ja', as he shrugged his shrunken shoulders and sighed. A sigh that told me, 'Yes, and this is how it always is. No-one will speak to me.'

> Most surprising thing about relocating? The freedom to walk alone at night and not be nervous.
>
> KB - Germany

In South Africa, sometimes two or more people a day would visit our house, in Riebeek Kasteel, seeking money or food. James would smile at the sound of the doorbell, and say, "slim pickings today, your buddies are at the door". After chatting with them for a couple of minutes I would ask what they'd like for dinner, offering polony and cheese sandwiches, or perhaps peanut butter and honey, or maybe warmed up leftovers from the day before. I consistently refused requests for money.

Sometimes, seeing my red car stop outside the village store, they would rush to greet my toddler son and I and engage us in conversation. I'd offer to take them inside with me to buy food but, coyly embarrassed, they would refuse to accompany me. Once a young man who was plagued by a violent stutter (and subsequently shunned by many villagers who believed he was drunk), decided to join me in the grocery store. As we meandered through the aisles buying my items, I attempted to pry information from him about his dinnertime wishes. We settled, after my pleading, on ham, cheese, bread and margarine.

Approaching the cash register the woman ignored the man and, turning to me, said, "What? What is he doing here? What are you doing? Why are you buying him food? He's just a lazy, drunk, layabout. Don't waste your money."

I was appalled that she spoke about him in that manner, especially since he was standing next to me in the queue. She did not greet him and he studiously focused on the floor tiles. "I'd appreciate it if you didn't speak about him like that. I'd also appreciate it if you weren't so rude. Please treat him properly especially if you want me to shop here in the future."

She looked suitably chastised, threw him a contemptuous look, and rung up the rest of my items. He would not make eye contact either with me or with her. Outside the store, he apologised for being the cause of the embarrassing encounter.

"I don't care about that. I care that you have something to eat tonight. I think she's rude and I don't like her. Just ignore it." I know that he couldn't do that. How can you ignore being treated in a sub-human manner or as a non-sentient being?

> *The biggest impact, I think, would be that I try to listen and understand more, and try to 'walk in the other person's shoes'. I think it has made me a better person.*
> 
> DDM - Japan

I miss the vagrants, the bergies and the street people who, facing the brutal reality of life, find themselves lacking and, find themselves abandoned by it. I miss our daily interactions. I would've liked my children to know them, to know their depth, their honesty and their simple needs and pleasures. I miss them.

∞ ∞ ∞

> *Most surprising was that we have met more racist or class conscious people from foreign countries than we ever knew in South Africa. In South Africa I could have a beer, a braai and a meaningful conversation with my gardener. Try that in India, England or Arabia and they think you've lost it.*
> 
> BM - UAE

∞

> *Initially when I arrived in Australia (after having left 'The Old South Africa') I wasn't prepared for the attacks on the political stance the government held and why I didn't do anything about it! I couldn't believe*

how they expected 'Little Me' to make a stand and expect to have an impact! Even more, they did not realize that I had a very limited view of what was really happening as the government had managed to censor the information that was being fed to its constituents.

JH - Australia

∞

I have huge amounts of hope and desperately wish for things to get better. My heart is in Johannesburg and one day I would very much like to do something that would help a great many people. I will do that someday.

JW - Japan

∞

How wonderful it actually is to live in a country that functions normally. No amount of money in the world is worth the very real possibility of getting that dreaded phone call that someone you love has been murdered or raped!

ND - UK

∞

I have found freedom to be able to walk in the forest alone quite safely, drive around alone at night, leave the house open / unlocked and not have to worry. I can get quite angry when I think about how security conscious we had to be in South Africa and thought that it was 'normal' and accepted it so easily.

BH - Australia

∞ ∞ ∞

# 35

∞

## America's Gift – My Children

*I am taking this knock for my babies.*
RVR - South Africa


**W**aking up, I stretch and yawn and wonder what on earth to do with my day. Should I shower and then make coffee? Decisions. Coffee wins. Twenty minutes later I am nursing coffee on the verandah and I wonder if the children are still sleeping. No matter, its 7:20 a.m. and Anna, my nanny, maid and housekeeper, will arrive by 8 a.m. She will wake them, dress them, and make their breakfast and, if needs be, entertain them too.

And so, what should I do today? Perhaps I'll have a facial, or go to the hair salon. My girlfriends might meet me for lunch or maybe I should just go shopping. I think I'll speak to Manie, my gardener, and find out if he needs anything from the co-op or the nursery. No doubt Anna could conjure up a grocery list, which would at least necessitate going to the shops....

This seems dreamlike now, but in Africa, this was my life – very colonial, very relaxed, the most difficult decision was what to wear each day and, of course, what to cook for supper. Anna would arrive each day promptly at 8 a.m. – wash the supper dishes from the previous evening, do the laundry, attend to the children and their needs and do the housework. Manie, her husband, would arrive at the same time and work full-time in the garden, tending the plants, picking the fruits and vegetables and seasonally planting more.

(Is it negative to say that I loved my maid and my gardener? No! I did, and I miss them as madly as I do the rest of my friends and family. And, despite what many would like to believe, not because they slaved to provide us with a neo-colonial existence of comfort and ease. I loved them because we shared much laughter and joy, they were like members of our family and we grew up with them, they grew up with our children. Anna and Manie are wonderful, honest, reliable, earthy people who formed a solid foundation for me and mine. For their sake, since I am no longer there, I want the country to heal so that they too, and their children, can live with true freedom again.)

My children seemed happy. I was terrified of spending too much time with them because I didn't know how to relate to them. Frequently I would pay Anna overtime to work on Saturday mornings, which left only Saturday afternoons and Sundays for me to be 'mother' (and I would count the hours). Subconsciously I realized how unimportant I was because each time they needed comfort, they would look for Anna. I remember a sinking feeling in my stomach when that happened.

> To be able to give my child a life where she could play outside, unafraid of being shot, get an education which actually meant something, and have the choices to be whatever she decides, I left!
> 
> LRK - USA

When we arrived in the USA in early 2002, I was thrust into a position of 24-hour responsibility for them. I had never experienced this before and they were already five and three years old. Fortunately, a full time pre-school nearby took care of most of the week for me and it was not as problematic as I'd anticipated.

In 2003, for the first time, I learned about home-schooling from a South African acquaintance. When she mentioned that she was home-schooling her son, my first reaction was horror – she must be possessed! I had never known that such an option existed. I had always assumed that my children would start school, I would have lots of free time, and my life would continue as usual.

One day, out of boredom, I was at the library and as a mainly non-fiction reader, I picked up a few books about the subject. The more I read, the more I consumed. I became voracious. And the more I read, the more I noticed my children. I noticed their reactions, their attitudes, their interests, their intelligence, their social interactions and I noticed their resistance to their schoolwork, their teachers and their complaints about the mean art teacher. It seemed that they were rather young to be feeling so irritated, hassled and bored at school. Where could they go from there?

As I noticed, I realized that I hadn't been listening to them for a very long time. I felt sad at having to send them off every day without having time to connect with them. I resented the morning arguments, the homework fights, getting them to bed, the 'in my face' feeling of school. We had no meaningful time without school-related issues being in our way.

I removed my daughter from kindergarten in 2005 and soon my son joined us. As James worked from home, things were rather cramped in an apartment with four 'strong' personalities in a small space. It was an interesting time of meeting new friends, learning new skills and enjoying many fun events all over Virginia. We discovered that we enjoyed being with one another and we used our time wisely. Driving to home-schooling events gave us time to listen to classical history CD's, discuss philosophy or try out maths concepts and test spelling. None of us tend to follow the 'mainstream' and home-schooling opened the world even wider for us.

Irrespective of the physical distance between the continents, and the differences in my lifestyle on each, I recognize an enormous chasm between who I used to be and who I am now. I have shifted as a person and as a mother and home-schooling bridges part of that divide. Wherever I live in the world, I can take the knowledge gained and the gifts given to me during my time here – those are priceless!

> *It really is a sad day when mothers and grandmothers like myself and recently my best friend are rejoicing when their kids and grandchildren move to another country.*
> IB - South Africa

America's greatest gift to me has been, and continues to be, my children. For that I would gladly change continents again.

∞ ∞ ∞

*I think the most surprising thing I have found is the fact that I was able to cope on my own for the first two months in a strange country with the three children, all of whom were struggling with the relocation in different ways, and not only coped, but held it together for them, so that by the time my husband arrived in the country, we were well settled, furniture in place and full acquainted with the day to day tasks.*

*The one other thing that surprised me, and which I noticed within the first couple of weeks, is the complete lack of stress in everyone's life. As an example, if you were doing your shopping at the supermarket in South Africa, inevitably at least half of every child or baby in the store would be crying or throwing temper tantrums (as would the mothers as well). Here in South Australia it is only on the rare occasion that you would see such a display, and when it does happen, everyone stops to see what is going on.*

AW - Australia

∞

*Most surprising thing about relocating? Not having to keep watching out for my sons. Going for bicycle rides in lovely green forests and not worrying about being too far away to call for help, or fear of being mugged! I was happy that my children could grow-up like I could in Cape Town, care free and without high fences!*

KB - Germany

∞

*I have found that the life outside South Africa is really great, there are some tough things being away from our culture and family and friends but the safety factor far outweighs that and I would have travelled to the other side of the world to give my daughter a safer, better future.*

RM - UK

∞

*We arrived in Dublin with our suitcases of clothing, not knowing a soul and not coming to jobs. Within two months, all five of us were working.*

SK - Ireland

∞

*On the down side of the relocation issue, we moved here, yes, for our children, for our children's future and to give them the best possible opportunities that life has to offer BUT at the same time we are depriving them horribly by removing them from their aging grandparents, aunts and uncles and cousins and friends who have chosen to stay OR have chosen to leave – but to somewhere else. This fact pains me and although my children*

are safe, happy, healthy and none the wiser, I cannot help but wonder if they will one day hold us accountable for having removed them from their loved ones!
LG - USA

∞

I've left a piece of me over there, but as I have a little girl to look after, I've preferred come back to the old Europe to make her have a safer life.
CT - Italy

∞

One of the saddest questions my daughter asked me once was, "how do I know it is any better anywhere else?" She is now a single mother with two small children living outside Durban with power outages three times a week – so of course, burglar systems are out. Can you imagine my anxiety?
MH - UK

∞

I don't believe that it's right to run away when times are hard and then return once people who have stuck around and worked hard to change things for the better. If this is your decision then I suggest that you stay where you are for the rest of your life. You've taught your children that they should run away when things get difficult instead of teaching them to stand and fight for what is right. There are MANY, MANY people here in South Africa who can take this easy route that you're taking but were not quitters like yourself. Stop using your kids as an excuse because you make it sound as if you're the only one who loves your kids. It's natural for parents to love their kids and to want them to be safe and you are not alone when it comes to that.
RP - South Africa

∞ ∞ ∞

# 36

∞

# Friends in Need

*I worry that we will not have any friends, that simply finding a babysitter to look after the children when we want to go out for an evening will be problematic.*
CH - South Africa

There are many things you don't consider when you decide to leave your homeland. As you begin the process of settling in to a new country, one of the questions asked on all forms is – who are your emergency contacts in a crisis? Forms that define your new life – pre-school forms, doctor's forms, school forms, extra mural activity forms, gym membership forms, field trip forms, summer camp forms. The list goes on and on and on. Yes, yes, yes – Mother, Father – who else can you add as an extra contact in the event that both are unavailable? There was no-one.

It is at that point that you realize the enormity of what you have done. We had to use my daughter's godfather's name – he lived in Illinois (a 14 hour drive) – or our friends in North Carolina (a 6 hour drive). I wasn't entirely sure what they could do if, in an emergency, they received a call from the school. There was Mary, my spiritual mentor from Cape Town who, fortuitously set up by the Universe, was on sabbatical and teaching at East Carolina University (a 3 hour drive). Mary was a lifeline in the early, traumatic months where we questioned our decision and our sanity. The happy times spent at her home filled many empty weekends. I dreaded her departure but her permanent teaching position at the University of Cape

Town beckoned. Our last link to Cape Town was broken.

What if something happened to us? What if we died in a car accident? What would happen to the children? I encountered a terrifying sense of isolation and a vision of our children being whisked to the UK (my sister) or South Africa (my mother) after waiting 24 hours for someone familiar to arrive. At such a young age, the children didn't consider any of these issues – it is only more recently that they have begun to question us.

> *It is a truly humbling experience to come from a country where you have financial security, a network of contacts and family support to one where you battle to have your application accepted for the most basic credit card with a conservative limit.*
> 
> SL - Australia

I did make friends at the gym – passing friends in that we didn't visit each other's homes but we spent a great deal of time at the gym talking and then we occasionally would have lunch together. During a time when we had no idea where to find money to pay the rent or to buy food, those same friends bought a $200 grocery store voucher for me. I don't know which one of them it was; I suspect it was all of them. They left a card at the front desk of the gym with the voucher inside it. It was as though I had found a gold bar, it was such an enormous amount of money. It made me cry.

In 2003, after two years, I finally made my first real friend. We met at a Christmas party and spent the entire evening talking beside the fire. It turned out that we lived almost within shouting distance of one another and our children attended the same school. Women are such multi-dimensional creatures and their companionship is a relaxant and a stimulant – I'm OK, you're OK, we have issues, we discuss them, we empower one another, life goes on, let's go and get on with it. She was my first moral, and emotional, support in two years. Suddenly, I had someone I could share things with again. There was another woman with whom I could share a female perspective, a backup, a person who would share child care, share secrets, someone who could understand the difficulties of being a mother and a wife.

After eight years, I know at least 10 people whom I could call on in an emergency. It's a small comfort and it has taken years to formulate the small foundation that you begin to call home. The stability forms even slower on an emotional level.

I have a diverse group of friends here, and these friendships have taken time to build. My American friends will never understand where I came from, nor do they seem inclined to find out. I don't think friendship is based on that. But the real bonus is having a person's name to put down as an Emergency Contact when asked to complete all those forms.

∞ ∞ ∞

*Emotionally, the sense of loss is compensated by the gain in security and support.*  AD - Australia

∞

*I wish that I could have read a book of someone else's experience of emigration/immigration, to educate myself in the emotional aspects of such significant change. I thought that I could handle the experience. Many times, I thought it was too high a price to pay. Sometimes, I saw the high price that other migrants paid, in broken homes, failed relationships, deep emotional scars. There we were, but for the Grace of God.*  ANJ - Australia

∞

*The biggest fear is finding a job and settling in without feeling like you're an 'outsider'. Having no family or support system or history over there and basically being completely alone in the world. The fear is there but when you compare it to living in South Africa you have nothing to lose by leaving because you live in an even greater fear in South Africa on a daily basis.*  CO - South Africa

∞

*We lived in an upmarket area in Johannesburg and would not be able to live in the Council Areas in the UK as I feel we have worked all of our lives for a decent standard of life and you hope to show this to your children – to make them want to work hard to live in a nice area and have a good lifestyle. This is why after six years we are still renting and have not been able to buy a house in the UK as we have chosen a nice area in England but cannot afford to buy only rent.*

*My children came from good schools in Johannesburg and the only schools to compare here are private and definitely unaffordable. They all*

suffered terribly and cried for South Africa for about six months but they are tough kids, saw their parents working hard and they did too and now they are all settled but still miss their home.

My husband and I still have not made friends here, only South Africans who are in the same situation as ours. We are different – not sure why – we are perhaps too friendly and it frightens the English as they are reserved people.

TS - UK

∞

You name them, I've been there – all the 'South African Reunited' type websites. After I arrived, back in 2002, I met some South Africans. I went over to their house for Thanksgiving. There were about 30 people, all from South Africa. I was really looking forward to it, but I was very disappointed. The thing is, I expect too much. I think I'm going to be instant best buddies with them because they are from South Africa, but they are just another bunch of strangers you meet who happen to be from South Africa. I never saw them again. I also met another big group of South Africans recently, had a braai with them twice and I don't think I'll see them again either.

IB - USA

∞

Most surprising thing about relocating? You survive!

CB - Australia

∞ ∞ ∞

# Part 6

∞

# Longing

*I do feel we have paid a price for leaving –
there is an underlying longing that never goes away.*

SC - Australia

# 37

∞

## Missing is Easy

### Introduction by James McIntosh

Even after all this time here in the US of A, people ask me whether I miss South Africa. In my early days here I was always surprised when I answered that I did not. So surprised, in fact, that I felt obliged to explore why I did not feel as if I missed South Africa. What I realized was that being in a new country is such a grand adventure, what with all the new sights, sounds and smells, that I didn't really have time to miss the 'old country'. Except, maybe, late at night.

One thing that moving to a new and strange country does is to you lock you in the moment. You become hyper-aware of your surroundings and the people. Everything is new and everyone seems interesting. You are in the moment, in the here and now… until the novelty wears off. Then you drift once again into living in the past or in the future, but not in the moment. When that happens, you start reminiscing. That's when I realized that I might not miss the place, but I did miss the people. Specifically, I missed having old friends who could experience this newness with me. Not American friends, because this was obviously not new to them. I missed my South African friends.

But I did not miss South Africa. Not really.

Today I understand the real reason why I don't miss South Africa.

For me, South Africa has passed into 'past'. I miss the time 'South Africa'; I don't miss the place 'South Africa'. Of course I miss the mountains and the sea and the vlaktes and the vineyards and the wheatfields and the beaches... but America has all those things as well.

What I miss are *my experiences* of those mountains and sea and vlaktes and vineyards and wheatfields and beaches. Because if I knew then what I know now, that those days would not last forever, that a time would come when I would not be there, I would have made sure that I experienced them more fully, deeply, richly, completely. I would have been more 'in that moment' of mountains and sea and vlaktes and vineyards and wheatfields and beaches.

Or so I think. But not too often, because thinking that I 'should have' experienced South Africa more fully, deeply, richly, completely when I had the opportunity, is the path to longing. I can handle 'missing', but 'longing' is something else again. 'Missing' is of the heart; 'longing' is of the soul. We Africans know that only too well.

∞ ∞ ∞

# 38

∞

# Belonging(s)

*Just back from a trip to South Africa and the feeling of being home is something I cannot explain, a feeling of belonging somewhere.*
RG - Australia

**S**peaking with a neighbour one afternoon, we were discussing our lives, where we had lived and where we had grown up. We were chatting about our families, and our friends. They had married in 1991 and were still living in their original home purchased at that time. Her boys were born and have grown up in that house, and in this neighbourhood. Their families and friends live relatively close to one another. Most of them live in the same state or within a couple of hours driving time from the place in which they were born, educated and married.

As she spoke, it struck me that she still has her place, her history, a safe space in time that is uniquely hers, a solid foundation....

When people talk to one another, they begin to know each other, they know their environment, they find common connections – be they people or places – their histories are entwined, and their memories are connected. They went to similar schools and colleges, they share similar life experiences, and they know some of the same people. This is their history.

Over time it has struck me and I've become more aware of how, living here, my history only began when I landed here in 2002. There's nothing I can share, nothing I can laugh about, when co-workers talk about the schools they attended, their high school achievements, the places they have been and the people they know. I put my head down and continue with my work.

In a new land, you have no familiarity and you have to build new traditions. The traditions we associate with our culture. The familiar repetitive actions we enjoy annually for birthdays, anniversaries and other holidays or occasions. These traditions are formed through a desire to commemorate events. They can be as simple as always baking a homemade cake for a birthday or eating out for an anniversary. For us, it was the summertime braais at Christmas. It was the tradition of seeing friends for Christmas Eve and family on Christmas Day. It was stopping at Coimbra Bakery after church on Sundays for fresh chocolate éclairs and canned pineapple. It was playing Balderdash with friends. And, for the children, it was Nana's scrambled eggs and visiting the Spur.

> *The loss of history is very sad.*
> LBM - USA

I envy my neighbour the solidity, the stability, the comfort and security provided in knowing your place, knowing where your place is in the world and having the support structure of family and friends around. I watch the neighbours as they visit grandparents, hold family get-togethers at Thanksgiving and Christmas, and I feel alone and lost. My children feel it greatly during the holidays, and they tell me, with tears in their eyes, that they wish Nana was here. I ask myself what did I do to them? Why did I do this to them? Have I really changed their lives for the better? They have no history prior to when they were three and five years old – they've never had a chance to be South African (no-one believes them when they say they are from South Africa) and they are not yet quite American. We, all of us, are caught between two cultures, still. We look American, if there is such a thing, but we don't sound American. Our children look American, sound American and yet are not American. I love to joke with people that one day we will be true African Americans. Most of them don't see the humour in my statement.

In May 2002, I put an end to my belonging 'somewhere', and an end to who I had been for 32 years, packed my belongings, and began anew, a child again. It was an end to my plans, for us, for the house, for our life in South Africa; it was an end to my foundation. It was the end of my connection to a past, and the beginning of an unknown future in free fall. By that time, Biddulphs Shipping had already packed our few remaining belongings. Those boxes were the only catalogue of my 'belonging' somewhere else. The analogy was not lost on me.

I'm glad I've opened our minds, and those of our children, to other cultures, to other opportunities and to the expansiveness of the world. I'm pleased that they are not insular, they are international in their outlook, they are searchers (like us) and learners (like us). Anyway, even if we were in South Africa, would we really spend time with family over the holidays – most of my biological family lives in Gauteng. As for grandparents, there is only my mother left and my sister lives in the UK. We had close friends, yes, but not much bonded biological family, so we would seldom have those family holidays with 15 people around the table – the raucous, noisy, fun, bonding time of other families.

> What do you miss the most about life in South Africa? The people, and sharing a common history – with strangers, as well as family and friends and people from school, university days, etc.     JW - South Africa

I justify our decision by saying it doesn't matter, we wouldn't have had it anyway, and I don't want to live a little narrow life in a small city, and state, my whole life through. I sometimes justify it by being critical of those who are happy in their existence. It is the only way I can make sense of mine. If I had stayed, I, too, would have been somewhat insular because I was living in the area – the Western Cape – in which I was born. Most of my family and friends lived within the province in which I was born. I, too, would have been happy and secure in my identity.

The first day of school after the 2007 Christmas holidays found me in the school library, an unusual occurrence, at 7:50 a.m. The school bell rang to signal start of the day, but the first order was to say the Pledge of Allegiance. I found myself emotionally overwhelmed, but saying the Pledge and really feeling it, for the first time, I almost cried. After six years in limbo, I had been somewhat accepted, I was on my way to 'belonging' again.

Even if I choose to sing the Star Spangled Banner one day, I can still sing the South African anthem. I'll always support rugby and not American football. I will always follow the cricket scores and not the baseball. Those things are not part of my being. I'm still a rainbow person from a rainbow nation, I've just added another stripe (plus star) to my colours. I call myself a citizen of the world. There is no anger in that statement – it is what it is. I have to weather the anger of friends who still live in South Africa and who have chosen to live in the eye of the storm. They are critical of America and its policies. Why would you want to be American? Why do want to ally yourself with them? Are you mad?

Yes, I will say the Pledge of Allegiance and I will feel proud to do so, just as I feel proud to sing N'kosi Sikeleli 'Afrika. Wherever I live on the planet, I'll support people and believe in people, not empty statements and warmongering and cruelty and anger. And, I'll find the goodness in people – whoever they are – and in situations – whatever they are. This is not confined to countries and governments.

The first time I was hit by a serious and intense longing was nearly eight years later, in December 2009. I was finally working – my first job in the USA – and my co-workers were talking about their family holiday plans, and we had none – we had no money and nowhere to go. What am I doing here when there are family, friends and sunshine in South Africa? I'm sitting on the brink of another cold, snowy, grey winter – a miserable indoor existence. It seemed that even those who apparently had no plans, were making no fuss, were still having a family holiday.

> My heart will always be in South Africa, but my brain always reminds me otherwise.
> MC - Cyprus

At night, I began dreaming intensely of the crisp warmth found in the early hours of the summer days, before the sun has actually touched the pavements of Cape Town; the moment of energy, of fullness and the joy of being alive, of it being warm and it being summertime.

∞ ∞ ∞

*One event stands out in my mind as particularly sad for us as a family. We were living in an apartment, (from a lovely farm) while trying to sort out a house for ourselves, and we had gone away for the weekend to a friend's farm. When we got back to our apartment, my son sat down and said he wasn't feeling well. I quizzed him on where he was feeling sick – is it your stomach or your head or your throat? But then he said the words that I will never forget and that still bring tears to my eyes: 'I feel like I am in the wrong place.' Isn't that a thought that we've all had?*
DM - Australia

∞

*Although sleeping peacefully every night is wonderful, I cannot shake that feeling of "something is missing". Something is missing and I don't know what. We have two boys and they seem fine. It's just me wondering everyday if I can make it (emotionally, of course) I miss home every day and wish things would change so that we can go back – just to feel a sense of belonging again….*

*We left a lot of friends and family behind. I guess I should stop feeling sorry for myself and do what every mother is supposed to do, and put her children first. I've been going through a bit of a depression lately. I want to go home, but know that I can't – for the sake of my kids. I have a great job here and so does my husband. When does it ever get better?* MO - Australia

∞

*I experienced all the things you would expect, missing my friends and family, but the part that is most pervasive is the part of me that was defined by South Africa. I didn't realize how much it made me who I was and how lost I would feel without it. Maybe I am glorifying it, but now that I look back, I feel like everything was more beautiful, fun, and exciting there…the culture, people and atmosphere. I now live in a world of accessibility…a world of strip malls and Wal-Mart, of conformity and a Starbucks on every corner…a world that lacks flavour and originality, and I fear that I have become soft.* OM - Colorado

∞

*The feeling of guilt at leaving behind my family, and the difficulty I would face in trying to bring them over to the USA.* AS - USA

∞

*Emigrating means trying to make yourself a home in a place where you have no history – no family – no true culture of your own – you are essentially a 'nobody'. And while you can make new friends, and thoroughly enjoy everything about say, Australia, you will never stop feeling that relief in your heart every time you land in the airport as you arrive home. And that's what South Africa will always be to South Africans who live overseas.* <u>Home</u>. *It's not something you can take out of a true South African.* JW - South Africa

∞

*Our roots and family and friends and our lifelong history and*

associations. These are irreplaceable. One has to learn to 'be at home' everywhere and 'homesick everywhere' at the same time, but more and more this is true of most global inhabitants. We are all part of the same human family, and one has to learn to become rooted and engaged 'with the few ounces of one's strength and resources' where one is ('glocally' as it were) and not to surrender one's roots and identity at the same time.  DW - USA

∞

Emotionally – don't go there! I am constantly depressed and crying! I hate being here! I am very angry for having to leave my country! My girls are very young and this is all they know so far so they are fine! But I do notice that they are outdoors girls and it breaks my heart that they are unable to live outdoors like they would in South Africa!  LS - The Netherlands

∞

We also arrived with suitcases and left everything material behind. It is a struggle. Our marriage has been affected. We were comfortable in South Africa. As you know this place is difficult. It is difficult for us all especially if you always prided yourself on being a positive person. Leaving was an acceptance that South Africa has a difficult future ahead.  AMS - USA

∞

Nothing can prepare you, you have to go and make the most of it, and deal with the homesickness as best as you can. But I guess good advice would be to expect your living standards to drop slightly. You go from being 'well off' middle class citizens, to 'just getting by' middle class in a first world country.

We were always outsiders – even when we had made close friends, we still did not enjoy the history and instant camaraderie that you experience with people from your own country. We struggled financially as well, despite having two good jobs. I think this is because we did not have the family to support us financially, nor did we have a lifetime of building ourselves up in Australia, whilst everyone else our age had, and had already accumulated their own wealth in the form of small houses, cars, clothing, etc.

But I constantly felt like living in Australia for the rest of my life was a prison sentence that I couldn't escape. You recognize that it is a better country – in that it is well run, safe, and a fantastic place for your future children – but at the same time you know that if you stay there permanently, you will always be uniquely alone, and that your children will not have a true extended family to enjoy or even know.   JW - South Africa

∞

Emotionally, it knocked me totally sideways having to leave rural South Africa and being thrown into German city life. The people seemed to attach more value to what material possessions one has, and I could not keep up in any way. After about nine months, I was being treated for depression, with medication and therapy. I am still on that five years later.   JB - Germany

∞

I read 'Third Culture Kids' while we were living in Holland and it made me want to return to South Africa immediately to give my children a cultural identity. My husband and I will always be South African, no matter where in the world we live, but our eldest daughter was born in Denmark, which didn't make her Danish or South African, and our youngest was born in Holland, which didn't make her Dutch or South African. So, we're here for a while soaking up South African culture and hopefully it will be long enough so that one day, no matter where in the world they live, they can always say they are South African.

I have a Dutch friend who so desperately wanted to fit in and integrate into Danish society. She spoke Danish fluently but every time she tried to speak to someone in Danish in a shop they would answer her in English and she would dissolve in tears. I so wished for her that she could just be a Dutch girl living in Denmark. I also have a brother in London who denounces everything South African, speaks with a fake English accent, supports English rugby and has married an English girl. Makes you want to shake him and remind him where he is from....   LP - South Africa

∞ ∞ ∞

# 39

∞

## Passion Lost

*I had one year of joy at the freedom from fear,
then two years of depression when I realised all that I'd lost.
Now, I look back with nostalgia, but know that the place I long
for doesn't exist any more.*
SP - New Zealand

Ignoring the background noise of the boisterous children cavorting in my lounge, I gaze vaguely out of the kitchen window. Our neighbour is cutting his lawn, again, for what will surely be the fifth time this month. How does it feel to grow old, watching the days while away and watching the grass grow? Where does one find the meaning?

The view of our adjoining garden must irk him tremendously. The mass of trees with unkempt greenery wantonly spreading underneath like a threadbare carpet, and the pervasive pansy-weeds. Pansies to me, but weeds to my neighbour – beauty is in the eye of the beholder. Their open purple faces gaze up from the shady spots at the base of the trees. Nature, in all her glorious element, has seized control of my backyard.

My unfocused thinking leads me to memories of my other garden. Memories that are mostly untended these days and left to their own devices because I visit them rarely. The images are too bright and the emotions run too deep. It's simpler to stay away....

*Searing sunlight blinds my vision as I poke and peer into the nooks and crannies. What gifts are there for me today? Popping points of greenery curiously emerge from the sodden soil. The long, wet winter is over. Apricots and plums are still green but plump and lush in velvet splendour. Soon, it will be time for plum jam, apricot jam, lemon syrup and candied figs. Every new day is an adventure in this garden for I never know what surprises are in store.*

*The water spurts strongly from the borehole and the old, gnarled Ficus tree complains that I am tickling his toes. I am used to this complaint. His loving, looming tenderness rules this garden kingdom. The Kasteelberg (Castle Mountain) provides a vibrant quilted backdrop as well as much-needed late afternoon shade and every day, around 4 p.m., could be counted upon to send a swishing, cooling wind down the slopes. This reliable breeze dashes through and cools the house during the stifling, hot summer dusk. Each afternoon we throw open our sash windows and welcome the gusts inside....*

Memories fade....

I fondle the smooth brown fruit, which resembles a small, ancient, cannonball. If it was truly ripe, it would be wrinkled, not smooth. The smooth ones are always sweetly sour. I remember, as a child, yanking one off the vine, feeling its heat against my palm, and bursting it with my teeth. Wallowing in the pleasure of sucking the juicy, slippery pips into my mouth, I would crunch them while their heated sweetness satiated me. That granadilla spent weeks absorbing the sweet warmth of the sun during its maturation time. This granadilla is cold.

> We want to go home!
> ANJ - Australia

"Ew, what is that? Is it a fruit or a vegetable?" Jeannie's response reiterates a fact of which I am often reminded – I remain an exotic import to this land.

"It's a granadilla. Umm, I think you call it a passion fruit." Always translating my life experiences into more understandable language takes a lot of energy.

"What do you do with it? How do you eat it? Are you supposed to eat the skin?" The rowdy children around the dining room table shout questions, an artillery barrage of sound. We're studying fruit and seeds and pips and reproduction as part of our botany course. Each of us was instructed to bring an 'unusual' fruit to discuss and eat. I cut it to show them a first glimpse of the uniquely thrilling innards of a granadilla.

"Gross, it's slimy!" "But there's nothing there, only seeds!" "What's there to eat?"

How do I expand my experience to include these eager children from another culture? "You eat the pips, uh, seeds!"

"Is that all? Gross! I don't want to eat slimy seeds!"

I know I will not be able to convince them to sample the unforgettable sweetness of the fruit or to crunch the pips between their teeth. The evocative feel and taste of a granadilla is unique to my experience of long, hot days under an African sky. Without transplanting these children, I cannot give them the fullness of the experiences I have had.

Carefully, I gather up the precious black, slippery gems and place them into a small plastic bag. These are too full of memories to eat and too expensive to waste. Idly, I wonder if I could grow granadillas from these seeds. Would they survive in this climate? Are they hardy, like me?

"I can't believe you eat that stuff. Weird!" Jeannie's voice has a bemused tone under-laid with humour and caring. Jeannie will always treat me like an exotic, hothouse flower from the tropics. When I am with her, I rather fancy myself to be a hibiscus, a frangipani or an orchid. Our friendship will never be based on shared life experiences but rather on our common values and humanity.

Talking to Jeannie and the children about the array of fruits that populated our lives in South Africa, I realize how blessed I was to grow up in an environment surrounded with such variety. Whether it

> *Do we miss South Africa? Not a single day goes by . . . .*
> NG - New Zealand

was climbing trees to pick loquats, plucking guavas off the tree outside my bedroom window or decimating mulberry trees on our way home from school, and arriving home with stained mouths, our lives were full of a bounteous supply.

Eavesdropping on my conversations, I find myself yearning for a friend who can understand that faraway life in Africa. I wish I could recreate those African childhood experiences and memories for my children.

∞ ∞ ∞

*In the 28 years I have lived in Australia there is not a day that goes by that I do not long for South Africa. However, I have just come back from a holiday there (after not being there for five years) and I have to say, I feel so sad to see what is happening to the most beautiful country in the world. There was not one person I spoke to that had not been affected by crime. Our family lives in different parts of the world. It is awful being separated from the ones you love and the country you love. I pray every day that things will change there so that one day I may go back to the country I long for.*

YW - Australia

∞

*We cannot share our innermost thoughts about the extreme sadness of not being among our own and although we have made friends who speak the same language, their eyes glaze over when we start on about South Africa. We have steeled ourselves not to try and offload our thoughts and wishes onto our new friends. New friends can never take the place of old and trusted friends. For myself, as a mother and grandmother when the longing to see, touch and cuddle the infants get the better of me, I retire to the study and force myself to concentrate on other matters often via the Internet.*

MH - UK

∞

*I'm South African and my husband is not. I met him when he was in South Africa for two years, and he fell in love with the country. We left South Africa with our three children in 2001 and have lived in Europe for seven years. I've just returned from South Africa, I went to spend time with my parents and the rest of my family who are still there. It is very hard leaving such a beautiful place, and after eight days of intense emotions of seeing family, friends, familiar places, and just being there, I sat on that plane returning to London and thought, 'what the hell are we doing in the UK?'*

*I'm completely torn in two. I desperately want to be there, to live there and let my kids grow up in the most amazing country in the world, to be close to my parents, but the question we ask ourselves every single day of our lives is, what must we do? It creates a very unsettling feeling on a day to day basis, because I cannot get myself to completely 'settle' here, with the* thought always lingering in the back of my mind that one day we want to go back. I guess we are in the same boat as so many South Africans living all over the world.

    I want to be positive because back home so many people are. I could live with a lot of things, including poverty, but the senseless violent crimes in South Africa will eventually cripple the country if they do not address the problem now. I thought I'm going crazy because of the chaos in my mind, but it is reassuring to know I'm not alone.

TH - UK

∞

    Sad, very sad! People can't believe I want to go back. I can't believe I want to go back. But I miss my family so much.... How difficult it is. The homesickness was awful the first year and I would not have come if I knew it was that bad.

LS - Ireland

∞

    It is funny, despite having settled and tried so determinedly to fit in, and having made a fairly good life here, I feel more and more African as the years go by. Although it's been 10 years since my last visit to South Africa, I still get tearful and miss those immeasurable things – the smell of the air, the sounds and energy of dawn in South Africa, the craziness and the complicated emotions of pride and guilt that accompany being a South African.

    Someone said that staying in South Africa was as hard as leaving, because the pace of change was such that everything was changing, and they had to constantly adapt. While I am glad we are here, where we can get on with our lives unhindered, I do feel we have paid a price for leaving. There is an underlying longing that never goes away.

SC - Australia

∞

    There are many broken-hearted South Africans and Zimbabweans living here. Like yourself, I know that every single South African friend I have here would head home TOMORROW should the crime be resolved. The issue is not about race, it's about personal safety. We are happy living our daily lives here without fear (which many South Africans have yet to experience!)

but, as you say, we still have a foot on each continent and we will never be completely whole again. When Africa takes a hold, it never lets go.

HL - Australia

∞

I had no idea of the extent of alienation I would feel here (Canada), especially in the first few years. I felt like my soul had been torn from my body – as if I had become empty inside. It has taken a long time to recover from that, and I would never advise anyone to experience it. Some people have described it as a fracture of the soul. I don't think it's an overstatement.

SP - Canada

∞

The first year was very tough, financially and emotionally. The first few months where some of the toughest, being alone with no money, I learnt to work through desperation and impending doom. I knew if I lost my job I would be screwed, but discovered that when I am in a corner I can deliver beyond what I ever thought possible before. All has ended well so far....

AP - UK

∞

Your article touched my heart! It made me cry, it made me mad and it made me smile as I identified so much with what you've had to say! I am sure you get many, many responses from people like myself, who just miss South Africa so much and who know that going back may never be an option again unless one is forced to. Yes, I feel as if I will never be whole again as you state in your article. I have just wondered how you manage to live with such a wound in your heart? Is this the way I will die eventually, missing my country and people so much?

HVG - USA

∞

I am going to miss so many, many things – the beautiful African sunsets, Highveld thunderstorms, wonderful people, wide open spaces, so many things that are purely African, and cannot be gotten anywhere else, but

*I believe that it will be worth the loss to ensure that my children grow up happy, healthy, educated and safe, with the chance to be able to live a life of their own.*
                                                                                CH - South Africa

∞

*I would do everything I could to go back. If I didn't have to worry about my kids, I'd be on the next plane back. The only thing that would stop me would be my children. I couldn't take them with me.*
                                                                                GD - USA

∞

*I think the people are friendly, outgoing and warm in South Africa and I would return in a heartbeat, if I felt that I would be able to make a living there.*
                                                                                FVR - USA

∞

*What do you miss the most about life in South Africa? Family and only family.... The loss of our family heritage and that my children only have limited knowledge of this heritage and culture.*
                                                                                JH - Australia

∞

*For my wife it was tough, and she came close to a nervous breakdown, the only thing that helped was letting her go back to South Africa to visit her sisters, only months after arriving here.*
                                                                                DH - UK

∞

*Homesickness for me was replaced by anger, then acceptance and sadness. The younger you are, the easier you adapt.*
                                                                                AMS - USA

∞

*I still struggle with my doubts. Did we do right thing ..... yes! Your writing makes it a little clearer and helps me to justify our escape. My children have totally integrated, have done very well and are happy, so we*

*have achieved our goal. Will I ever be truly happy in this still alien land ....
no. Your words touched me deeply, you seem to put my thoughts into
words.*

GS - Canada

∞

*My parents and our best friend. Its impossibly hard, as everyone
knows that you might not be coming back, and it's as though someone in the
family is dying. It is completely heartbreaking.*

JW - South Africa

∞

*I have a seemingly subconscious internal remembrance of my life in
South Africa, good and bad, that plays out in my head, in my mind's eye,
almost constantly. It's extremely painful. I probably have post-traumatic-
stress-disorder.*

EN - Arizona

∞

*The most surprising thing still is that even though we live a much
better life now than what we had in South Africa, I still long to go home,
smell the dust, see the "donder-wolke" rolling in from the Jo'burg area and
everything that is Africa.*

PVDR - Australia

∞ ∞ ∞

## 40

∞

## An Imported Product

*I have come to the conclusion that once Africa
gets in your blood it never leaves.*
PM - UK

**I**nitially the most difficult times of all for me were those spent buying produce (I would call these fruit and vegetables) – a fairly innocuous task. Since leaving South Africa, it has become an exercise fraught with emotion. I was unprepared for the headiness of the grief I experienced for the first time, in a grocery store. This was the most unexpected experience in the most impersonal place. On finding a box of clementines labelled 'Outspan – Product of South Africa' and a Clanwilliam address, I remembered the vacuous boredom I had felt, while driving the road to Clanwilliam and passing miles of citrus groves to my left and right – the heavy, heady slightly spicy citrus scent blending with every ounce of oxygen breathed. I stood transfixed wondering if, on one of my visits, I had passed the very grove that gave birth to this fruit. I would hold the clementine in my hand and gaze at it as if by holding it, I could somehow imbibe those days and recreate them for myself – transport myself back home again.

I wanted to buy them, but not to be eaten or used, just to have something real and alive from Africa – some part of myself which I had left behind. While holding one, feeling its cool skin, I tried to absorb the intensity of the energy – knowing that this fruit, too, had travelled a long distance to end up in this place. And watching people around me, going through their daily motions of shopping, wondering if I should tell them, "Do you know where I come from? Do you eat this fruit? Do you know we've both come so far, and neither of us know why? Do we feel similar to you? Can you believe that we were both birthed in the hot intensity and soil of Africa? Do you care?"

The sudden, suffocating bouts of emotion caught my breath in my throat and tears threatened to overwhelm me. What would you think if you saw me crying hot, silent tears over the clementines? Would you notice? Would you call security? Those moments of divine madness were few and far between. I shut down and didn't allow myself to feel them.

> There are so many broken-hearted South Africans and Zimbabweans living here.
> HL - Australia

The apricots almost did me in, though. Reserved for the area allocated to the expensive, exotic fruits, they sat alongside passion fruit (granadillas); I held the ripe apricots gently in my hand and appreciated their warmth of colour, their slight fuzziness, their happiness and I remember – I remember those apricot trees in my garden and how few we could actually eat, it seemed the worms took most of them.[22] Occasionally, on a truly lucky day, we would pick one that was ripe, warm, sweet and untouched and eat it. The flesh soft as a baby's skin would melt as a warm virginal sweetness in our mouths, and we would appreciate having the apricot trees. Anyway, the birds loved them and at dusk, the fruit bats loved them too. Their tiny wings flapped furiously as they swooped and sped through our garden, squeaking wildly.

That was enough. Holding an apricot, in a grocery store in the USA, in my hand, I would remind myself of where I was, I would remind myself not to cry – it was, after all, only a piece of fruit – and it was not necessarily grown in Africa. I fondled the coldness and remembered lengthy, heated days and the warmth of the same fruit as I picked them in my garden. I cupped their smooth velvety exteriors and thought about buying them. I, too, was imported – we shared a common bond – and I held them hoping somehow to transport through space and backwards in time. Would I change my decision? I still didn't know!

Lemons are expensive here, and they are all the thin skinned variety,

---

[22] Soon after moving to Riebeek Kasteel, the local municipal representative informed us, the city slickers, that the best time to eat apricots directly from the tree was at night, because you can't see the worms in the dark.

not the thick pithy skins of home. Again, I would remember the lemon trees that produced such prodigious bounty that I would beg friends and family to fill a grocery bag to take with them. This was after I had produced lemon marmalade, lemon syrup and candied lemon peels. My kitchen shelves were always laden with jar upon jar of homemade preserves.

I don't see many figs – I suspect they do not transport well and do not last long enough to make a profit for the stores. I recall the deep, burgundy, sensual inside of the red 'Adams vy' (Adam's fig) that made rich fig jam – with the unique fig flavour which cannot be imitated by any other fruit. And then there were the plain, hard green figs with their white interiors. They were the poor cousin, they took longer to ripen and never had the same lushness as the red figs. Our garden was blessed with both varieties. Many days, in my impatience, I settled for picking the plain hard green figs and boiling them in sugar syrup, waiting for the moment when they would turn into evanescent candy. My hands became raw from exposure to the irritating fig juices as I scrubbed the figs to roughen their exterior, then slashed a small cross across their swollen posteriors to allow the thick sugar syrup to penetrate their core.

> *I am sitting here crying and knowing, truly knowing, that we are all so dislocated from the home that we have loved and left... It is the precious figs – when I can find them – that do me in! And no one can understand if they haven't left another life behind too. Just going back this last month has left me gasping again, for those vineyards, even just the sun. It's different there!*
>
> DM - Australia

I don't buy plums here... will plums ever taste the same to me again? Plums with a rich dessert flavour as though they have been brewed on the tree. Making thick plum jam was a pleasure although we had only one tree and gleaned a few jars each year. And, if I was lucky, there would be some for my lunch preparations. As my baked onions (wrapped in foil) were nearly finished cooking, I would baste them with plum jam (the rich sweetness oozing into the much tamer sweetness of the onion).

The granadillas (passion fruit, I suppose) always seem like hard and shrivelled musket balls, the same rusty brown-grey colour, very unassuming to look at. Who could ever believe that inside they hold the nectar of the gods. On hot summer days sitting in the shade of the lemon trees, we would pick a granadilla – unpretentious passion fruit – and use a stick to force an opening in the tough, shrivelled leathery skin (they were only ready to eat when they were seriously shrivelled) and squeezing the fruit, suck out the magnificent sweet, sometimes a little sour – scrunching up your eyes sour – hot juice with hundreds of small, crunchy black seeds – a teaspoon or two that generated the heady happiness of summertime. I no longer buy granadillas, they are too expensive and, having lost something in translation, they do not encapsulate the energy and pleasures of a life in Africa any more.

Plants don't grow easily in my rented garden here, the winters are too cold and the summers too humid. This ground is clay. I remember my mother-in-law sighing over the glorious, peaty earth in Riebeek Kasteel. I find it difficult to compromise; I want to recreate the garden of Riebeek Kasteel – fruit trees and vegetables, and perhaps a little mountain for good measure.

What have I become? A sporadic gardener on someone else's land.

∞ ∞ ∞

*We are having a tough week, very homesick. We had a family discussion last night and decided that we would consider returning to South Africa. Our hearts feel so empty, here.*   AMS - USA

∞

*'South African' is too deeply rooted in my identity for me to abandon and ignore without discomfort.*   PB - South Africa

∞

*We left South Africa 30 years ago with two children at the tender ages of five and seven. We are still South African citizens, and remain torn after all these years. I read the South African newspapers daily to stay informed. My heart belongs to South Africa and I live for the day we return.*   ADP - USA

∞

*Most unexpected thing was dealing with the unfamiliarity of the most simple items. Even yoghurt looks different. When my wife and I returned to South Africa for a brief visit we went to a grocery store (just a normal Pick*

and Pay) and when we were surrounded by familiar products we almost burst out crying.

EL - Ireland

∞

We left South Africa in 1999, definitely the most difficult thing we have ever done. I read your article today and I cried my eyes out, I never knew how much pain I was still carrying with me, I too will always be split in two.

CP - USA

∞

I wish I had never moved as it was too late for my children to make a change – but we have made the best of our mistake and our four children are making the best of all opportunities here. I too will go back tomorrow with my four children if they sort out the crime – as if the crime goes – in will flow the investments, which will mean our white children will be able to find jobs and create a future for themselves in South Africa. Until that happens – I battle as a wife and mother with the hard UK life and miss my country, family and friends desperately. I'm sure I'm not alone.

TS - UK

∞

I also left 'The Land of Green and Gold' just over six years ago in search of a better existence, quite strange really because I've returned to settled in the land of my forefathers (Bonnie Scotland) and must be going through the same emotional transitions as they went through all those years ago when they settled in South Africa, torn between the emotional state of belonging and the yearning of their Motherland, to quote yourself being 'a cultural alien'. I've had the good fortune of travelling the world and it's amazing the comradery and connection that exists between us South Africans.

JHM - Scotland

∞

We're South Africans who have returned to Cape Town after spending some four years in Denmark and Holland. We're career expats so neither our moves abroad, nor our return back home has had anything to do with the

South African situation, but more with my husband's career and our financial future. And our future moves will likely be determined by the same factors.

We hear of a lot of people leaving South Africa now to 'secure a future for their children'. Who knows, perhaps those that stay are ignorant or don't have your level of self-preservation. On the other hand, I think of all those poor people who fled this country 20 years ago and have ended up miserable, homesick and, perhaps even worse, unable to return for whatever reason, while we have largely continued to live well here, albeit with all the security and safety compromises we must make. How they have missed out on 'being home'!

LP - South Africa

∞

We emigrated from the UK in 1976 and returned in 2000. My wife has settled back here, feeling safer, but I fear that I never will, I have come to the conclusion that once Africa gets in your blood it never leaves. After experiencing the UK for five years I feel that there is a simplicity of life in South Africa that you can never find anywhere else, I don't know how to explain it, it's just a feeling that I have. I don't think that you can really appreciate anything until you have lost it and what I know now I would never have left South Africa.

I was highjacked in 1977 before it became fashionable but fortunately it was knives then and not guns. My wife was held up in early 90's at gunpoint. I know that has had a lasting effect neither of us was injured and I know very lucky as many of our friends didn't get off so lightly.

I miss the times when as a pipeline inspector I worked in the bush miles from anywhere and seeing the incredible sunsets when travelling home, listening to the sounds of the night out in the bush when staying over, these memories I will carry forever and hopefully if I can make enough money here I will be able to spend summer in UK and winter in South Africa then life would be really great.

Have just been looking at some old videos of braai's past and friends of old and it stirs up so many emotions that I can't do it too often, the days when we had big house, two cars, swimming pool, boat, huge garden, I feel that I had so much to be grateful for but wasn't at the time.

Have often thought that I would like to go back and do some sort of aid work and give back a little of what the country gave to me, but at moment I am tied in the UK with financial commitments, hopefully this will change shortly and I can fulfil my dreams.

Once again loved to read your view on South Africa. Thanks a lot.

PM - UK

∞

It gets better, the feeling of being a 'displaced person' eventually passes, and one becomes one with the new community. I am happy now. I have embraced our new life, I have learned to smile when the Americans don't understand our accent immediately. I have gotten bold enough to tell a few of them that everyone in America has an accent, and many of them have smiled with me about that. Life is good, it is as good as we allow it to be. I wish for you and your family happiness, and a sense of belonging. It takes time, but it will happen.

MW - USA

∞

My wife has been here two years, and is only just starting to settle in.

AS - USA

∞ ∞ ∞

# 41

∞

# The Immigrant

by Heather Claire Scott

A stranger in this huge New World of States
These seven years.
My childhood was not theirs, these people hurrying by,
My teens were lived in another country
I have no peers.

I should assimilate - I know I must,
They laugh and share their memories of days and years ago
Should I tell them of mine? Would they want to know
Of days spent in sunshine, blue skies, no snow
A sub-tropical paradise, flies and dust
Will they listen? Can I trust?
I don't think so.

So I hurry on too, to catch the train
In streets dirty and grey, dripping with rain
We sit together, these people and me.
A mutual youth so hard to find.
But I live in my own skin
Closed, and within
The world I remember, and left behind.

Copyright © 2007 Heather Claire Scott - Used with permission

# 42

∞

# The Missing Mountains

*Each country has its beauty
but one cannot live in two countries.*
PD - Belgium

**D**o you know what you're doing? Aren't you going to miss everyone? This will tear your family apart? What about your mom? Won't you miss her? What about the dogs? The questions wore me down until I figured out my constant refrain about this being our 'Most Grand Adventure'. As most people can't relate to the instability of tossing everything to the wind (fear included) and going on an unplanned journey, those words tended to stop the conversation and questions. They smiled wryly, their expressions clearly saying how naïve, deluded and silly I was to be doing such a crazy thing.

No-one ever asked me whether I would miss the scenery or the mountains hence I didn't realize how integral they were to my existence. As a child, growing up in Cape Town, I took the mountains for granted. They were always there! There was tea at Kirstenbosch Gardens on a Sunday and then climbing through the shade of Skeleton Gorge. And slowly, scaling the mountain until we found a grassy field, a running stream to sit beside and drink the cool, clear, cold water. My father produced apples and chocolate bars – huh! This was impromptu event so where did those come from?

In Cape Town, everywhere you go, the mountains form a backbone and a compass and of course the enormous existential presence of Table Mountain is central to everything in the city. Standing guard over Cape Town, Table Mountain is a spectacular nature reserve surrounded by a city. The mountain is designated as one of the world's Floral Kingdoms. The smell of fynbos envelopes you as you walk in or on the mountains around the Cape. This is a full-bodied mixed spice, with hints of sweetness, and the density of marinated cloves. It is indescribable and is a scent that is never forgotten.

I may not have known which road to take, but I always knew where I was, thanks to the mountains. Over years they became an unobtrusive background scenery to my life, and were ignored. Living in the Southern Suburbs as a child – Kirstenbosch Botanical Gardens for tea, Newlands Forest for walks, Constantia Nek for braais and hikes – all our social events were defined by the mountain.

There were also the mountains around Hout Bay and Fish Hoek and frequent visits to friends in Clovelly. Their house was halfway up the mountain and had a glorious view across Fish Hoek and the beach. Once, while visiting them, I remember a fire on the mountain. As good old South Africans were wont to do, men were outside at the braai and the women in the house. Firefighters and Mountain Club volunteers were slowly bringing the blaze under control. A short while later the men came in proudly to tell us that after they had each peed on the fire and the problem had been resolved.

Weekend drives over Constantia Nek, towards Hout Bay, and onward to Fish Hoek meant that there might be the fun of stopping for a troop of baboons. They would climb onto the car, bat on the windscreen, make faces, push each other around and provide endless amusement. I'd pray that they would be on the mountain whenever we'd go for a Sunday drive, a drive which would culminate with a Flake 99 soft serve ice cream in Diep River.

Living on the slopes of the mountain in Sea Point, James would awaken at 5 a.m. and go for an early morning hike. Living on the slopes of the Kasteelberg in Riebeek Kasteel, we had a pet mountain in our backyard – ready for attention whenever we wanted to bestow it. We would climb it on Sunday mornings and stop to admire the vista spread beneath us. I would walk the dogs on the slope of the Kasteelberg. Opening my front door in Riebeek Kasteel, I'd gaze across the wheatfields to the distant ranges beyond stretching towards Ceres.

When we left, I didn't give a moment's thought to their presence or to the lack thereof. They were just there – unprepossessing giants that were simply a backdrop to my life. In Cape Town, I didn't need a compass; the mountains always provided my bearings. I never developed a sense of direction because I didn't need it.

In Virginia I've been lost metaphorically, and literally, more often than not. When a highway sign says South or East, I don't know if I live West or North. Mostly, it's a potluck guess and I hope to take the correct exit. I've learned to master the art of the U-turn. Someone said 'just look at the position of the sun in the sky and orientate yourself like that'.

> We have been here for almost two years in the USA. I certainly am nowhere near settling in here.
>
> HVG - USA

Hmmm. Yes, the sun is in the sky, exactly where it should be – apart from that, I have no further comprehension. For the first three years of living in the USA, I took the long way round to get everywhere. Once, caught between a web of one way roads, from which I couldn't seem to extricate myself, I phoned a friend and asked her to help me get out of the city. She laughed but I was serious.

I avoided the highways and would find every other route (Americans say *r-ow-t*) to take that was not a highway. A drive of 20 minutes by highway would take me 1,5 hours. It was amusing to James but educational for me. I proudly state that I know more shortcuts around our city than he does. And for the first six years, I avoided the toll highways because I didn't know how the toll booths worked.

I'm pleased to say that I have now developed a sort of sense of direction – Washington DC is north of us, North Carolina is south. If I go east, I'm driving towards the city and thereafter to the Atlantic Ocean. If I go west, I'm liable to eventually end up in West Virginia or somewhere that way – Shenandoah Mountains maybe. We live in the West End, there's an East End on the other side of the city and Southside across the river. Slowly, slowly I've sorted it out in my head though much of the learning has taken place from necessity (a desire to frequent yard sales or pick up items from Freecyclers). Homeschooling also meant a great deal of driving and I slowly learned to find my way to activities and friends all over the state.

Jennifer is now available to help me. My cellphone has a GPS function who is named Jennifer and we play very nicely together. I look up the route on Google Maps and get an idea of my general direction. I give the address to Jennifer and see if her directions tally with my ideas. As I'm driving, if I feel she's taking me the 'long way round', I change according to what I think or know. Vaguely I hear her sigh 'recalculating route...'.

The analogy is not lost on me. In South Africa I had a true sense of direction and everything in my life was in its place. Here, I was (am) directionless, and have no compass and no sense of self in relation to my environment. I had to grow past a childlike fear of my unknown surroundings and venture out into the wider world. It's taken me years to rebuild a semblance of that confidence.

> *Most surprising thing about relocating? How depressed I have been – I thought I am very adaptive person and quite easy going – NOT!*
> LS - The Netherlands

Recently, I climbed to the summit of the Humpback Rocks in the Blue Ridge Mountains, and as I sat at the top, I looked across the Shenandoah Valley and realized how much I miss my mountains....

∞ ∞ ∞

*Emotionally, a never ending story. Some days are good and some days you ask why you ever left South Africa. I am looking for the beauty of Cape Town in my life, all the time. I find it in summer sometimes, and certainly in the garden when the flowers come out. I have a past, which was a beautiful period of South African history, spent as a child living in Newlands, Cape Town, as my ideal of life, which no longer exists in the New South Africa. I know if I visited my childhood neighbourhood, I would be shocked at the huge walls and security all the neighbours have put up?!*
KB - Germany

∞

*In Geneva in the early 1990's there were not many black people to be seen on the streets and I will never forget seeing my first black face there: I wanted to rush over and greet the lady like a long lost friend!* AM - Austria

∞

*I so wish someone had told me that I would miss my home so much, that I would be in a state of mild depression for a number of years. Although English is the spoken language here, and the weather is the same, there are so*

many subtle differences that one has to navigate a new life very carefully. This was surprising as I always imagined it would be just like South Africa....

DM - Australia

∞

    Yes, we miss South Africa. But we have come to realize that the South Africa that we talk about with each other so often just does not exist any more. That does not prevent us, however, from looking back with nostalgia to the land of our birth. We will always miss the easy relationships with friends and family there. We still wish for braais under the trees of a large garden at Christmastime. We speak to each other often about how one could just 'drop in' at a friend's home on a Sunday afternoon, and be assured of a welcome and scones for tea. We look at photo albums showing faces of dear friends whom we will probably never see again, and we ache.

    The country is still there – Table Mountain still towers over the Mother City, and the harbour opens its arms to sailors from other lands. The Drakensberg is just as magnificent as it ever was, and always will be. Governments and criminals cannot change the unique beauty of South Africa. The hot, red soil of the Highveld will not change, even though the feet that tread there now are no longer ours. The 'vlaktes' of the Free State no doubt still put travellers to sleep with boredom as they drive through it, and those who live there probably still pretend that the climate is the healthiest in the country.

    But we do not live there any more, and less and less of the people we knew when we lived there, are there now. They are in Australia, New Zealand, England, and even spread throughout our new homeland, America.

HS - USA

∞ ∞ ∞

# 43

∞

## Gatvol is not American English

*I don't think that you can really appreciate anything until you have lost it and what I know now I would never have left South Africa.*
PM - UK

Ek is gatvol, gatvol, gatvol!

There! I've said it. Not as often as I'd like to have said it. There have been many occasions when I have longed to tell someone, "I am GATVOL" but I can't. I'm a stranger in a strange land and they don't speak my higgledy-piggledy mix of English and Afrikaans. Sometimes the longing surfaces and I feel compelled to tell someone that I am 'gatvol' and then I am compelled to try and explain and translate the term to them. Unfortunately, direct translation ('hole full') sounds rather risqué and rude (in a nudge-nudge, wink-wink sort of way). The closest explanation has been to say 'full up'. I am 'full up'. Oh, you understand, it doesn't sound the same, the intensity is not conveyed properly, not in the same way as,

"Ek is die moer in en ek is gatvol met hierdie plek!" Even if you say that with a smile on your face, another South African will understand the depth of the exclamation.

I miss Afrikaans. I often listen to our Afrikaans CDs. Ek verlang so na die taal en wil graag net luister na mense wat Afrikaans praat. I miss David Kramer en Anton Goosen en Laurika Rauch en Koos Kombuis en Johannes Kerkorrel en Pieter Dirk-Uys en Leon Schuster ens.

An unexpected culture shock is not hearing familiar languages any more and not being able to mix languages any longer. I had become accustomed to speaking a mix of Afrikaans and English to everyone. I grew up with English, Afrikaans, Xhosa, German and sometimes Yiddish terms thrown into sentences. I miss hearing Afrikaans in daily life – thick 'brei' of the Swartlanders and the uniquely expressive Afrikaans of the Cape Coloureds.

> How people are so expressive. We express ourselves, and it is magic.
> JW - Japan

I miss my time spent at home with Anna, my maid and helper. She was an extremely grounded, kind, caring person who filled my days with pleasure and interesting conversation. I enjoyed being with her. We would sit together on the back verandah and peel vegetables from the garden, for my preserves.

"Anna, los die werk! Kom. Kom ons gaan sit op die stoep en die groente skoonmaak."

"Nee, Bronwyn, Meneer het gevra dat ek die wasgoed vandag klaarmaak."

"Ag, los die wasgoed, Anna, ek sal met Meneer praat en sê dis my skuld. Kom ons gaan sit op die stoep, die son skyn en dis lekker buite. Maak vir jouself koffie, bring die beskuit, en kom rus n bietjie."

We would sit outside and discuss men, children, life, family and being a woman, we'd watch the children, drink our coffee and 'skinner' about people in the village. Anna was a wonderful filter for those who came knocking at the door, ostensibly seeking food or money but with a long story to accompany the plea. She would often draw me aside, provide insight to the real hardship or the real story and, through that, allow me to choose how to further deal with the situation.

> I miss getting into an elevator and greeted by all, especially the Africans. And Mellita, my maid. I dream about her.
> LBM - USA

My Afrikaans was maar 'altyd swak'. My husband said I spoke a colloquial form of kitchen Afrikaans, much like a Cape Coloured, because I learned my Afrikaans from the staff. I loved to speak it because it is musical and expressive language and there are some untranslatable words which I still use – seven years later. Hey Anna, maybe one day we can drink coffee on a stoep again.

Sometimes, during homesick days, I trawl YouTube for videos of South African comedians, humour and songs. And that is how I found

Wayne McKay.[23] This is one of those truly South African stories. The South African clip I've watched the most on YouTube has to be the one of Wayne's stand-up comedy routine at a Vodacom event in Cape Town.

Can you imagine, in the USA, approaching a public figure – finding his number in the phone book – and having a long, 'gesellige' chat (another 'lekker' Afrikaans word that is just too untranslatable) and inviting him over for coffee? I don't think so. This is exactly what my mother did, being the enterprising South African soul that she is. During her visit at Christmas 2008, I showed her the YouTube video. Both of us, me again for the umpteenth time, howled at Wayne's perfect imitation of the contrast between white South African and Coloured South Africans, when placed in similar situations. I asked her to find out if he had a DVD available in South Africa. She went home, could not find anything in the stores, duly found the only W McKay in the Cape Town phone directory and called the number. A long chat later and he offered to visit her for coffee and bring an autographed DVD for me.

> We did not have a common background with our close Australian friends, and could never relate to their jokes, reminiscing or tales from childhood.
> JW - South Africa

They say that South Africa has some of the friendliest people in the world. I'd have to agree. This was a convoluted long distance connection, yet still a connection, and I now watch my very own Wayne McKay DVD whenever I like.

Hey Wayne, maybe I can have coffee with you in person one day.

∞ ∞ ∞

*Ja, ek is 'n boer en mis maar die ou moedertaal.... It's been quite an experience going from speaking Afrikaans for 22 years to speaking English 24/7 - and they don't understand me! I'm sure you've had that too, but being English you wouldn't have such a heavy accent as I do. Some days I wonder if we even speak the same language! SO many words they don't know, hey? You know what I'm talking about, I don't have to give examples! But I've learned what words to use (and sometimes how to pronounce them, which I hate doing) so they understand me the FIRST time around. I'm crazy*

---

[23] Here is Wayne's website address: waynemckay.co.za

about Afrikaans music and my friends back home send me the latest Laurika Rauch or Koos Kombuis. It's food for my soul.

IB - USA

∞

    I laughed as I read about your maid, nanny, gardener and days in South Africa! How familiar that all sounds. My precious Jane was my 'mother', maid, nanny and mentor and comforter on many days. Tempelton my gardener and I would discuss the politics of the day with real depth and he would berate me for not getting the compost and plants there in time for him to plant, so he would just bring some himself the next day. Yes, Bronwyn, those precious people I could never replace . . . not here anyway!

HVG - USA

∞

    I wish I had known what the culture in my chosen country would be like. I had no idea of the extent of alienation I would feel here (Canada), especially in the first few years. I felt like my soul had been torn from my body – as if I had become empty inside. It has taken a long time to recover from that, and I would never advise anyone to experience it. Some people have described it as a fracture of the soul. I don't think its an overstatement.

SP - Canada

∞

    Another issue that I encountered when trying to meet people and make friends was that, when I told them I was from South Africa, they immediately thought one of two things: That since I'm white, I'm racist, or that I'm not really South African... I must be from somewhere else. A lot of people seem to find it hard to accept that I am a white South African, saying "But where are you from originally?" I had never had my identity, my heritage challenged like this and I felt like I was being denied part of who I am. I would generally reply:
    "Well, where are you from?"
    "America," they would say.
    "Are you native American?" I would ask.
    "No..."

> "Then you're not really American, are you?"
> "I am!"
> "You're right....and that's how South African I am"
>
> OM - Colorado

∞

> Expect to feel completely empty inside. That it's normal to be so homesick that seeing a plane flying across the skies will send a pang through your chest and a yearning to be on that plane flying back home. That no matter how long you're away South Africa will always be home.
>
> CL - UK

∞

> After having lived in Australia for 18 years, I was planning my first trip back 'home' and an associate introduced me as "She's a South African, but don't hold that against her!" I was mortified as I felt that I had assimilated into Australian society and didn't like being labelled as different. A few weeks later when I was in South Africa, I was introduced as "My Australian cousin." These two experiences made me realize that no one wanted me. I was not a South African or an Australian.
>
> JH - Australia

∞

> Family and I came to New Zealand 14 years ago and I still feel as though I have one foot in South Africa. And I still wonder if I made the right move!
>
> DD - New Zealand

∞

> I have been living abroad for eight months now, this is the longest I have been out of South Africa my whole 29 year life. I am aware of two things, firstly, I am struck by the peace of mind that one can experience in other countries and am worried that I have become too complacent and if I will be able to adjust to the culture of fear that is part and parcel of the Johannesburg lifestyle. Secondly, I do however miss South Africa – being a resident there my whole life – 29 years. It is the only world I really know, albeit a fragmented mishmash of Western, Colonial and South African

*cultures. The difficulty in trying to adjust to a new culture makes me long for the familiarity of home even with all its problems so yes I can say that I am indeed torn.*

SK - Japan

∞

*I'm contemplating a move back home as I miss my family and friends who will always understand me and I can understand them.*

RG - Australia

∞

*What can I say? Your words are my words. I too have left my home, my family and my roots. I have two young daughters and wanted to give them a better life. So here we are four years later in the UK. I struggle here, I can't put down roots, I want space, I want the bush. But, I do sleep at night, I don't worry when we are at the park, I don't feel anxious in the car, I forget to pack the bikes away and they are still there the next day. Imagine that. If only things would get better, if only I could go home....*

NM - UK

∞

*It has been a very difficult move. We are not the same people. We are aliens in this place. We cannot even understand the English they speak and vice versa. We still think about going home all the time. My son, just turned 18, is going to South Africa for a holiday this summer – it is one of the only things that keeps him motivated.*

AMS - USA

∞

*To come back to your article. All three of us feel as if we live with one foot in Germany and one foot in South Africa. We are cultural chameleons who decorate our homes with bits of South African flare and bright colours to make us feel at home. We speak English to each other and German to everyone else. We sadly watch the developments in South Africa and wonder what if we had stayed, and hate hearing everybody say how lucky we were to have gotten away!*

*So yes, we made the right decision to leave, but at heart we will always be South Africans. After 13 years in Germany, we have made it, but I still find myself reading the Pretoria News from time to time via the Internet... as homesickness is always tucked away at the back of our hearts!*

KB - Germany

∞

*Feel like I am in a zoo when I travel around the USA. 'You can't be from Africa – you are not Black!' The States is a big place, with lots of different ethnic groups, so it is quite easy to blend in. Just wish they would learn to braai (with charcoal). The USA has no real class discrimination in the workforce. By that, I mean that whatever job you do, be it sanitation engineer, construction worker, waiter, sweeper or doctor – everyone is regarded as doing an equally important job.*

CS - Thailand

∞

*Ek kan maar net sê dat daar so baie van ons is wat so voel, ek is steeds in 'n proses van aanvaarding na drie jaar in Australië en sukkel om te glo dat ek my erfenis in kultuur, taal, en alles wat daarmee gepaard gaan werklik moet afsterf, net omdat ek sonder 'n konstante bedreiging wil lewe.*

RO - Australia

∞

*I'm listening to Highveld Stereo through the Internet and wish I could be home tonight!*

IB - USA

∞ ∞ ∞

# Part 7

∞

# Lasting

*Everyday we are faced with the decision
to re-affirm ourselves to South Africa.
Some days are easy and some are difficult.*

*And I really think that it is the same for you too,
no matter where you are.*

TW - South Africa

# 44

∞

# Beyond Torn

### Introduction by James McIntosh

**O**nce upon a time I was charged by a lioness. That episode, like so many 'happenings' in my South African life, had sunk under the weight of new memories added helter-skelter to reduce the dull ache of 'torn-ness'. I call it creating 'ancestral amnesia'. However, in trying to make my way financially in America, I had to find that part of me which made me stand out enough to be noticed. I needed to remember what made me *different* so that I could *fit in* more easily, if you understand what I mean.

What made me different, really different, not just I'm-from-Africa-different? The fact that I was charged by a lioness and lived to tell the tale. When something typically ridiculous happens here in the USA people often say 'Only in America!' Well, being charged by a lioness, I realised, was an 'Only in Africa!' event. And so I learned to tell the tale of the lioness, of how she scared me into seeking meaning in my life. In my story I explain that the first thing we did after getting away from her was to re-tie our bootlaces, because we had almost jumped out of our shoes with fright. I remind my listeners that life has a habit of doing that to you. It is a way of getting your attention, a way of waking you up, a way of bringing you back to what has meaning (for you).

In many ways, living in South Africa is a daily getting-your-attention, a constant waking-you-up, an ongoing back-to-meaning experience. On so many levels it is a fantastic way to experience 'life'. But do you know what? Even though the lioness never actually caught up with me, I got tired of having to tie my shoelaces so often.

Once upon a time I had to run with elephants. Yes, another true African adventure story, but with a different message. We had stumbled into the herd probably because we were so relieved at having escaped the lioness that we let our guard down. South Africa today is not the sort of place to let your guard down. Nor is Africa. History has taught us that much.

History's purpose is to get you where you are now, but depending on how you see it, history can hold you where you were. Legend has it that elephant trainers don't bother to tether their adult elephants to large stakes; they know that small stakes will do just as well. As babies, these elephants grow up being tied to strong stakes from which they cannot pull free; as adults they have stopped trying, for they still feel the 'weight' of their baby stakes. It is not the stake that secures the powerful animal, but the power of its memory. The elephant does not realize this, and so remains trapped by the nonsense in its head.

Seasoned travellers know that travelling light makes border crossings easier. The same trick applies if you want to get from torn to not-torn easily – carry less history. Some travellers weigh their suitcases and pack accordingly. Again, the same trick applies to getting to beyond torn. Weigh your history to know what to put down and what to carry. A diver with a weight-belt struggles to walk on dry land, because the lead of the weight-belt serves no purpose. Undoubtedly, the weight of your history once served a purpose and helped you to reach your current state. Can you now feel where the lead weight has become dead weight?

In basic psychological terms, you are an accumulation of your stakes and tethers. You carry with you all that you once were: your experiences, education, memories, hurts, joys, hopes, and so on. You also carry perceptions of who you are: what you think you should be, what you think others expect of you, what you think dependants need from you, and so on. The greater their influence, the heavier your history, the bigger your stake. Only once you realize that you have the power to pull out the stakes are you free to choose to stay or to leave. To be torn or not.

Let me now remind you of what I wrote in my introduction to this book. Being-against or being-for holds the clue to being-torn or being not-torn. We are torn when we *leave* something; we are less torn when we *go to* something, willingly. Ask yourself, did you *leave* or did you *go to*? Think carefully, because it holds the key to crossing from torn to not-torn. Knowing what you are against makes you want to leave; knowing what you are for makes it easier for you to settle down, wherever your leaving has taken you.

As you approach the end of this book, my wish for you is that you will find your way to loving where you are now (whichever place or country) as you stop longing for what you left behind (whichever place or era). The one is present; the other is past. And the future? It exists only as a promise in your state of mind. May this book help you to never confuse the three.

And if ever you are confused about who you are where you are, hold onto this thought. What made me different enough to stand out is what, finally, made me fit in. Or, if you will, what initially made me feel torn is what made me whole again.

∞ ∞ ∞

## 45

∞

## Attitude is Everything

*We have our brains; we have willpower; we have a solid work ethic.*
*With those three things, anything is possible.*
AH - USA

Some people start their writing careers with the sole focus being the satisfaction of their creative energies. Others begin with the ulterior motive of financial benefit. Me? It's a little simpler than that. I need to make sure my kids can afford their school lunch payments. Desperate times call for desperate measures. I opened my purse this morning to realize that it was either paying for school lunches or paying for household groceries for the week – either way, my kids would be missing some meals.

Since I function best under stress and I don't have time today to forage for roots, shoots and berries; I figured that I'd better use whatever skills I do have in order to cover those missing meals. I don't think anyone appreciates the extent of their survival skills until they are in a similar position.

During the past eight years, I've kept food on the table in a variety of ways – sewing furnishings and doing alterations (a soul-destroying activity), upholstery (a self-taught skill from library books), painting wall murals, sales of various items – books, clothing, jewellery, CDs and such – on eBay and, I ran my highly successful Amazon book selling business with books obtained at no cost. I've marketed and cold-called for a catering business, taught yoga classes, done data entry, office management for an insurance brokerage, sold discount health plans, written a few articles, and along these diverse paths, taught myself to create web sites and do online marketing. As a bonus, I realized what a multi-dimensional, enthralling, dynamic and self-reliant person I am.

Our life here has been forged with blood, sweat and tears. There was blood on my fingers as I worked until 3a.m. to finish an upholstery job, or sewing alterations, in order to generate income for our weekly groceries. There was sweat, that poured off me, after driving in an old Mazda, without air conditioning, when the temperature was 100°F, and humid. There were the tears of desperation, desolation and depression and the overwhelming weariness of drawing effort out of myself when there was no energy left inside.

> I sometimes feel I'm prepared to wash the streets with a toothbrush, if only some country would give me permanent residence.
> MC - South Africa

During the worst times, I was looking for house cleaning jobs to do. I was willing to work as a gardener and to clean people's toilets and bathrooms. I was willing to do anything to keep a roof over our heads and food in our stomachs

I found that the strangest things sustained me, words remembered and resonating inside me – long ago motivational cassette tapes played by my father during a 20 minute drive to school each morning. At the time, I hated them, I resented him trying to brainwash me, and I set myself against their messages. Despite the rebellious reactions, the phrases must have permeated my being at a cerebral level. Those same words and messages rose up from the depths of my despair in our first years here, and supported me, giving me security in the knowledge that I could make whatever I wanted, I could be whatever I wanted, and I could have whatever I wanted as long as I believed in the power of myself and my attitude.

My life, so external in Africa, became so internal in America. In the USA I had to turn my focus inwards to who I really was, what I really wanted and what I really believed. I had to find my intrinsic value and make that my foundation. I didn't do that for myself, I did that because I wanted a different future for my children. I couldn't bring them here and then bemoan the fact that I was unable to recreate my life as it had been. I brought them here for a different life, I just hadn't qualified what 'different' would mean but the onus was on me to make it the best kind of 'different' that I could.

If a different life meant that I had to work as a maid, a municipal worker, or a gardener, in order to keep us clothed, fed and a roof over our heads, then that is what I would do – living here sorted my priorities. I no longer have aspirations of grandeur beside food on the table, a reasonable car and a house in a safe neighbourhood. Leaving South Africa and learning to survive in another country and culture, exposed my inherent snobbery and forced me to get back to grassroots and to what was really important in my life.

The most unexpected benefit of this process was finding my self-reliance. I've only scratched the surface of my skills. There are so many more things I'd be willing to do – gardening, housekeeping, waitressing, retail, selling my own artworks (yes, I'm not yet an acclaimed artist, but that's a minor point – after all, I can be... anything I want to be). Losing a job isn't the worst thing that can happen, nor is losing my house or my possessions. Losing my self-respect and my self-confidence would be the direst of circumstances. That hasn't happened yet and isn't likely to today. So, I'll get on with whatever I can do for this moment and keep foraging for those hidden skills that lurk inside me and are desperately seeking their moment to shine.

> *I feel I have suffered the most, not feeling sorry for myself, but as a mother and wife, I too had to work, sort the four kids out, clean, cook, drive, pay bills and try to enjoy my new home which I couldn't as I was too exhausted. This country is never going to be like South Africa as it is a much harder lifestyle as you have no maid, no gardener and no time – that is the problem – in South Africa you have help and you have your own time to see your friends, go to gym, watch your children play sport, etc.*
>
> TS - UK

Our story sounds sad and part of it was. I found an iron resolve inside myself that I'd never known in Africa. I'd become soft, life was easy. I had a maid-nanny-housekeeper; I had a gardener; I had a beauty therapist; a massage therapist, I had everything I could materially desire and I was oh so, so bored. Did I leave Africa out of boredom? I asked myself that question a number of times. Perhaps. Among other reasons, of course.

This period may have been hard, but it hasn't been without its fun moments – it has been a period of intense learning and growth, regrouping as a person and a time of becoming someone else or perhaps just scraping off the veneer and becoming 'real'. As Margery Williams explains (through the voice of the Skin Horse [24]), becoming real doesn't happen all at once. It takes a long time and "once you are Real, you can't be ugly, except to people who don't understand."

If I had stayed in Africa, I don't know if I would've ever really been real. And would I have recognized real? I've had to turn inside, view my internal landscape, recognize myself, my value and the solid foundation that underscores my being, accept my choices and their results, create something where there appears to be nothing and let go of material obsessions. I have had to realize the true simplicity of happiness, how little I need, and how much I have.

Here we are, eight years later. I have learned that pride and arrogance don't count, but self-reliance and confidence (act it, even if you don't feel it) go a very long way. Nothing will ever seem difficult to me again. During our initial years of hardship (emotional and financial), I likened our situation to those war-torn people who left Europe after WWII. They had to settle in a new land, often with large families and no belongings. I took books from the library and read their stories and I decided that if they could do it, then so could I. We were in a far better situation in many ways. America had opened her doors to us and we had to seize the opportunity.

Basically, it boils down to motivation. That 'get your ass out of bed and get on with it' feeling in the morning. I have learned that the biggest hurdle is attitude, getting out of bed in the morning and making it work – smiling and appreciating what the day contains, making it the kind of day you want. I brought my children to this country for a better life and have sacrificed myself to that process. Having come only halfway with them, I'm not about to give up now and let them starve this month. Eight years later and they haven't yet missed a meal. It hasn't been plain sailing and it hasn't been cordon bleu but they have the chubby cheeks to prove they haven't starved.

> I hear comments of "you are so lucky to be away from here". No luck about it, it has taken a lot of hard work and determination to restart our lives in a new country.
> MS - UK

∞ ∞ ∞

---

[24] *The Velveteen Rabbit* by Margery Williams and illustrated by William Nicholson.

*I feel guilty sometimes because I found the transition so easy. So many of my friends have had a really tough time of it.*
SS - USA

∞

*I think because I knew I had to be the one to adapt, I made it work. Living out of large urban areas, I have found the folk very friendly once they get to know you – which is probably universal. What are the differences in lifestyle? In some ways here, I feel as though I had stepped back 20 years when I arrived in the Shenandoah Valley. Especially as far as the treatment of black folk. It was quite an eye-opener after having experienced the whole 'apartheid' stigma from Americans earlier. And before coming here, I hadn't really thought of Virginia as being a 'southern' state. Interesting turn of events.*
CF - USA

∞

*We have no interest in ever going back. We had everything materially in South Africa. We've always built everything ourselves from scratch. Our families don't have much by way of money or possessions. We both had good careers. We had our dream home and we both had great cars. When we emigrated, we eventually had enough money to put a down-payment on house and small cars, but we literally started from scratch again.*

*We have our brains. We have willpower. We have a solid work ethic. With those three things, anything is possible.*

*Even if South Africa became a crime-free country, we have a life here that we are happy with. We've created that future we wanted and we believe firmly that one can never go back. It was challenging in the beginning but we always took a positive approach. A big part of adjusting is one's attitude. If you are willing to overcome obstacles and see them as opportunities, everything has a way of working out.*

*The most difficult part was missing our parents, but we call them every Sunday and that contact helped the emotional adjustment. I will always miss them but it makes our annual trip even more special.*

*Financially, we have always been very disciplined about our finances. We've never accumulated debt. In fact, any debt we had has always been* short term and our goal is always to live within our means. So, adjusting financially was no problem. We just lived simply.

Our family goal was to settle into our life in the USA. All three of us were on board from the very beginning. Our son settled in school fairly easily. We didn't encounter any problems at work any different to what might encounter anywhere else. We always displayed a respectful attitude to people around us.

We found it very easy to adapt because we embraced it. If you're willing to stay open it isn't difficult at all. The cultural differences have enhanced our experiences. The differences in lifestyle are not common to every family. People adopt certain ways of doing things based on their particular environments. The big differences, which are more of a general nature, are that people here are not dependent on maids – though there are house-cleaning services. You do your own gardening and mow your own lawn (you can hire gardening services). It takes a few months to get used to the different grocery products until you find the one that you like or something that's similar to what you were used to.

The really great things is that you have the freedom to be the family you want to be – the spectrum is extremely wide – you get to choose where and how you fit on it.

AH - USA

∞

I know what you are saying about cleaning house etc... Our first year here I met a woman at Church and she was going away, the guy she normally gets to clean her place was away, so she approached me, at first I was embarrassed, but after she told me how much they pay and how many people do it, I jumped at the opportunity. It seems to be the same in America where they hire services to clean the place, the Australians are not like us South Africans, we are not scared to get our hands dirty. One of my friends were shocked to see me cleaning my windows the one day, I just laughed at her.

NH - Australia

∞

Financially it's been much easier than in South Africa because of the job opportunities. Emotionally it's been tough – people need to realize that it's not all paradise overseas – it's a culture shock and hard when you miss your family and friends. That being said, you need to immerse yourself in your new life, and the most successful people in their new countries are the ones that embrace the new culture and 'when in Rome, do as the Romans do'.

EC - Australia

∞

We left South Africa with nothing, left the smallholding and our two cars as is. We had to start all over again, living in a tiny flat with a small social welfare grant which had to support the three of us plus our daughter we left behind in South Africa to finish her matric. Emotionally it was an absolute disaster.

JB - Germany

∞

The thing I have found difficult is that the Aussie people are not as warm as South African people. To hug a friend here is a bit foreign. I think it depends on your attitude. I have been willing to adapt myself to the local environment as I realised I cannot expect this country to change for me. So I've adapted the way I come across in business making sure I don't come across as arrogant, because South Africans here in Australia have a bad reputation of being arrogant.

IM - Australia

∞

Another self-serving reason I'm very glad to be out of the USA is that it is the centre of the black hole (slight exaggeration!) into which the capitalist system has begun to implode, as I have been warning my friends for years now. And before the dust has settled, the situation in the USA is going to become very ugly indeed. Yes, it will get ugly wherever the capitalist disease has been dominant (including South Africa), but I doubt whether any country will pay as high a price for its exuberant greed and arrogance as the USA. In addition to the self-interest that will keep me in South Africa, I also want to try to make a positive contribution to the inter-related problems of crime, corruption and capitalist greed. Exactly how is still the top of my agenda. I am well aware of the fact that whatever contribution(s) I may be able to make will probably remain even less visible to the naked eye than my contributions towards the ending of apartheid. Some things, however, are not susceptible to weighing and measuring. Some things are worth doing for their own sake. And the effort, of which everyone everywhere is capable – the effort to become a humane and compassionate neighbour, is an end in itself worth striving for. And it is an effort that can be made, not only in South Africa, but even in the USA!

KC - South Africa

∞

Financially, I had nothing when I arrived here, and was lucky in that I could stay with my brother when I arrived. I got no help from the State, and walked for miles to go to the Job Centre, as I could not afford the bus fare. I walked looking downwards in case I saw any loose change lying on the road or pavement. But I got a reasonable job within weeks, and have not looked back.

DH - UK

∞ ∞ ∞

## 46

∞

## In Helen We Trust

*I feel safe at night, safe to walk around, day or night for that matter and that's what keeps me going.*
A - Europe

The first Helen entered our lives in the months prior to our arrival in the USA. She was the immigration attorney who managed the original visa applications in 2002, through James's first employer, and successfully obtained them. She was in our lives in September 2004, as our first 3-year visa wound down and there were only a couple of months to find a new sponsor for James.

A South African friend, opening the *Sunday Times* on October 10 2004 to find my published reply to President Mbeki, said, "….but will she be able to come back to South Africa now?" When the question was conveyed to me, I thought, oh good, perhaps that's the solution to our visa sponsorship; we'll apply for refugee status. Helen said, "No, that's an arduous process with little hope of success, unless you've been chased out of your country by gun-wielding madmen."

A fortuitous meeting at an after hours business networking event brought James into contact with the owner of a consulting company. Over the next couple of months they explored how the two of them could work together on projects and so, when she found out that our visa was about to expire, the owner asked James to join her company as a part-owner.

Helen approved this plan, but warned us that as James would be a part owner of the consulting company, this company would not be able to sponsor the application for our green card. In other words, if the company was approved as a visa sponsor, we could stay another three years, but not indefinitely. Helen shepherded the second process and obtained the visas within a very short time frame, which soothed us yet again.

In 2007, facing the end of our second 3-year visa period, we approached Helen. We believed that the magic wrought by her, for our visa applications, would extend to our green card application and the pursuit of that elusive Permanent Residence. Stage 1 of our first 'green card' application was submitted by Helen in April 2007 through a new company, coincidentally also named 'Helen' (based on the owner's name).

When it seems that there is no hope on the horizon, you have to make up stories to soothe your psyche. You clutch at threads to give yourself hope when times are difficult – portents, omens, signs that this too will pass, things are about to get better, and on the other side of this desperation, your life will be settled again.

In May 2007, we decided to replace the old $1 Mazda 323 which I had been driving for 3 years. It had no air-conditioner so, in summertime, I would arrive freshly sauna-ed at every destination, sweat pouring off me. Winters were marginally better because the heating worked, albeit sporadically. I learned to bundle up with three layers of clothing and a coat and gloves, in order to keep warm.

We called her the '$1 Mazda' because she cost $1.00. Close friends we made in our first months here – my son's kindergarten teacher (his surrogate grandmother) and her husband – decided to buy another car for their daughter when she graduated. They knew that our shared car meant that each appointment required a marathon of careful planning and scheduling. They offered us the old, grey, unassuming Mazda. Unassuming was an understatement. She drove as though she had a cracker in her exhaust. I often admired the expensive tires on the brand new SUVs at the traffic lights (since I was sitting low enough to do so). Then, I enjoyed watching the expressions on the faces of the lofty SUV owners, as I left them in the dust as I accelerated when the lights changed.

I craved a minivan (an American contact calls them a 'Mom-mobile'). Since James was a dedicated and happy Hyundai owner, he agreed to buy a Hyundai Entourage and we test drove a top of the range 'Entourage Limited Edition' – a golden, brand new van with leather seats, tinted windows, heated front seats, two single captain's chairs in the centre row, front and rear separate air-conditioning and heating controls, and 15 cup holders. The children counted the cup holders during the test drive and for them, this was the selling point; it was a seriously impressive car. For me, the best was that the back seat folded under into the base of the car, and the middle seats folded up, which would give me enormous transport space for my Freecycle© acquisitions.

We were certainly not able to afford this mammoth girl with all her fancies and foibles so we chose the basic model, which I wanted in Burgundy. The dealership umm'ed and ah'ed and said they would find out if another dealership had such a car in stock. Later, they called and said they were unable to find the vehicle. But wait, they said, you can have this gold Entourage, top of the range model and, because you are repeat Hyundai customers - yadda yadda - we will sell her to you for the bottom of the range price. A better woman may have been be able to say "no" when offered such an obviously brilliant bargain, but since I couldn't find a reason to do so, I agreed to take her.

She arrived with 100 miles on her odometer and I named her Helen. The act of naming her was one of those clutched-at straws to which I previously referred. She was big, beautiful and golden blonde. We spent a long time climbing in and out of the car checking features and cooing over her beauty. We called the neighbours to come and sit in her too, so that we could listen to others sighing over her style and new smell.

The reason for her name, besides my needing a personal relationship with my car, was that I had decided that it would be a Helen that would keep us in the USA. Stage 1 of our green card application had been submitted in April 2007. The sponsor company was named Helen and the owner of the company was named Helen. The contact person at one of James's corporate clients was named Helen and she was also exploring ways in which her organization could sponsor James. Our immigration attorney was named Helen. Her assistant was named Helen. We would need to remain in the USA in order to pay for my car, Helen. One way or another, it would be a Helen that would cause us to stay in the USA - a client named Helen, a sponsoring company named Helen, an immigration attorney named Helen, an assistant named Helen or a car named Helen.

Secretly, something I never shared with my family, I thought that should we ever be homeless, and unable to afford to pay rent, there was enough space for everyone to sleep in Helen. Through our YMCA membership, we would still have somewhere to shower and spend our afternoons and evenings.

In July 2007 we attended an event hosted by The Brett Jones Memorial Foundation, founded by one of James's clients, to raise funds for children with cancer. Each of us received an elastic wrist band with a metal charm, engraved with the word 'Hope'. As none of my family wanted their bands, I appropriated them and created another story to soothe my overwrought psyche. Each time I tied my hair with a 'Hope Elastic' wrist band, I noted mentally I was keeping 'Hope' with me every day. As long as I had Hope, and Helen, we would be fine. I tied my hair with Hope, and as I brushed my teeth each morning, I mentally visualized the words, 'All will be well' written across the clouds.

By early August 2007, apart from my Helen being a sublime pleasure to drive (and an excellent listener), we were ready to book our tickets to leave the USA on 31 December 2007 (the expiry date of our second visa). We tried not to think about the cost of the tickets because we didn't have any money. I spent time on skyauction.com watching the bidding and pricing our options. I was toying with pulling names out of a hat to pick a country. New Zealand seemed appealing – we loved Lord of the Rings because of the scenery; Canada was closer, but cold; Australia had great cricket and weather; anywhere in Europe sounded civilized – I fancied myself back in a small village buying produce at the local farm; Botswana – I'd just read *The No. 1 Ladies' Detective Agency* by Alexander McCall Smith; perhaps an outlying island with eternal sunshine – nope, what about global warming? Anywhere in South America sounded exotic – but what about drug cartels and violence? (I'd love to live near the Amazon, but I imagined mosquitoes the size of small birds); England – my sister lived there but didn't yet have citizenship; or Ireland – but I'd already tried that route. I slowly watched our options dwindle. I thought 'it may yet end up being a life of working, and walking, around India' which was something I'd considered in South Africa, six years earlier. On the plus side, I was a newly qualified yoga teacher and I would happily 'ohm' my way around India with fragments of my serenity intact.

> We have investigated and visited the Netherlands (my country of birth), Peru (wife's home country), France and Sweden. We have investigated Norway, Finland, Spain, Argentina and Uruguay. We have a cupboard full of books, reports, statistics and other information on these countries.
> JVD - South Africa

Had we not progressed at all since 2002? Again, we sat at night with our cups of Rooibos tea, and looked at each other wearily. We discussed worst case scenarios. If we didn't have the funds to leave legally when our time was up, would we consider staying and becoming 'illegal immigrants' and secretly blend into the masses? That option troubled us because, thus far, we had been model citizens.

We had to go forward; we had nothing to go back to in South Africa. However, if we went 'illegal', we might be arrested and deported. And of course that would mean a free air-ticket. It would also preclude us from entering the United States for the next 10 years. We smiled at our level of desperation and, most of the time, were able to hide it from the children.

The permanent residence process was arduous. Stage 1 meant that the United States Department of Labor had to confirm that there was a skills shortage in James's line of work; the employer had to advertise the position and explain, and prove, that it had not received any suitable resumes, apart from the candidate seeking sponsorship. The Department of Labor would hopefully approve Stage 1 and agree that the employer could sponsor the candidate (which would lead to Stage 2).

Way back in 2002, the owner of Helen-Company had introduced James to his first 'real' client. Since then, James has advised the founder and his management team, and he had even worked directly on projects for *their* clients. When they heard in 2007 that we might have to leave the USA they offered to employ James full-time as a means of securing his ongoing services. After carefully vetting the company and the job opportunity, Helen-Attorney submitted them as a sponsoring company, triggering the same process previously described, namely the vetting of the skills shortage, the advertising of the position, and so on.

The sitting and waiting began again.

If we received no response to either Stage 1 filing by November, Helen-Attorney suggested we file Stage 1 for the third time, but from a different angle. James would sponsor himself and would need to justify why he should be allowed to stay, live and work in the USA. It would be an exceptionally difficult route and could possibly end in an appeal court with her arguing and defending our case. She held all our hopes, fears and dreams in the palm of her hand and we had to trust absolutely that if Helen-Attorney couldn't achieve this for us, then no-one could.

∞ ∞ ∞

*Emotionally it was the hardest thing I ever had to do. It came close to destroying my marriage.*

LRK - USA

∞

*I am so grateful for the security, peace and freedom I have found in England and know that there is no other choice for me because I can't deal with the pain to innocent and helpless people. I no longer feel threatened or frightened. I have totally recovered from my post traumatic stress disorder but it has taken a while.*

*Before I left South Africa I made a promise to myself to remember to say thank you for my safety every day of my life. Safety is a great gift and something people who have never experienced would never be able to appreciate. I believe that one is not free if one is not safe. One has to have safety to have freedom. South Africans are not free.*

SVB - UK

∞ ∞ ∞

# 47

∞

## Are We There Yet?

Although this chapter may seem long, and the sequence of events makes for labourious reading, I've written it for all those people who wrote and asked, "How can I get a green card?" Many correspondents appeared to believe that if they could gain entry to the United States, on an approved work visa, they were guaranteed 'Permanent Residence'. No, it is not that easy. Not at all. I have heard too many stories of people who arrived, their visas in hand, and were either turned back at entry or those who could not find a sponsor for their green card and had to return to their country of origin when the visas expired. – Bronwyn.

Our children adopted a new refrain, as most children who travel anywhere do, and "are we there yet?" punctuated our journeys with moments of irritation. Although it quickly became an annoying chorus from the back seat on any trip we undertook, I often felt the same way. Are we there yet? Our journey began on September 29$^{th}$ 2000 and seven years later, we still had not arrived.

Another September arrived, Labor Day passed by, and with summer officially over, our stress levels rose noticeably. I eagerly awaited the 3rd of October; the opening date for entries in the US Diversity Visa (Green Card) Lottery. Since 2000, I had entered the 'contest' every year and, like a desperate gambler, every year I believed that this year was 'it'. This was our year.

## Scene 1: Taking a Gamble

In mid-September I sat down and finally collated our 'green card file'. All the documents, carefully applied for before we left South Africa[25], were carelessly stuffed helter-skelter into a folder. I spent time filing and labelling so that everything was nicely sorted. *One never knows,* I thought, *be prepared.*

I dragged the family on October 2nd to have digital passport photos taken so that I could complete the entries online at midday on opening day. The photos were only one of many arduous regulations that govern the entries. They had to be specially cropped and resized to fit the US Government specifications on the Department of State 'Diversity Visa Lottery' website. Entrants had to be from specific continents, or areas of the world. This is meant to balance the intake of immigrants into the USA, in order to ensure 'diversity'. Only 50,000 visa 'winners' are chosen each year and this is divided between the various geographic regions of the world.

## Scene 2: The Call

At 7 p.m. on October 3rd, I was checking our entries (yes, I take a long time, checking over and over to ensure that all details are correct) and I was about to hit 'Submit' when the telephone rang. James and the children were at soccer practice so I deigned to answer instead of ignoring it as I usually do, because we receive too many calls at night, from telemarketers.

It was Helen, our immigration attorney, calling to say that she had received notification that our second Stage 1 application had been approved – within six weeks. The usual time-frame is about three months and as our time was already short, we had been simply praying that the application process would be would be shorter than that. I was speechless for a moment. I told her that I was about to submit our green card lottery application. She laughed and told me not to bother because Stage 1 approval is equivalent to winning the lottery. Until you complete Stages 2 and 3, there is no guaranteed 'green card'. The lottery merely gives you a foot in the door.

---

[25] I began applying for these documents before we left South Africa, which was a process within itself. We needed copies of each birth certificate, our marriage certificate and James's decree of divorce, each with an original Home Affairs pink stamp certifying it as a true copy; and our South African police clearance certificates.

## Scene 3: Frantic Activity

Our next step was to have our individual medicals with a Certified Civil Surgeon. From a list of eight local civil surgeons provided online, all unknown to me, I chose a Dr. Narang because I liked the poetical sound of his name. We spent an entire afternoon with him discussing our medical histories, having our physical examinations, having our vaccination records checked, blood tests taken, TB tests done, and James and I were tested for HIV and syphilis. After satisfying these requirements, Dr. Narang completed our medical forms which were to be submitted as part of our Stage 3 filing.

Helen-Attorney told us that Stages 2 and 3 could be filed simultaneously because there was no backlog. Stage 2 required a great deal of information about the sponsor company who had to prove that it was a bona fide company with enough income, history, and current employees. A company representative had to complete a myriad of forms and submit copies of payroll reports, financial statements and tax returns for the previous few years.

Stage 3 was all about James and our family history and details. Collating the information meant that we had to submit almost 50 pages of copies and details for each of us. Helen-Attorney required a completed questionnaire giving every date related to our parents' details; our personal details; our marriage; James previous marriage; details of his divorce; every passport number; date and place where original US visas were issued; the date we entered the country and the number and form allocated to us on our entry date. Photocopies of our marriage certificate; letters of reference from every employer for the past eight years; details of all our residential addresses during that time; copies of every page of every passport, even the expired passports and the blank pages; our Police Clearance certificates; all pages of our South African identity documents; copies of our tax returns; our bank statements and of course the passport photos.

Three weeks later, all the forms were finally completed.

Once we had submitted the information, Helen-Attorney prepared the papers and then we had the arduous task of checking another 50 pages of BCIS (Bureau for Citizenship and Immigration Services) forms to ensure that every number, address and detail was correct. Any mistake would trigger a question which could lead to a delay or rejection... the end of this road for us. After I checked, double checked and triple checked everything, we officially signed all our forms on November 7th 2007.

Fedex delivered the package of forms and copies to Homeland Security in Texas on November 13th. BCIS cashed our checks on November 16th, which meant that our application had been accepted. Our Acknowledgments of Receipts arrived on November 27th. These were the most important documents for us, at that point, because Homeland Security's acknowledgement that our application was in process automatically extended our visas indefinitely until final approval or denial of our permanent residence. Each Acknowledgement assigned an 'Alien Number' (yes, we would call it a Receipt Number). We relaxed noticeably.

Helen-Attorney had advised us to expect the Biometrics Notice (appointments for fingerprinting) after three months. They arrived on November 28th, far earlier than anyone expected. "Your designated appointment is set for Friday December 7th at 2 p.m. at the Homeland Security office in Norfolk, for fingerprinting and photographs." As it was only two weeks after filing the papers, I thought perhaps the 3-month time frame had been a joke. I was surprised that during the major 'holiday' time of year – Thanksgiving – the process was so speedy. "Calm down. Don't get excited", Helen-Attorney's office responded to my excited email communications. "Homeland Security does things in odd ways. This is no indicator of an easy process." I was still clutching at straws that would indicate a smooth road.

Visiting the Homeland Security offices was unexpectedly enjoyable because, despite my state of nervous anticipation, they were not busy, and the offices featured an open-plan, relaxed layout. Everyone was in a happy, Friday afternoon, chatty mood. I monitored everything I said because I was afraid that any minor verbal inanities might be reported to their superiors and jeopardize the process. However, when my 'official' asked about my sweater, we had a girl-to-girl discussion about clothing, and I relaxed. *OK, she's real, there's a person under there, not a robot,* I thought. When she offered to take a couple of photos of me so that they could use the one I liked best, I knew she was a real woman. That was a sure sign of a woman who understands!

December 7th 2007 was a Friday so I decided that the background checks would probably begin on Monday 10th. Spanning generations back past my father and grandfather, all the way to my great-great-great-grandfather, at a time when my ancestors lived in Cornwall, there were stories of them being involved in privateering and pirating off the coast. I trusted that this would not be held against me and prayed that the Interpol records didn't extend that far back.

As Stage 2 (Advance Parole and Work Authorization) was expected to take three months, according to the attorneys, I anticipated that it would be the end of February 2008 before we were told to attend an interview or to supply extra documents and information. And Stage 3 – Application to Adjust Status (from visa holders to permanent residents) – usually takes between 6–18 months. I tried not to think about the stories told, by other South Africans, of green card applications that had taken between one and 10 years and the morass of legal fees and filing problems they experienced during that time.

I enjoyed the efficiency of the BCIS website because with the Alien Numbers (Receipt numbers), I could check the status and progress of each application. Being an A-type personality, I had decided that I would not allow myself to check the site until January and then, only twice a week because, being me, I would check the website three times a day, every day.

The Advance Parole travel authorizations arrived at Helen-Attorney's office on December 17th. Another step completed, and yet I didn't really care since I couldn't travel anywhere. Helen-Attorney's office notified us on December 21st that our Work Authorizations were approved. Huh? Three months? We had been cautioned not to expect either of these authorizations until, earliest, February 2008. Obviously they hadn't found details of my pirating ancestry. This was only two weeks after fingerprinting. I smiled and thought, *two weeks from filing until we received receipts and fingerprinting notices, two weeks from fingerprinting to receiving the work authorizations and now, what will happen in the next two weeks. Could it be possible? Nah, don't be crazy. Forget it.*

The official Work Authorization cards arrived via US Mail on December 26th. My greatest dream was to be able to work in the USA. I spent the morning of the 27th at the local Social Security office registering myself and the children. Having a 'social' (as they are referred to in the USA – isn't that some kind of high school dance event?) gives you credibility and a bona fide identity. Suddenly, when you have a 'social' to write onto any application you become someone, a real person, again. You have an identity. One never knows when the children may need to be seconded into child labour, so it was important to register them as well.

Biding my time at Social Security, I noted that I was breathing again. Breathing in and out and I was watching my breath with a single-minded focus. I felt much more relaxed because this was actually happening. I was trusting the process again and not allowing my fears to suffocate me.

## Scene 4: The Final Minutes

The following description of events are so clearly etched in my mind that I found myself reliving them, and my emotions, as I wrote them down. And yet, these intense moments lasted only a few minutes of my life. This is what happened.

Friday, December 28$^{th}$ 2007, the children and I had spent all day with home-schooling friends in another county. We arrived home around 7 p.m. It was winter; it was dark and it was cold. My son fetched the mail and handed it to me. There were four window envelopes with the Homeland Security, Texas address. All the other receipts, notices, acknowledgements and cards had arrived from this address with the same style unassuming window envelope.

*Oh dear*, I thought, *this is where the difficulties begin.* I am breathing in; I am breathing out; I am calm. *Do we need to go for an interview? Do they need more papers or must we answer more questions? Crikey!*

It's late. The children are hungry and tired after a long day. They are excitable and, together with James, are having a very loud conversation in the kitchen – everyone is speaking at the same time. Me? I'm ignoring them. I always open our mail so, gingerly opening the envelopes, I am mentally preparing myself to expect a list of questions or requirements for each of us, or an appointment for an interview, or what else it could be?

I find a card inside each envelope. My brain goes into hyper mode. What? We received cards two days ago. Why do we need another card? Is this to prove that our application is pending? Do we need this to prove our status is pending? Stupid bureaucrats; it's the holidays; someone duplicated the work cards. This has our photo, and our fingerprint. Surely not, what *is* this?

I am panicky. It is Friday night and I can't reach Helen-Attorney. Why do we have more cards? I forget to breathe in and out. Calming down slightly, I think it must simply be another thing for filing. It is OK. We are on track, we are fine, this is working, probably another formality – a duplication or something.

Each envelope has the same content but differentiated for each of us. A thick credit card with a photograph, fingerprint, alien number and bar code. I am studying them closely, looking from one to the other. James is not paying attention because he's still participating in a chaotic conversation with the children. I'm muttering, "What is this? I don't know. Why did they send us more cards? These must be duplicates. Helen never told us anything about these."

He turns to me, sees the look on my face and he says: "And now, what's that? Just leave it, you can call Helen-Attorney on Monday. Come on, the kids are hungry. What's for supper?" Typical man, I'm having a conniption and he's talking about food.

I ignore him and I keep staring because the cards are very official looking and it says 'Permanent Resident.' I keep turning them over and over until I note the date stamp 'valid till 2017' which was the final clue. I know that 'green cards' are valid for 10 years. I begin to cry.

I have never seen a 'green card' and this card is not green. It is beige and although it is the same size, it is heavier than a credit card. It arrived in a folded cardboard slip like a credit card received in the mail. A mini tri-fold brochure saying, "Welcome to the USA, as a new Permanent Resident you …" and detailing rights and responsibilities. No bells, whistles or anthems. I look. And I look and look. There are our Homeland Security photos, our fingerprints, bar-coding and on the back a gold strip, about one inch wide, with holographs of the US landmass, our photo and our signature.

Finally, I manage to say, "James, I think these are the green cards. That is not possible! Surely not? How can they be here already? There must be a mistake." I rush to check the immigration website. I check each application under the I-485 (Stage 3 – Application to Adjust Status). Every application stated "26 December – Application Approved. Cards mailed."

(As I write this, I feel every ounce of emotion experienced during that half hour, as if it were now.)

I cried over the keyboard, while I emailed everyone who might have a remote interest, and probably a few who didn't. James phoned as many American friends as he could find on a Friday evening. Appropriately, one of the original Helens and her husband arrived within 20 minutes with a bottle of champagne.

I was incoherent because I could not stop crying. I could not put the green cards down because I felt they might dematerialize. Seven years of my life were wrapped into four small cards. There was such desperation, anguish, exhaustion, fear, hope – so many prayers, and unspeakable emotions contained in these cards. I slept with my card on my bedside table because I was determined to protect it with my life. I wanted to see it first thing in the morning to remind myself that it had not been a dream. I don't think the children did get their supper that night.

The application took 30 working days to process, during the Thanksgiving and Christmas holidays. Being born and bred in Cape Town (and Capetonians are known for their extremely relaxed attitude to life), I believed that the holidays would slow our application considerably – people take vacation, companies run with skeleton staff, businesses close and everyone goes shopping, or so it seems – and add at least a month to the processing time….

To say I was astounded would be an understatement. The attorneys were also amazed at the speed with which things happened. Helen-Attorney told us that, in her entire career, she has only had a handful of applications completed so quickly.

I believe we had the best immigration attorney in the state. She laughed and her staff said, "if that is so, then why are our other client applications not completed as fast?" They say ours was a clean case because we had no criminal record, no parking fines, speeding fines or drunk driving incidents on record either here or in South Africa. The employers were all solid companies and we had been model citizens for the past six years.
Some cynical souls believe that my maiden name, 'BUSH', combined with the forms being filed in TEXAS, was critical to the speed of the approval. To that, I say, you should never listen to rumour mongers.

I haven't met anyone who can say that the US Government gave them the best Christmas present ever. And yet, like one of those tacky musical cards, the cardboard sleeve could at least have sung the *Star Spangled Banner* when opened.

Are we there yet? Yes. Finally, we are.

∞ ∞ ∞

*Now I am truly privileged. Privileged that my family is safe. Privileged that my skills are needed. Privileged that we got out before something terrible happened. Privileged to simply feel wanted.* SDT - Australia

∞

*I cried when I read your article. Firstly because I feel the same and secondly because I was denied my green card three days ago after trying for seven long years to stay here in the US legally. I am out of options and am forced now to leave the country. I am asking the question to myself, "Would I rather live in a prison of 52 big states illegally with a future and kind of freedom until the real ID act catches up with me? Or do I go back and live in fear daily of being tortured and murdered with hot water like I have read recently, or become a paraplegic because I was shot in the spine for a cell phone?" What a big decision. But now I do not have a choice any more.*

CVDW - USA

∞ ∞ ∞

# 48

∞

## Staying the Course

*I don't look back any more . . . .
I have started to live and breathe again.*
YL - Australia

**W**e arrived here with nothing. Well, OK, not really nothing. Six suitcases and, courtesy of Biddulphs, three months later we received 19 boxes of rugs, toys, clothes, bedding and some kitchen items. The boxes were only 48"x48" but, when they arrived, they were unpacked with reverence and the pleasure of being able to touch familiar items. We brought no assets, no 'settling in allowance', financial cushion or financial plan, and no idea about our future. Our motto was 'To Infinity and Beyond' (a la Buzz Lightyear in Toy Story).

During 2001, it was easy to sit in the rocking chairs in Riebeek Kasteel and watch 'Winnie The Pooh's Most Grand Adventure' while titillating the kids with thoughts of our own forthcoming most grand adventure. In the wake of my father's passing later that year, we were trying to keep the excitement of the 'adventure' uppermost in the children's minds. One day, shortly after my father's death, my son, then all of five years old, turned to me and said, "But Mama, who is going to take care of Nana now that Gampa's gone?" Did this make me reconsider? No. I knew my father would approve of this move, irrespective of the cost.

There were people to whom I said goodbye, on a superficial level, because I expected to see them again. There were people to whom I said goodbye and I knew I would never see them again. James's mom passed away in 2003 and we were not there. A nephew passed away in 2006 and we were not there. My uncle passed away in 2006 and we were not there. From a distance, we have watched family and friends deal with divorce, physical illness, and emotional crises and we could not be there to support them. We have not been there to celebrate the birthdays or the milestones.

The underlying reasons that we ended up here are the basics of life in a 'civilized' country. A safe lifestyle and economic opportunities for the children, access to excellent public services (medical, education, security) and I think that there is a big price to be paid for that. We meet many Americans who complain about taxes and are surprised when we explain that we are happy to pay our taxes. We appreciate everything we receive in return for the monies paid to the county, the state and the federal government. The systems work.

We have enormous suburban parks which we visit safely at any time of day – they close at dusk. We have a 911 facility which means that for any emergency, the police, an ambulance or the fire brigade – sometimes all of them – will arrive within 5 minutes. We have a city where, if the murder rate reaches 90 victims per annum, people will call for the resignation of the police chief. A city where, when five years ago, a family of four was brutally murdered, the public was outraged. Within four days, the police had arrested and charged the perpetrators.

Yes, it does feel sterile sometimes. It's a lot quieter than Africa, a lot less exciting and much less stimulating. I've lived on the edge for too much of my life and I'm happy to enjoy the quiet.

On reflection, I think I may have under-estimated the 'cost' of emigrating, but I never gave it much thought once we were committed to the idea. It was just a case of moving on to the next phase. I didn't expect it to be easy, I expected it to be exciting and new and I expected it to be better. I didn't plan for much because I like to travel light.

> *When in South Africa, I enjoy every moment and wish I have never left. When in Canada, I enjoy every moment and am glad to be back home.*
> RC - Canada

Emigration makes you behave in ways you never anticipated. I have always been a shy person. In grocery stores my ear would pick up nuances of conversations in a foreign language. Unobtrusively moving closer, or following them down an aisle, I would listen carefully in case it was Afrikaans. It never was. Whenever I saw a South African flag bumper sticker on a car, I found myself wanting to wave down the motorists. Would you stop your car, or roll down your window, to talk to a lunatic waving and gesticulating at you from her minivan? I've accosted strangers in parking areas because their license plate reads 'bakgat' or 'windgat'.

One sweaty morning, in a crowded Body Shape class at the YMCA, I spotted a heavily pregnant lady with a South African flag design on her T-shirt. Much to her consternation, I almost jumped on her during a 2-minute break in class. She's from Durban, we had a short chat about South Africa – she came over as an au pair and married an American – and our connection was over.

Relocation is made more difficult when people build a social circle almost exclusively around South Africans. This leads to the 'when we...' trap of making comparisons with another life in a distant land. To spend all your time focussing on the past makes it impossible to enjoy the present. As soon as you begin to compare your new life with an old life elsewhere, the new experiences lose their lustre. It is as if you have to draw a curtain down inside yourself and, instead of hankering, look at this new world through the eyes of an excited child, excited to be given the opportunity for this experience.

Psychologically, it's more challenging to find a way to meet, and make, new friends from another culture. We are here, we are living in their culture and their land and we should open ourselves up to that. You have to 'invest' yourself in life in a new country. Much of our survival was directly related to the fact that we made American friends and contacts. It wasn't easy and it took longer than anticipated but it has been worth it. I have one very close South African friend, met in Richmond. When she, James, and I had dinner recently, I found myself shrieking with laughter at the stories of Jo'burg and Hillbrow shared by the two of them. It struck me that it was one of the few times we have ever shared a 'when we' moment with another South African. We enjoyed ourselves, we enjoyed the moments and then we went on with our American lives.

The energy to keep going was often generated by small moments created by people I've met in strange places or in unusual situations. There was a chance conversation with a lady in the portrait queue in Wal-Mart who told me about a South African tax consultant – who has done our taxes since 2002; a librarian who gave me a short motivational email to read when, sensing my bleakness and desperation that day, she reached out to me; George in the produce section of the grocery store, who spent time talking to me about the exotic fruits and vegetables; a sales associate at the hardware store who offered to sponsor our green card; the clerk at the post office who knew my name and spent time explaining the postal idiosyncrasies, each time I went to mail items; many of the friends, clients and strangers who channelled work to me when they knew I was in dire straits financially; a lady from Eritrea who chatted to me at the DMV (Department of Motor Vehicles) while I was waiting for my driver's license; my son's kindergarten teacher who, becoming a surrogate grandmother in his first year, made a huge difference to his settling into a new life; the friendly grocery store assistant who's practically related to me. It's a joke between us because she's from Nigeria and we laugh, we're definitely more closely related to each other than to the Americans. The corner café where I buy gas (petrol) and found, in their small wine stock, a wine called 'Sebeka' bottled by Swartland Cellars outside Malmesbury. Of all the strange places to find a tie to home, not just a tie to South Africa but a tie to the very cellars close to our home.

These small moments add up over time and, brick by brick, build the foundation of a new life. All the interactions, however minor, contribute to a feeling of 'OK, I think it will be fine, I can live here'. It was four years before I finally felt that emotion.

I discovered that a batch of home baked crunchies creates a lot of goodwill (Americans have renamed them granola cookies). I've baked them for our immigration attorney, the librarians, the bank clerks, the post office clerks, business associates, friends and acquaintances. I've lost count of the number of times I've been asked to share the recipe.

> *South Africa's emigrants are a sad, but resilient people.... We will make new lives for ourselves and our children as our fore-fathers did in South Africa, so many years ago....*
> 
> DM - Australia

It is not possible to replicate our lives when we relocate overseas. Economic affluence doesn't create a life. People arrive, with financial assets, they buy a house, a car or two, have a job and expect life will continue again. It doesn't because of all the emotional and cultural change. Your head spins with so many different things. The economic affluence doesn't change the vague disconnect with other people who feel like cultural aliens to you. You have to re-establish yourself on a whole new level. You are a toddler again, learning to walk and speak, and not everyone understands you or your intentions.

I wouldn't recommend that anyone does this the way we did it, throwing caution to the winds, unless you are very brave and totally committed. I didn't think about it that way. I counted on my determination and tenacity. My sister once described me as a bulldog (no offence intended toward the breed) because once I take hold of something, I am tenacious and I never let go. My husband, having to live with this virtue, might not agree, but I think this is the greatest compliment I have received.

Many years ago, I read one of Dr Wayne Dyer's books in which he made the point that if you believe in something, you really want to achieve something, you will put everything you have into the idea, you will relinquish everything you own to follow the dream, you will be willing to give up everything to make it happen. And that is what we did. I kept that uppermost in my mind. People will commit to an idea, which sounds a good one, but often they are not completely willing to throw their heart and soul into it.

A recent revelation caused all the fractured pieces to slip into place. These eight years have been a 'setting up phase' of creating the right environment for our children. We didn't bring them here for a 'different' life when they were toddlers or pre-schoolers – at those ages, children are still closely bound and their environment is easy to manage. It's once they reach pre-adolescence and begin to expand their boundaries, that I knew I would feel uneasy about their life in Africa. These years have set the foundation for them. It would have been difficult to uproot them as pre-adolescents but they've only ever been to school here; their social and cultural interactions have been American, yet their foundations are international.

"It's gonna take a lot to take me away from you, there's nothing that a hundred men or more could ever do…" 103.5 FM seems determined to persecute me. They play this song every single day during my drive home from work. I was in Tower Records in London on Monday 23rd July 2001. My sister and I were browsing DVD's and CD's when "Africa", by Toto, began to play over the stereo system. She turned to me and said,

"You know, this is the Expats song."

"Really?"

"Yes, in London this is known as the Expats song."

I forgot the conversation until, living in the USA, listening to the song on the car radio, it hit me again. This time I <u>was</u> an 'expat'. I was a stranger in a strange land. Yes, it did take a lot to take me away from you, Africa. I have these same thoughts every time I hear the song. Sometimes, sitting in the 5 p.m. traffic, I begin to cry. Yes, it did take a lot to take me away from you and yes I knew that I must do what's right – for my children, at least. Sometimes I wonder about my wisdom and about doing what was right for me.

Who I am these days? Who have I become? I am different. I am connected. My emotions run close to the surface and, despite that, I am stronger, wiser and older. Am I happier? Certainly, sometimes I am, in some spaces. That is all I can hope for, to have spaces of happiness and contentment inside myself. No, I remain a cultural alien and on some level I will always be severed and lonely. I watch my children grow and I know it is worth it.

∞ ∞ ∞

No. No. No! When I watched the furniture removers pack 39 years of my life in South Africa into 63 cartons, nothing will make me ever pack up again. Far too traumatic, so I'm here to stay!   KLB - Ireland

∞

I read your article and you have said everything I feel. It really struck a chord. I have lived outside of South Africa since 1995. In 1993 I was caught up in a shooting at a bus stop relating to taxi wars (Cape Town). In 1992 I witnessed my friend's car being hi-jacked right outside of the bank where I was working. (There was nothing I could do.) We are street wise in a lot of ways. I was attacked once, almost raped, but luckily a car came along and scared the individual off. I was about 20 at the time. An experience that changed my life and I never looked at the world as a safe place again for a long time.

After all the years in the UK I was planning to move back in January 2006 to South Africa to start a new life with my family and then 8 month old baby. It took me three days after arriving to realise I had made a mistake. A BIG ONE IN FACT. Not one of my family members living in South Africa bothered to tell me about the baby rapes. I found it virtually impossible to find a place to live since I didn't feel safe anywhere. My husband and I called the UK stopped our personal items from being shipped, which wasn't much, but photos, linens and a few things that meant the world to us. We sold our house and gave a lot of things away.

I was never happy in the UK but I think it was the first time I appreciated the freedom and safety that that country offered me. I have never before appreciated not having to worry about looking over my shoulder and thinking about if I wake up will my child still be there in the morning. The reality of what had happened really changed the way I feel about South Africa. I am now past the stage that I feel like it is my home. It has taken me 11 years to get over the sickness for a place that no longer exists.

We flew back to the UK two weeks after we landed in South Africa. My family and I are in Australia now. It will almost be a year to the day we landed here. Strangely enough the first day we drove down to the Gold Coast (near Brisbane) my husband and I both said that it feels like we have come home. We are finally where we are supposed to be. It's clean, the people are friendly. No need to run red lights at night or to look over your shoulder. A stroll on the beach is a wonderful stress free experience. My children will have a great future here.

I miss my family in South Africa, but I don't miss South Africa. I regret that my mother and father will not be able to be proper grandparents to my children, but I believe I have done the best thing for my kids. And I have no regrets. I don't look back any more . . . . I have started to live and breathe again and my world has a lot of colour to it.  YL - Australia

∞

At the time I left I thought it would just be an adventure and I never left thinking I would never go back. That just happened. But I know now I will never go back there. Never.  RG - USA

∞

Whenever we are a little down we go onto the internet and look at a few South African websites and any minor issues we have at the time, pale into insignificance right away.  IJ - Australia

∞

I, too, felt that safety, prosperity and self respect were the obvious and overriding reasons behind my decision never to return to South Africa. I believe that those that have stayed have closed their hearts to the love they have for their own lives and those of their loved ones. I believe they are in a permanent state of denial. Their personal dishonesty makes them blind to the creeping lowering of standards on every level in the country. I go back every two or three years for a short holiday, but my heart has a cold part too. It has truly been broken. However, now I honestly love my life and my loved ones, safe and free from anger, paranoia, fear, disappointment. My mind and my family can prosper here. All it took was a little respect. For myself. And from my fellow man.

JH - Ireland

∞

Creating a new life in a new country is not easy - but if I may pass on some words of wisdom and encouragement. Once the mind is ready the rest is easy. This is a good case in point when one eliminates the things that cause the most pain, and at the end of the day, the freedom one experiences when the value one added to a specific thing has no more value!

T - USA

∞

I just can't justify going back and living in constant fear if I would be murdered today or a few days from now, statistically speaking it's bound to happen to me or a loved one at some time.

GK - UK

∞

I can't really say that I miss anything from South Africa – perhaps it is too soon for that. We did not have much life in South Africa – being cloistered behind high walls and locked gates the whole time. The most surprising thing about my emigration experience was just how easily I felt at home. I really expected to battle to settle. I have not really experienced any serious homesickness or longing for my 'old' life. Perhaps this will come later once the honeymoon period is over.

SDT - Australia

∞

You hit the nail on the head when you say that you will never be whole again. We are in Florida, have been here for six months having just returned from trying to live in South Africa again. We moved back three years ago and for the first year kept saying that things were getting better when in fact they were not. We had our car stolen within three weeks of our return. We went back and started a parrot farm and had 100 pairs of African greys. In February of this year I was in an industrial area buying food for our parrots, and was involved in a brutal cash heist. I was lucky to survive and it was then that we decided to leave South Africa for the last time. SP - USA

∞

    A retired Danish executive who has been in the country for 30 years told me that he, like I, has studied what it is that makes a successful immigrant (ie, one who does not pack up and go home when the going gets tough). He said that he has tried to study whether it is temperament, culture, education, class. He has come to realize that it is only incredible and stubborn determination that makes one stay until things work out. LH - USA

∞

    Homesickness is mostly memories. We miss the good times we had. Being homesick helps us to forget all the bad and unpleasant things - like the crime, the fear at night, not being able to sleep with windows wide open, riding bicycle with no fear of it being hijacked etc and etc.
    But we South Africans are a tough lot, and will 'tolerate' all the negative things because we appreciate and love all the positively beautiful things in our beloved country! JB - Germany

∞

    I visited South Africa six months ago and it was an interesting change that I experienced – MOST people (family and friends) now told me that it was the best thing that we did and they wished that they had the courage to do it when we did what we did. RC - Canada

∞

    I will never return to South Africa. I don't believe that most people appreciate just how quickly your life can change. I don't miss anything about

*South Africa. The sirens, gun shots, dead bodies, motorcar accidents, bank robberies etc. etc. compared to a normal life style like Australia is worlds apart. It is not surprising that the Aussies don't comprehend the stories we tell them.*

CS - Australia

∞

*Ultimately it is not about our happiness, but about a future for our girls. Wishing it could be different! Wishing I could tell you that I am so glad we left...but it is not so. I mourn for my land, its people and my family and friends.*

HVG - USA

∞

*We went back to South Africa for a holiday at the end of last year mostly because our children wanted to see South Africa again, not to mention visiting their Grannies. It was a surreal feeling to be back. I felt like a foreigner for the first week. The mountains were even more breathtaking than I had remembered, the food was good and restaurants cheap and of course I enjoyed the break from domestic chores. After a month we were all grateful to be home. Home is where the heart is and ours belongs right here.*

SL - Australia

∞ ∞ ∞

# 49

∞

## Tapestry

*I miss the sunsets over the grasslands, huge and colourful,
like an artist's paint set tipped over and smeared by the hands of a child.*
ML - New Zealand

When you are young you don't think about life. You don't realize that you are collecting. Collecting memories all the time. You are collecting the moments that will never be caught again.

And then, one day, you turn a corner somewhere, invisible somehow, and you try to look back and all you can find is your collection – the curtain is drawn and you only see a faintness of the path you have walked.

You begin to face your own mortality.

You find yourself turning over those precious memories like treasured seashells after a week at the beach. Touching them, tasting them, drinking in and imbibing their colours – a collection of brilliant hues; a tapestry.

Before we left South Africa, an especially close friend and mentor said to me, "Take lots of photos, you'll want them, you'll need to look at them, you'll be sorry if you don't." I was too busy – talking, researching, packing, organizing the remnants of our life – and I didn't do that. And now, yes, Mary, I am sorry.

Photographs don't capture the essence of those jewels, the memories, but at least they colour them and they provide a framework for them. I try to remember the fullness of the colours and the variances in the valley scene which spread before me, like a tapestry, as I drove over Bothmaskloof Pass.

I stand at my easel, pick up my watercolour pencils and I don't remember the colours. I can't quite capture the deep violet shade of the sky, before a thunderstorm, standing at my front door and looking across the wheatfields towards Porterville and the Groot-Winterhoekberge. I wish I had a photograph to compare, a small substitute for the lack of depth in the mental pictures I carry inside.

I know that scenery as though it were tattooed onto my soul. But the colours lack clarity and I had to use Google Maps to look up the name of that mountain range . . . .

My memories are faded.

∞ ∞ ∞

*I wish I had saved more stuff like school magazines and brought more stuff that was typically South African, stuff I had taken for granted and hadn't known how much I would appreciate here.* SP - New Zealand

∞

*I know deep down we have made the right choice, but Africa will always be with me.* NH - Australia

∞

*My heart will always belong to South Africa, but the reality of living there is just too difficult at the moment!* LH - UK

∞ ∞ ∞

# 50

∞

## The Way it Should Be

*We never locked our front door behind us. Isn't that wonderful?*
AMS - USA

8:35 p.m. It is a Friday night in the summertime. Dusk and a peaceful afterglow to the end of the day as the sun sets on the heat and humidity. My son and his cat are playing outside in the front yard catching fireflies in a jar with the lid poked with holes for air.

My daughter and her best friend have walked down the road, in their pyjamas, to fetch blankets and pillows for a sleep-over. Neighbourhood children are slowly gathering – one, two, three, five, seven, maybe eight – because the best game for summer evenings is playing with a lighted, luminous Frisbee and tossing it across the road from one house to another and back again. There are no fences around these yards to hinder the game. The neighbours come out to watch, and sit on their steps while drinking cocktails. We are invited outside to join the fun.

This is what childhood should be, a relaxed freedom of expression and energies focussed on the small pleasures of every day. My children have never known anything different.

Am I still torn? Yes.

Do I still feel split between two continents, one foot on each shore? Yes, but I'm looking forward now, not backward. We make choices; we live with them; life goes on – forwards.

Would I change my decision given what I know today?

This scenario clearly answers that question. I brought my children here for a better life; I've given them that opportunity; I've given them back their childhood. For this, I've made great sacrifices.

When did I start feeling again? I don't know if I ever have nor do I know if I ever will.

My children are happy. All is well in our world. No. I won't be going back.

∞ ∞ ∞

*So... one can fully understand your move as it relates to your children's safety and the peace of mind and safety of your family. When my children were growing up, they could ride their bicycles anywhere, play in the local parks safely, catch trains all over the peninsula to attend all sorts of events in total safety. Today this is no longer the case. Children have to be ferried everywhere by car, even those attending local schools. If they ride their bicycles in the suburbs (all children – black, white, brown) they stand the chance of being mugged, the bicycle stolen and whatever else of value they may have on their persons at the time. Often these muggings are accompanied by violence and injury.*  JH - South Africa

∞

*Now that we live in the UK and I am 18, I feel free. I don't worry about walking across the park at night on my own in my town, I don't hesitate to get on a bus in case we're shot at, I don't walk around the empty house with a cricket bat when I'm on my own.*  SM - UK

∞

*It is always said that Africa is not for sissies. I believe that is a simplistic way of looking at it. Or perhaps I have become a sissie. I prefer to*

think that we have become used to living in a society with living standards that are more appropriate to what they really should be. Yesterday afternoon my wife and I went for a walk in the beautiful spring air to Dairy Queen. We never locked our front door behind us. Isn't that wonderful? I remember not fetching the mail from my mailbox, behind the eight foot wall with the electrified fencing that surrounded my garden in South Africa, without my handgun in my hand, loaded with one in the breach.   AS - USA

∞

We used to rush to work, praying that we would not get hijacked, work long hours with the constant fear of being replaced by a government enforced BEE initiative, rush home hoping that we would not get killed on the road by an unlicensed driver and lock ourselves in for the night, gun close at hand. And we were supposed to like that because we were considered privileged. Well, I now live in a place where my children can play in the streets, where I do not even own a gun and where I don't live behind barbed wire and security systems. That is a civilized and progressive society.
SDT - Australia

∞

South Africans living in South Africa will never know what it is like to sleep with windows open with only fly screens between you and the night air, or to leave your house accidentally unlocked for a month's holiday away and return with everything still intact and accounted for or leave the car accidentally unlocked in the supermarket car park and return with your stereo and CD collection, etc still inside.   JH - Australia

∞

I don't know exactly when it changed, but I remember reading the online local Port Elizabeth newspaper about a year ago, and I saw an article about a man who was hijacked and shot dead at a particular intersection that I used to drive by all the time (and still do on the rare opportunities when I get back for a visit). And it just hit me that death is so random and senseless there. There is nothing you can do to protect yourself from it. All of a sudden I felt deeply, deeply saddened. There was a sense of loss that I hadn't felt until then – not even when I first departed. And then I thought about how I have felt living in America for the past few years – not having the constant shadow of fear infecting every part of my life. There was no comparison. I realized I don't ever want to go back to feeling that way again.

RS - USA

∞

I know that every single South African friend I have here would head home TOMORROW should the crime problem be sorted out as the issue is not about race, it's about personal safety. We are happy living our daily lives here without fear (which many South Africans have yet to experience!) but as you so beautifully say, we still have a foot on each continent and we will never be completely whole again. When Africa takes a hold, it never lets go.

HL - Australia

∞

We still have family living in South Africa but the remaining few are seriously considering immigrating due to the fear of crime. My family has experienced five hi-jackings, nine house break-ins were my brother almost lost his life because of trying to defend his home, my step dad was hospitalised for three months after defending himself from an attack by four armed men that broke-in to our home in Johannesburg... and I have lost half-a-dozen friends due to violent crimes.

We have decided that we WILL NOT give up on South Africa! We WILL return one day. One day when we know that our children will not have to carry fire-arms on them for self protection.... Well, will that ever be possible?

LM - Ireland

∞

We are living a life that is not continually interrupted by gunfire and maniac taxi drivers swerving out in front of you, plus the fact that in the event of me forgetting to close the front door I don't get uninvited guests waving guns at us, plus the fact that the few times I have stupidly left the garage open neither our car nor other possessions have been touched or taken, plus the fact that we can enjoy an open air meal at a sidewalk eating establishment without fear of being attacked, robbed or harmed, plus the fact that when a crime has taken place the police actually investigate it immediately, plus the fact that after an evening meal we can safely go for a stroll through our suburban streets without even taking some form of protection, plus the fact that we don't have to worry about house or car alarms going off suddenly, plus the fact that the air is clean and not polluted by hundreds of grass fires, light for no reason whatsoever, plus etc, etc.

BH - Australia

∞

I don't know how to explain it, but some days I feel a little guilty for just packing up and leaving, almost like turning my back on an old friend. I have a good life here blah blah blah, but I would still like to fight for that old friend, but when, where and how, I don't know. But with all its problems, I still think it's worth fighting for.

IB - USA

∞

When I started travelling, I soon realized how different other lifestyles were overseas as opposed to ours back home. There just seemed to be so much more freedom and so much less fear. Houses didn't have electric fencing and alarms. Instead kids did play in the streets whilst community members chatted. It was a complete wake up call at the age of 20 compared to what I was used to. You become so ingrained to a certain type of living that you can't see any other lifestyle. I have now become determined to change this.

KK - South Africa

∞

Few sirens; no action-man stunts required; able to travel on business and know the wife could leave the windows open and the door unlocked and be safe.

BM - UAE

∞

Now when I hear about South Africa, I feel a surge of horror when I realize that, in a way, I am glad I'm not there, and I'm not sure if I could go back. I used to say "It's worth it" when people asked me why I stayed in

South Africa even though it was dangerous. And I was proud of myself, but now I look at people like that and I feel like they are deluded. It's not worth it! Then I feel sick with myself for thinking that, knowing that I will never truly belong anywhere again, knowing that I will never be entirely happy where I am, but that I can never go home, and if I did, it wouldn't be home any more.

OM - Colorado

∞

I believe that one is not free if one is not safe. One has to have safety to have freedom. South Africans are not free.

SVB - UK

∞

What will it take for ALL the people of South Africa to demand more than political rhetoric in solving the unacceptable level of crime which has reached 'civil war' proportions? I wish I knew.

AMS - USA

∞ ∞ ∞

# Invictus

The poem, *Invictus*[26], sustained me through traumatic teen years. I read and re-read it until I knew the words and then silently recited them whenever I needed the sustenance – my mantra. A fact unknown to me that Nelson Mandela, only a relatively short distance away, was reading the same poem to sustain himself.

My son and I went to see the movie, *Invictus*[27], on its opening day. It felt a little too much like a documentary but I think, having read the book and lived the moments, I appreciated it as so much more than that. I could feel my son's boredom. I'm not given to public outbursts but, to his embarrassment, I actually jumped in my seat and cheered when South African scored the final goal in the world cup tournament. I lost myself for a moment, forgot where I was, and then stopped myself from crying from the intensity of the pure emotions that ran right through my soul in those seconds. He thought I was mad.

I had a vivid, searing memory of the day that we watched that same match, real-time, on a television set at our neighbor in Riebeek Kasteel. The nervous butterflies and breathless hole of fear in my stomach in those last few minutes, that we weren't going to 'pull this off', we weren't going to win. Afterwards, walking home, across the road, with James, the bubbly elation

---

[26] The poem *Invictus* was written in 1875 by the English poet William Ernest Henley (1849–1903).

[27] The film *Invictus* is a 2009 biographical drama directed by Clint Eastwood about Nelson Mandela's life during the 1995 Rugby World Cup in South Africa. It is based on the John Carlin book *Playing the Enemy: Nelson Mandela and the Game That Changed a Nation*.

filled me as if I was walking on an airy surface – of the planet but not quite on the planet.

We did it! We Did It! WE DID IT!

I wanted to yell it to everyone (except they already knew) and twirl whirly circles around and around until, still spinning, I fell dizzily back to earth. At that moment, you could have asked me to do absolutely anything for South Africa – anything – and I would not have given a moment's thought to the idiocy of any request.

Look at us, look at what we did, watch what we can do, we can do anything, it's only onward and upward from here.

If all of us felt that way, where did that go?

∞ ∞ ∞

My sister-in-law, Jenny, inadvertently gave me
the appropriate ending to this book:

*We are fine.*

*Our country is not.*

*What can we do but pray?*

# Acknowledgement

For my husband, James, who has always been my navigator. Although I often choose the path less travelled, despite your misgivings, you always keep me on course. And so it is with this book – I could not have created it without you. You provided my backbone and stability and you plotted the route. I love you.

∞ ∞ ∞

For Jules (Julie Hattingh), who is a patient editor and a dear friend. I've argued mentally with you the whole way through this book as I made your changes. I thank you for your time and dedication to this project. Upon completion, all I can say is "Vrystaat!"

∞ ∞ ∞

www.torninthenewsa.com

# Cast of Key Characters
(in rough order of when initial key impact was made)

The following people either precipitated our initial thought process, participated in our mental transition, facilitated our physical move, kept us strong emotionally or, once we arrived in the USA, reached out to us in some way. In so doing, they assisted us to stay here. And now we thank them...again.

(As always in life, there were many other people along the way. Small morale boosters came in many different forms and helped us to create the foundation of a new life here in the USA. We thank them also.)

John Bush
Jean Holland
Jan van Zyl
Mary Simons
Anne Oliver
Helen Konrad
Gill Kerchhoff and Jonathan Kaplan
Marilyn Bush
Jenny Cleland
Anna Lazarchic
Lynn Spitzer
Rebecca Woody
Rowan, Linda and Aidan Mickleburgh
Dave Burnham
Fitness for Ladies (the group of friends)
Roy and Diana Johnson

Karin Kruger

Fred Moore, Margaret Price, Jan Crable and Terry Taylor (of Big River Advertising)

Tyrrel Fairhead

Kim Leibowitz

The Real Jim Wilson

Blythe Park

Elizabeth Roark

The Freecyclers (in particular: Chris Sheehy, Elle Merkle)

Joe de Fazio

The Homeschoolers (in particular: Lois Curling, Amy Anderson, Teresa Parr, Jeannie Wiant, Connie Lapallo, Cheryl Stern)

Dr. Wally Johnston

Dr. Omprakash Narang

# Biographies of Main Contributors
## In order of appearance

**James McIntosh:** *Telling Stories* and *Introductions*

James is the CNO (Chief Nonsense Officer) for NonsenseAtWork.com. He was born in the middle of South African wine country, earned three degrees drinking red wine, was chased by a lioness, had to run from elephants, got bored, and moved to the USA seeking adventure. As a business consultant and executive coach specializing in strategy development and execution, he has seen a lot of nonsense at work. That's why he now shows senior executives how to make the nonsense at work work for them. When this gets the better of him, he retreats to writing and public speaking until his confidence returns. He has been repeating this cycle for more than 25 years without seriously hurting himself, his clients, his audience or, most importantly, his family. His current books are available on Internet bookstores: *Crossing The Nonsense Divide: Steps to Finding Your Path to a Successful Life* and *Make the Nonsense at Work Work for You*. You may also read his blog at blog.nonsenseatwork.com


**Eve Hemming:** *Out of Love*

Eve has contributed a wide range of articles for publication in South Africa. She and her husband reside in Auckland, New Zealand, where Eve is an educational psychologist. They, too, suffer from a torn family, having children and grandchildren in South Africa and New Zealand. Eve grew up on a Free State (South Africa) farm, where she developed a passion for the wide expanses of African sky and landscape. She takes her passion into her work in the expressive arts and in specialised education. *Out of Love* was originally published on 12 May 2008 as *Leaving South Africa on a Jet Plane* in *The Witness*, a South African newspaper.

**Michelle Leech:** *I Miss*

Michelle was born in Springs, on the East Rand of South Africa. She is a young mother with a toddler, another baby on the way and a New Zealander for a husband. At the time of writing this short bio Michelle had been living in New Zealand for just over two years where she writes, edits and proofreads.


**Rob Dickens:** *F\*\*k You, Emigrant*

Rob has been a slacker since Grade 2. That's when he learnt how to write...and he's been trading on that talent ever since. He's run the full gamut of wordsmithing from ICT PR to online casino content management, Dimension Data copywriter to ZOO Weekly features editor, FHM digital editor to ISP webmaster, as well as feeding his love for poker as Group Media Manager for BLUFF Magazine. Having had two print magazines pulled out from under his feet, he now harbours a vehement grudge against the troglodytic print industry. Rob currently lives in Johannesburg (but is soon 'semigrating' to Pretoria) where he heads up his own digital marketing agency called Cattleprod Media & Marketing. He still snarls at emigrants.


**Anthony Krijger:** *Leaving Cloud Cuckoo Land*

Anthony grew up in Natal, South Africa, reluctant scholar at Michaelhouse, an even more reluctant student getting a useless degree in knitting at Leicester. Failed textile tycoon at age 25. Interest remains as an armchair follower and critic of Fashion TV. Has been self employed ever since as a successful spice merchant, trucker and self-taught global mustard expert and salesman. Now a modern day 'carpetbagger' peddling dry mustard flours and seeds to food ingredient users anywhere he can find them on the planet. Suffers from perpetual rash induced by other people's children and pets. However, recently became closet dad to teenagers Ashley and Lauren when he fell in love with their mom, Sharon. Commutes between home in Westville, South Africa, work in Brunkild, Canada and enjoys the family holiday home in Bali whenever he can escape.

**Alison Wolfson:** *To Those Who Aren't Concerned*

Born in Cape Town, for the first 46 years of her life Alison stayed within the confines of the land of her birth, during which time she had been a paralegal, sheep farmer and builder, but finally broke free from her self-imposed, blinkered non-existence, and discovered that there is indeed a right to life and a life of rights awaiting her and her family elsewhere. She is not a writer, nor an artist, not even a business person of any note, but just an ordinary, honest, hardworking, middle-aged woman, living, breathing and loving every minute of her new life as an Australian citizen with her husband, Joe, and their four daughters in the Adelaide Hills, South Australia, and wondering why the hell they didn't make the move years ago. She now runs a family-owned chocolate and dessert café in the town of Hahndorf in the Adelaide Hills.


**Kate Richards:** *You have to stay, Ben*

Kate and family used to live with their six dogs and a cat in Hilton. Leaving South Africa was traumatic, and leaving pets was one of the most difficult hurdles. The Richards family now lives in Auckland but sadly no pets are allowed in their rented home. Kate wrote for *The Witness* and *Midlands Life* as a freelancer. She also writes short stories (see *Celebrating ten years, Shuter & Shooter*) and a blog titled, *A new life in New Zealand* (katesrichards.blogspot.com). *You Have to Stay Ben* was first published in *The Witness* on 9 November 2009.


**Heather Claire Scott:** *The Immigrant*

Heather Claire Scott, prev. Albon, nee Howson, was born in Port Elizabeth, South Africa, in May of 1944. She grew up in Pretoria, educated by the Irish nuns at Loreto Convent, where she learned her love of writing from wonderful teachers. She has three children, two of whom now live in Virginia, USA, and her eldest lives with his family at The Hague, in Holland. She and her husband Ken have seven grandchildren. The couple became US citizens in January of 2006.

It has been a time of tumult and upheaval

A time of losses and gains

A time of loving and hating

And it has been a time of living laughing being doing and becoming

A time for pain anger grief and longing to be replaced by acceptance wholeness and healing

A time for planting seeds and uprooting dead wood

It has been the time of my life

    And yet it has been...

                      ...just a moment in time

Bronwyn McIntosh

www.ingramcontent.com/pod-product-compliance
Lightning Source LLC
Chambersburg PA
CBHW021957160426
43197CB00007B/164